GOING MUTANT

"In a world gone batty . . .

there was one bat who could save the world."

Dr. Barry Leed, PhD (MBS), Neil McGinness,
and the editors of
Weekly World News

SCRIBNER
New York | London | Toronto | Sydney

SCRIBNER
A Division of Simon & Schuster, Inc.
1230 Avenue of the Americas
New York, NY 10020

First Scribner trade paperback edition September 2010

SCRIBNER and design are registered trademarks of The Gale Group, Inc., used under license by Simon & Schuster, Inc., the publisher of this work.

For information about special discounts for bulk purchases, please contact Simon & Schuster Special Sales at 1-866-506-1949 or business@simonandschuster.com.

The Simon & Schuster Speakers Bureau can bring authors to your live event. For more information or to book an event contact the Simon & Schuster Speakers Bureau at 1-866-248-3049 or visit our website at www.simonspeakers.com.

Designed by Tom Deja

Manufactured in the United States of America

10 9 8 7 6 5 4 3 2 1

Library of Congress Control Number: 2010008932

ISBN 978-1-4391-5700-8

ISBN 978-1-4516-0909-7 (ebook)

"While it is true that we in this nation remain free to be idiotic, it does not necessarily follow that we must be idiotic in order to be free."

—Mumford Jones

This book is dedicated to the big man who first introduced me to Mumford Jones.

CONTENTS

GOING MUTANT
The Bat Boy Exposed!

Written by
Neil McGinness
Dr. Barry Leed, PhD (MBS)

With additional material from the editors of *Weekly World News*:
Karl Benjamin and Jonathan Shipley

Nick Thornton, Bill Creighton, Dack Kennedy, Dick Siegel, Joe Berger, Jack Alexander,
Dick Kulpa, Conrad Morse, Deuce Collins, Nick Mann, Alex Morgan, Ernst Craven, Rex Wolfe,
Ahmet Farouk, Vincenzo Sardi, Miguel Figueroa, Lois Castini, Joan Yung, Mike Foster,
Wayne Diaz, Larry Mulder, Michael Chiron, Will Shivers, Darren Davenport, Ian Merkins,
Mark Miller, Michael Forsyth, Tanya Broder, D. Patrick, Wolf Landrum, Kevin Creed,
Cliff Linedecker, Scott D. Peterson, Brett Goldberg, Ron Nicholson, Laura Sterritt,
Brett Anniston, Daniel Guzman, Ed Anger, Dallas Smith, Sandra Lee, Donna Santos, Joan Ryan,
Peter Bagge, Dorian Wagner, Nigel Potts, Nikki Long, Jeanne Kelly, Tim Jones,
Erin Magner, Brian Magner

Design
Tom Deja

ACKNOWLEDGMENTS

Weekly World News would like to thank the Frozen Santas: Ketch, Ihsan, Ponge, K-Sev, the Pizza Man, Mr. Apple, Petro, R. G. "the Rock" Rochester, AC Reilly, Señor Flaco, Ed Slink, Cobra Beck, C.S.W. Ketch, Che Garnett, D. C. Collins, Laura Sterritt, Leslie Grossnickle, Fat Willie, Frankie, Vlad, Freaking News, E. C. Skwiblet, Benson Bunniepanz, M. H. Meancey, Charlie Pikels, the House, M. A. Twineball, Professor Greenjeans, Mowdy Gogo, Dallas Commagreens, Rob Mier, Merlin D. Tuttle, Chin Strap, the Bishop, Dennis Kucinich, T. D. Bati, Ben Jovi, Ed Anger, and the Angriest Generation.

Thanks to Susan Moldow

Special thanks to Brant Rumble and Jake Elwell. This book would not be possible without these two intrepid young men who were recently found alive.

For Burnsie, my superhero

W.R.II.IG #1: I.A.IIE.IT D..IGE.

This book contains classified, personal, sensitive files concerning Bat Boy that have never before been made public. If you purchased this book without a cover, you should be aware that this book may have been stolen property and reported as "unsold and destroyed" to the publisher. In such case neither the author nor the publisher has received any payment for this "stripped book." The cause of this "stripping" is likely Bat Boy.

Bat Boy has a vested interest in halting distribution of this private material. Rather than pursue appropriate legal channels, the mutant has decided to bite the cover off the book wherever possible.[1]

In the probable event that Bat Boy mauls this book, the reader is strongly recommended to wear animal-trainer-approved padded mittens[2] while reading.

Beware, and enjoy.

WARNING #2: USE OF THIS BOOK AS AN AX

Kafka once remarked that a book should serve as an ax to break open the frozen sea inside us. If you have a frozen sea inside you, please do not use this book in an axlike manner to break it apart. Instead, remain calm and seek the advice of a medical professional or certified MRI technician.[3]

If you are being attacked by Bat Boy while reading this book as referenced in Warning #1 and would like to use this book as an ax to fend off the mutant, you should do so only at your own risk and only if equipped with animal-trainer-approved padded mittens.[4]

---

[1] Knowing that Bat Boy would likely target innocent readers of this book, *Weekly World News* had recommended that the book come equipped with a mirror attached to a telescopic antenna that could be extended during reading so that the reader could easily detect oncoming danger. The mirror would function like those wide-view mirrors that you see nailed into a telephone pole on those blind driveways that are really hard to pull out of with your car. *Weekly World News* was informed that this would not be possible. Sure, we can make Kindles that whisper-sync downloadable e-books in more than one hundred countries with GSM/EDGE wireless modem connectivity, but somehow we are still unable to affix a metal antenna with a mirror on your everyday book to prevent attack from mutants. So much for progress.

[2] Sold separately.

[3] If you are claustrophobic and resistant to the idea of an MRI, or if you are heavyset and do not fit into traditional MRI chambers, please be advised that new advances in MRI technology have allowed walk-in patients greater freedom of movement during the procedure. In many cities, a new technology called stand-up MRI is available. This is equipped with a motorized patient-handling system that allows a patient to be scanned while in a normal upright standing position. The freedom of movement during this procedure is remarkable and many patients can get scanned while watching television or reading a book. In the event you decide to consume media during your stand-up MRI, we prefer that you choose to read a book. In particular, we recommend this book.

[4] Sold separately.

FOREWORD

Bear Grylls is an idiot.[5] Grylls, a popular television host, disparages bats every chance he gets. Popping his head outside an Ecuadorean cave in the Andean jungle: "If there's one thing I don't like, it's bats." Inside a cave deep within the Panamanian rain forest: "I don't like bats. They bite and have rabies." In his interview with **Outside** magazine: "I hate bats."

How can an outdoor expert who injects himself into the most untamed areas of Earth make such inane comments? How can he spread dangerous misinformation on bats to the millions of couch-bound Americans watching his choreographed mock-struggle to survive?

As responsible members of this planet's ecosystem, we cannot tolerate Bear's "battitude." Sure, it's okay to delight in watching this telegenic, strapping young man traverse jungles eating elephant dung, mealworm grubs, and discarded decaying animal carcasses to survive, but when the man disparages bats, that must not be taken sitting down.

Bats save our planet nightly by eating millions of tons of harmful insects. Should something happen to our bat population, as you will see in this book, the consequences would destroy our ecosystem. According to the ATEX Institute, if the bat population were compromised, the resulting destruction of food crops from insect damage would plunge ninety-three countries into famine over-night—and that's in Africa alone.

If Bear Grylls wants to capture the true hero of our wild planet, he should instruct his director to turn the camera away from himself to film bats emerging at dusk to devour bugs. Without bats, Bear Grylls would not have a show because he would be devoured alive in the wild places he likes to roam.

We need more public figures who will stand up to profess their admiration for these noble creatures that save our planet.

One public figure who dares to take this stand is Bat Boy. As you are about to read, this American hero, when faced with a raging pandemic called white-nose syndrome, took the disease head-on without regard for his personal safety. He fought valiantly and saved our planet even when our own president could not. In the end, Bat Boy's sonar provided the audacity as well as the hope.

     Glenn Windeatt
     Senior Bat Conservationist

---

[5] Forewords these days are typically reserved for glowing comments about a book from some kind of celebrity. Foreword author Glenn Windeatt and **Weekly World News** decided to turn that on its head by disparaging this otherwise harmless television sensation: Bear Grylls. In fairness, this decision was aided by the fact that the numerous requests to write forewords that were submitted to Simon Winchester, Noam Chomsky, Soupy Sales, Hugo Chávez, Bear Grylls, and Batman all went unanswered. Mr. Grylls is not an idiot. Additionally, he is powerfully built, and when he strips down to a mere loincloth he possesses what appears to be a diver's body that makes us want to spread his nation's national treat, spotted dick pudding, all over his interstitials. Grylls also claims that he spent time in the British Special Forces. That alone is enough to make our Argentinean Falkland Islander staff member cower in our coat closet muttering, **"Dios mío,"** and wishing we were never linked to the comment above. Still, we should all agree that American television airwaves should be restricted to natural citizens and not misappropriated by British hams such as Bear Grylls, David Attenborough, Simon Cowell, Angela Lansbury, Laurence Olivier, and Thomas Selleck. Exceptions to this rule would apply in the cases of Kate Beckinsale (for obvious reasons) and Marty Feldman (posthumously, as he had Bat Boy's eyes). Nonetheless, we do agree that Grylls needs to study bats and stop crying like a little pantywaist whenever he comes into contact with these noble creatures that save our planet every night.

A Letter of Introduction

When the author of this book, Dr. Barry Leed, first entered our office, we regarded him with some suspicion. He was, after all, attempting to sell us private information on our own stock-in-trade, Bat Boy. It was also not a convenient time for a discussion. My management team was working around the clock on our bid to buy the **Boston Globe** and my two ace reporters had headed north to get the story on the Shroud of Cobain, a startling formation of dust on a Canadian playground that bears an uncanny resemblance to the late grunge singer.

As it happened, our deal on the **Boston Globe** unwound at the eleventh hour thanks to a duplicitous, fee-grubbing banker who is currently doing seventy-five years upstate. Simultaneously, Dr. Leed came back to the table and offered to dramatically reduce his price for us to buy his story.

With time, then, to focus on this Dr. Barry Leed, or Dr. Squealgood, as he was known in his substitute science teaching classrooms, we performed a thorough background investigation. He checked out. Indeed, he had graduated with a PhD (MBS) from the University of Indianapolis, had served as a graduate research assistant in the lab of Bat Boy's discoverer, Dr. Ron Dillon, and had also guest-lectured in many well-known caves around the East Coast. The documents that he showed us, now contained in this book, were remarkable.

Our rancor-filled negotiation behind us, you now hold in your hands the most complete collection of Bat Boy's personal mementos, writings, art collection, personal recordings, private space photos, and Facebook updates. And thanks to the work of Dr. Squealgood, we now have proof that Bat Boy has shaped the course of modern events (and also knows how to bake a mean mosquito pie).

Yes, this book was published without Bat Boy's cooperation. We recognize that by publishing this work we shatter Bat Boy's privacy forever. But we do so with the noblest of intentions: to show the world that Bat Boy should be loved as one of us. For, as you will learn, mutant bat species are living creatures just like us. Perhaps even more like ourselves than ourselves.

Neil McGinness
CEO
Weekly World News
Grand Central Station
PO Box 3081
New York, New York 10163

CHAPTER 1
SIGHTINGS

At 3:21 P.M. on a cool December day north of mile marker 63 on I-95 just south of Richmond, Virginia, Amanda Lethbridge checked her rearview mirror and noticed an unusual figure clinging to the grille of the Peterbilt truck in her rear. Lethbridge, a thirty-seven-year-old resident of Richmond, switched to the right lane to let the truck pass. She caught a glimpse as the truck passed by at seventy-five miles per hour. The creature had his head bent back and was snapping at insects in midair.

A week later, on a clear, balmy night in Sarasota, Florida, Chris Caddick's cocker spaniel, Meat Loaf, became agitated by something in his backyard. Caddick stepped outside to investigate. Meat Loaf led his owner to a banyan tree where Caddick saw an animal crouching on a lower branch. Caddick grabbed a broom and attempted to prod the animal from the tree. In a second, Caddick was mauled. His two hands were bitten clear to the bone. Hours later, from his hospital bed, Caddick told the investigating officer that the animal's teeth were like "tiny daggers." Meat Loaf was never found.

Later that month, outside Ely, Nevada, a young woman named Lucia Rickards left her house around dusk to look for her cat, Cookie. Rickards spotted what appeared to be a small boy standing behind her car parked in the driveway. The boy did not see her. Rickards watched in horror as the boy lifted up her Honda Accord with one arm, grabbed Cookie from underneath the Accord, and ate her.

Then, without warning, in Seattle, Washington, Lionel Boldy came within inches of losing his life. Boldy's chilling encounter was recorded by the Seattle Police Department in an official witness statement: "I was sitting on my patio eating a pizza and drinking a beer when I heard scratching in the bushes. What I saw froze my blood. My first thought was, 'My God! It's Dracula.' I could actually smell his breath. The creature looked like he would be extremely dangerous if he felt threatened. There was no way I was going to threaten it, whatever it was. He stood there staring at the piece of pizza I was holding. His eyes were as round as saucers. I figured he might be hungry, so I threw a slice to him. He grabbed it right out of the air and disappeared behind the bushes. I discovered the next morning he'd spit out the anchovies."

The sightings were growing frequent. Too frequent. As the nation grew worried over its fate, the climate changed. Climate warming dropped out of sight. Climate fear took over. The president scrambled every available agency, including FEMUR (Federal Emergency Mutant Undercover Recovery), which hadn't been scrambled since the Teapot Dome scandal of 1922. FEMUR failed to allay the growing fear. The situation tormented reds and blues alike. Glenn Beck cried in prime time. Then, a night later, so did Anderson Cooper. Our country didn't need this. Not now.

> **I was sitting on my patio eating a pizza and drinking a beer when I heard scratching in the bushes. What I saw froze my blood...**

Ex. 1.1
Albino Bunny
Cat/ABC

had found in a discarded beer cooler. Gradually, people tried to go about their business.

Ever since the "Bigfoot in a Balloon" episode, I had learned not to trust CNN. No way was this an STO or an ABC. Maybe the work of an eagle-headed hare, or EHH, but I doubted it. I had good reason. I had seen this attack pattern before, and it didn't fit with an EHH. For me, the culprit needed no introduction. As a young doctoral candidate in mutant bat studies, or MBS, I had first laid eyes on the ornery beast known as Bat Boy in Dr. Ron Dillon's lab in 1992.

The nation would not want to believe that Bat Boy was behind the attacks. The government had declared him a hero for his service in the Middle East. He had returned home from

Not with escalation in Afghanistan, economic instability, child vaccination uncertainty, and Regis Philbin still on television.

Most media outlets promptly placed the blame on a rabid albino bunny cat gone wild. CNN located a primate biologist named Devon Pickstock, who had surveyed the attack scenes for DNA and bite radius samples. Pickstock went on-air and quickly ruled out an ABC, or albino bunny cat, and confidently identified the culprit as a shaved saber-toothed ostrich. The saber-toothed ostrich, or STO as Pickstock referred to it, would be quickly trapped and shot.

CNN declared the case closed and focused the bulk of their attention on the discovery of an alien mummy fetus that a Kentucky man

Ex. 1.2
Saber-toothed
Ostrich/STO

Saudi to a hero's welcome and then tried to keep out of sight. But around the time of these recent sightings, I had intercepted chatter on the wire indicating that Bat Boy's shell was beginning to crack. Signs of post-traumatic stress disorder, or PTSD, had surfaced. These recent attacks were either a poorly veiled cry for help or an angry assault on the citizenry that made his postwar re-entry into society so difficult. I hoped for the former. Either way, something needed to be done before it was too late. Innocent lives hung in the balance.

Ex. 1.3
Eagle-Headed
Hare/EHH

I took off to visit the scientist who had first captured Bat Boy, the high priest of mutant bat studies, the Wheeling Wunderkind, the Mammal Messiah, Dr. Ron Dillon.

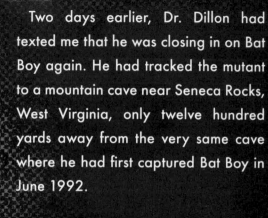

CHAPTER 2
THE MAMMAL MESSIAH

Two days earlier, Dr. Dillon had texted me that he was closing in on Bat Boy again. He had tracked the mutant to a mountain cave near Seneca Rocks, West Virginia, only twelve hundred yards away from the very same cave where he had first captured Bat Boy in June 1992.

Early in his career, Dr. Dillon had earned respect within the scientific community for his work on natural color selection among winged mammals. Then, in 1992, he found Bat Boy in the heart of the Appalachian Mountains. Dillon was two miles below Earth's surface in a cave complex when he heard a faint squeal of pain. As it turned out, Bat Boy's foot had wedged into a crack between two rocks. With Bat Boy temporarily immobilized, Dillon was able to sedate him with a tranquilizer dart. Dillon took the creature to his lab in Wheeling for observation. Dillon's life would never be the same. The acolytes in his lab called him the Mammal Messiah. Every researcher in the lab felt as though they had hitched their petri dish to the next Charles Darwin. When Dillon hired me in 1992 as a research assistant, I was on summer break from writing my doctoral dissertation in mutant bat studies at the University of Indianapolis. As an eager young doctoral candidate, I gained Dillon's trust and was granted second-class, or supervised, access to the creature.

My memory of that first day in Dillon's lab remains with me to this day. Dillon assembled the staff to introduce me and began to speak in his trademark scientific tone that dispelled all mystery. "This, ladies and gentlemen, is young candidate Barry Leed. He is to have full access to all of your findings, and you all are to consider his inquiries with the expeditiousness that you do mine. He is here because he is what you all routinely fail to be: perfectly, incorruptibly, and passionately aware of what would befall the human race if our bat population were to ever be compromised. I have never known a young scientist of such purpose—with, of course, the exception of myself. You are all to consider him my Moses."

Dr. Barry Leed

I couldn't have predicted that my dissertation work on the relevance of bats to the human ecosystem would strike the chord it did with Dr. Dillon. My professors back in Indy treated my work with skepticism. My adviser warned that my theories relied solely on hyperbole and worst-case scenarios. "Beware of the temptation to invent the catastrophes you hope to prevent, Mr. Leed. History tends to treat this kind of scientific/martyr complex with enduring scorn. And the decision makers in the grant department tend not to fund them. You should also know that this so-called Mammal Messiah, Dr.

Dillon, is rumored to dabble in mutants just like a Bigfoot hunter. Watch yourself out there, Mr. Leed, or you'll end up teaching remedial science to a bunch of illiterates at Podunk Middle School."

Instinct compelled me to leave Indy. In my gut I knew that the Mammal Messiah was no circus act. Yet my heart wanted to stay put. In those first weeks, the swirling lab smells of formaldehyde and other chemical agents couldn't shake the lingering scent of sweet Marie in my bed. It killed me to leave her back then. Years later, even after all of the deceit and humiliation, I still catch myself drawn back into those early days of our romance, in Indian-no-place, Indiana, of all places, sucking back cold beers down in Broad Ripple in between marathon lovemaking sessions on those oppressively hot Midwestern summer nights. Johnny Freakin' Mellencamp in a dirty lab coat.

Dillon despised the innocence of my uncomplicated, beer-swilling, Midwestern youth. The doctor knew that in the back recesses of his lab prowled the one thing that would shatter my innocence forever: on the morning of September 19, 1992, Dillon took me to meet Bat Boy.

Dr. Dillon led me through his main lab area, where we passed by his staff of tight-lipped, anal white coats and the petri dishes they dutifully manned. No one looked up as we moved toward the back of the lab. Dillon was a taskmaster and a vicious perfectionist; his staff never made eye contact with him and pressed on with their work as if it were the Manhattan Project for bats.

At the back of the lab, an addition had been made to the building. The gaps of ceiling panels above and the differing vinyl floor surfaces that joined together unevenly beneath my feet suggested that the addition had been done hastily to make room for an unexpected, special purpose. In the middle of the threshold of this newly created addition, a janitor sporting a name tag that read SCHMING swept patches of scuffed plaster into a central pile.

"Morning, Doc," the janitor greeted Dr. Dillon. Dillon walked on without acknowledging the sweeper. The hallway grew darker. I noticed that the fluorescent light tubes had been removed from the ceiling fixtures and that someone had placed cardboard boxes over the windows and taped them over. We reached a steel door flanked by a guard sitting in a folding metal card-table-style chair.

Perched in the chair outside the door with a wooden baseball bat in his hand sat Alan Thrush. Thrush wore taut fatigues and oversized aviator glasses, and had a nine-millimeter gun strapped to his side. I could smell wet tobacco. Thrush's jaw had an uneven jut that suggested some kind of shrapnel incident. This was a man who had stuck his chin out too many times. "Thrush here is in charge of security, Mr. Leed. Thrush, Mr. Leed here is being granted second-class access."

"Boss, you sure about that? You ain't known

the kid too long. How do you know he ain't with FEMUR?" Thrush peered over his shades to make eye contact with Dillon. Dillon nodded. "Nice to meet ya. Call me Thrush," the guard said as he waved the bat in front of my face. The bat came from a Cooperstown souvenir shop called the Hall of Fame Bat Company. THRUSH was branded on the side. Underneath, the second brand read KONTRA KILLER. Lab scuttlebutt later informed me that Thrush had served as some kind of mercenary before Blackwater made that line of work glamorous. Thrush fancied himself the Sultan of Sandinista SWAT. On his coffee breaks, Thrush could be found in the lounge doing check swings with his souvenir bat, bragging loudly to unimpressed females about what he called the Thrush & Ollie show, a reference to his Sandinista-thumping, back-jungle Nicaraguan adventures with contra supporter Colonel Ollie North. Thrush now earned his keep running security for Dr. Dillon.

"Thrush, I don't pay you to question my judgment. I pay you to kill anyone who tries to enter this door without my authorization. Mr. Leed, you have now met the *real* Bat Boy, our rent-a-cop Alan Thrush. Thrush, just add Leed to the short list, please. As for anyone else, it's—"

"I know, Doc, I know, two in the chest and one in the head. And you don't have to tell me how to do my job." Thrush picked up a paper coffee cup and fired a sluice of tobacco juice into it. He then stood up to begin unlocking the three dead bolts on the steel door.

With the dead bolts cleared, Dillon stepped forward to use his keys to open the first steel door. He led me into a dark anteroom. Thrush poked his head in and handed two cylinders to Dillon. "Here are your bugs, Doc." Then Thrush reached out to me offering two earplugs. "Kid, you're going to want these. Bet you haven't heard a squeal this loud since prom night. Hell, I ain't heard a squeal that loud since I stuck a

Sandie with my bowie down in Nicky Gra-Gra."

"That'll be all, Thrush," Dillon ordered while he secured a miner's hard hat to his head and turned on the headlamp. Thrush retreated and closed the door and began fastening the dead bolts. Dillon tested a penlight by pointing it into my eyes. "For the time being, you are not to be trusted with any flashlights. The slightest mistake with a flashlight and you'll set him off." Dillon then handed me a pair of thick protective mittens. "You'll want these on as well. These are animal-trainer-approved gloves."

Mind you, all I knew of Bat Boy that summer was what I had read in *Weekly World News*. Unverifiable smatterings had been printed about the sighting of a potential missing link in the Shenandoah Mountains, but as I stood there in the dark, suffering a rash of very real paranoia that Dr. Dillon had not-so-platonic motives concerning me—he was, after all, awfully appreciative of my talents—I didn't know whether to dirty my shorts or cry for help. What the hell was I getting myself into? Dillon pushed us through a low-ceilinged alcove and began to futz with more locks and yet another door.

"Stay calm, Mr. Leed. Life is about to become very interesting for you. You are about to meet my Chiropteran Tot, or Bat Boy, as the press corps has labeled him. Whatever you do, keep your arms and fingers to your sides. Don't tempt him with any sudden movements. You'll get only a glimpse from the penlight. Bat Boy's not so fond of daylight, or any other light, for that matter. Temperamental prick. Trust me, you don't ever want to anger him. The little guy's stronger than an ox on steroids."

As we passed through the second set of bolted steel doors, all external noises ceased. It was dead silent. Dillon put his shoulder up against a large iron bar and slid it back to unlock another large steel door. The door swung open. Using the door as a shield, Dillon hid behind the steel to make sure the mutant was caged. Convinced he was enclosed, he inched forward. Inside it was dark, pitch-black. Dillon waved the weak light beam across the creature and I caught my first glimpse of Bat Boy.

He moved in a rush, a quick, pale sixty-five-pound blur of motion. Dillon pointed the flashlight toward him again, and it seemed to dazzle him for a moment. Bat Boy froze and I caught him clearly. The creature had a haunting white lantern of a face that looked to be the unholy by-product of a one-night stand between Nosferatu and Mickey Mouse. His bulging eyes darted back and forth. When his bulbous pupils moved, the whites of his eyes shone wildly in the darkness. I could feel his core torso muscles tighten and detected his large ears prick back just like a horse when it senses danger. Suddenly the bat child let loose a bloodcurdling scream. My eardrums nearly burst and my pants soaked instantly. I had forgotten to insert the earplugs and dropped them to the floor in fright. The scream had to register over 120 decibels. "Sweet Marie, get me out of here," I said to myself, longing to be back in the flat Indiana plains pressed against the acreage of her rolling curves. Dillon used the penlight to open a large cylinder that he had brought with him. It was packed solid with mosquitoes, and they started buzzing around the room. Bat Boy went to work darting about devouring the bugs. He was caged but you could feel the air move and hear the swish as he sprang back and forth inhaling his protein with wings beating. Dillon then reached into his lab coat pocket and threw five frozen dead mice into his cage. "Here you go, Tot. I didn't forget dessert."

Dillon motioned for us to back out of the room. On the way out, his headlamp flashed near Bat Boy's right ear, causing another shriek. While he chewed hungrily on his mouse-icle, I saw what looked like an earring.

The chiropteran bared his teeth and hissed a stream of liquid at me. My cheek felt the splatter of warm goo. Dillon grabbed me by the arm and pulled me out of the room. "It's his natural anticoagulant. Don't worry, it's harmless—unless he bites you. If he bites you and injects that anticoagulant into your wound, you'll never stop bleeding. When he spits, that means he's ready to eat. Let's get out of here."

As we emerged, Thrush pointed his bat toward me, on the end of which he had placed a soiled towel. "That mutant got you pretty good, kid. Here, take this to clean up." Not wanting to offend the guard, I grabbed the crusty old oil rag. Warm urine dripped down my pant legs. Loud ringing obscured my hearing. In the space between my two damaged ears, a warm, filmy goo coated my face. My eyes started to sting. My heart pounded with a disorientating fear. My dignity crushed by this caged creature, I hobbled back toward Dillon's office, sliming the lab hallway with a snail trail of wetness.

Back in the safety of Dillon's office, I regained some composure. I toweled off and spoke to the doctor. "Was he wearing an earring?"

"Good. You noticed that. We had to sedate the hell out of him to get that in. It's a transponder. I am hoping that it'll give us the opportunity to track him one day back to the race of people he left underground. I am hoping this little guy leads us to his tribe. You did good in there, candidate Leed. His appetite is insatiable. I really don't have enough to feed him.

A·T·E·X
INSTITUTE

BAT BOY INITIAL OBSERVATIONS September 1992

BACKGROUND FILE — CLASSIFIED

SCIENTIFIC NAME: Chiropteran Tot

NAME: Bat Boy

SPECIES: Mutant

ORIGIN: Genetic splice: half-boy/half-bat

PLACE OF BIRTH: Unknown cave

PLACE OF RESIDENCE: Pharmaceutical laboratory

RESIDENCE: Outskirts of Stony Bottom, West Virginia, Seneca Rocks Region (GPS coordinates strictly classified)

AGE: Unknown; discovered in 1992

HEIGHT: 3' 8"

WEIGHT: 65 pounds

EYES: Bulging blue, size of Ping-Pong balls

EARS: Pointed, size of Little League catcher's mitt

TEETH: Razor-sharp pointers

HEAD: Tilted back, usually with mouth open for the purpose of scooping mosquitoes or high-pitched squeaking

TONGUE: Brillo pad consistency

ECHOLOCATION FREQUENCY: 47–53 kHz

EDUCATION: Cave schooled

FOOD: Mosquitoes and moths, diced fruit, featherless lizard chickens, frozen mice

MATH SKILLS: No mastery of sorting, patterning, or basic numerics. Addition, subtraction, geometry out of the question. No faculty for estimation. With work, the subject could possibly grasp basic currency and potentially use a number line.

HANDWRITING: Subject ate both pens and pencils when presented. Currently no ability to print or create any legible printing. Basic handwriting out of the question at present.

LANGUAGE SKILLS: Complex squeal pattern. Working on deciphering. Creature appears to use mix of short-vowel and long-vowel sounds. **No** r-controlled vowels or vowel variants. Squeals do not contain inflected endings. Aggressively loud. Earplugs recommended during observation. Catherine Peake booked to evaluate.

READING SKILLS: Are you kidding? Mutant has no ability to read books or maps, or determine any words by sight. Despises being read to at night. Even oversized book with large print was rejected. No sign of critical thinking, effective inferrals, or oral communication abilities of any kind.

AURAL SKILLS: Loud shrieks exceeding 100 decibels

SLEEP: Hangs upside down to sleep. Has precise biological time clock that functions even when deprived of natural light, as in current lab state. Creature still on regular sleep pattern via sunlight hours.

INTERESTS:

Eating mosquitoes

Political pundits — James Carville, Lee Atwater

Water polo

Politicians — Al Gore, Clement Attlee, Yasser Arafat

LIKES:

Pictures of construction sites

Featherless lizard chickens

Gothic architecture

The Cure (music)

Soldiers

Gnats

Count Chocula Cereal

DISLIKES:

The sun

Ringo Starr solo albums

Feathered lizard chickens

Disco balls

Flashlights, laser pointers, miner headlamps, any objects w/bright glare

Jazz

Modern art—Picasso, Rothko in particular; however, a picture by Joseph Stella drew no reaction whatsoever

Cher recordings post-1984

Peaches—Subject displayed a violent reaction to this fruit

POLITICAL AFFILIATION: Independent

FAVORITE HOLIDAY: Halloween

LEAST FAVORITE HOLIDAY: National Feathered Lizard Chicken Day

OFFICIAL MOTTO: God, Country, Mosquitoes

QUICK FACTS: Can consume 1 ton (2,000 pounds) of insects in less time than it takes to play a round of golf (4 hours). Bat Boy can appear good-natured (though not around peaches).

That feeding you witnessed is merely a fraction of the bug intake that he would consume in the wild. I am waiting for my bug shipment to get here."

Dillon was understandably obsessed with the creature. He refused to think of Bat Boy as a mutant, as most others did. Based on his knowledge of natural selection, Dillon believed that Bat Boy belonged to a new species of subterranean cave dwellers. I remember him telling me, "Find one mutant and get your name in the paper; find an entire new species and you're Charlie friggin' Darwin."

He told *Weekly World News* in his famous interview announcing the discovery of the creature, "His eyes are twice as big as they should be, and his ears are like satellite dishes. This boy clearly belongs to a race of people who live miles beneath the surface. It's my belief that they evolved batlike features to enable them to survive in total darkness." He went on to explain, "Bat Boy almost certainly strayed from a much larger pack."

The doctor pulled open a steel file cabinet door to show me the records he had begun to compile on the creature. To this day, I remember seeing that initial file and knowing then and there that I could not retreat to the Hoosier hospitality of my native state and the pinup-pretty Marie. This was the front line of everything that I had studied for and I had just glimpsed what they can't teach you in school. Just like Dillon, I found myself en-snared under Bat Boy's spell. The buzzing in my ears melted into a rhythmic whoosh as an ethereal calm came over me. I was disoriented, my pants were wet, my hearing cut in and out, and warm goo was crusted on my face, yet somehow my anxiety dissipated now as it all sank in. My muscles relaxed as though I had ingested a strong benzodiazepine. Bat Boy was my medicine. Everything felt soft and fuzzy, even Dillon's pointy fifties-style glasses. In that moment, I knew I had fallen off the precipice into a life-altering free fall. Sorry, Marie, there would be no turning back. My life was about to become the cave I had always wanted it to be. I was in it, beautifully lost in a subterranean alternate universe, where I found myself seated at the right hand of the Mammal Messiah himself. As I scanned the documents Dillon handed me, he began speaking in excited tones about how close he was to communicating with the creature. He told me that within months he would locate Bat Boy's lost tribe, that there were other species out there to be discovered. The tingling sensation in my ears made my hearing itself seem more acute. It was as if I were hearing for the first time. Everything began to make sense. My eyes bore through Dillon's glasses. We locked eyes as I held the file close to my chest and listened intently to his spellbinding theories. I had become a disciple of the Mammal Messiah.

CHAPTER 3

THE SCHMING THING

Over an intense observational period, Dillon studied the creature intently and attempted to communicate with him in an effort to locate the rest of his race. This quest drew Dillon inward and made him less communicative to his underlings in the lab. He grew distrustful of those around him and began to guard Bat Boy zealously. His security guard, Thrush, actually bugged the cage area so that he could eavesdrop on Dillon when he went into Bat Boy's holding pen alone. On two occasions, Thrush allowed me to listen in on Dillon during one of his speech therapy sessions. Dillon was trying—unsuccessfully—to communicate with Bat Boy. The session was nothing more than a squeakfest. Dillon would start with three short squeaks followed by a long one, and Bat Boy would echo him. Dillon could get Bat Boy to parrot him, but that was all. The dialogue (if you can call it that) reminded me of the sad exchanges between a delusional parent who believes his one-and-a-half-year-old has started to talk when in reality the child merely babbles.

Dillon grew more exasperated as his attempts to deepen communication with Bat Boy met with failure. Then he located a speech therapist named Catherine Peake. Peake billed herself as the "lisp fixer." She also took pride in correcting unreconstructed Southern drawls. She spent several days attempting to "squeak it out" with Bat Boy. She lasted only three sessions before she ran out of the room red faced and vowing never to return. Many in the office believed that Bat Boy may have exposed himself to her. Others took the position that Dillon exposed himself to Peake. Thrush boasted that he knew what really went down but wouldn't cough up the information unless someone paid him two hundred bucks.

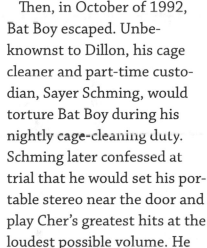

Sayer Schming

No one took Thrush up on his offer. Instead, someone leaked incriminating security camera footage of what happened when Catherine Peake left the lab that day. Misplaced conspicuously on the coffee lounge bulletin board where they would certainly be discovered, the grainy black-and-white still shots showed Peake beating Thrush back with a femur that she had dislodged from the lab's skeleton.

Lab controversies aside, Dillon went out of his way to please the creature. He ordered a diverse collection of bugs from an insect supplier. The company supplied Dillon with tons of mosquitoes and gnats and fourteen different types of flies. Mayflies and scuttle flies were Bat Boy's favorites. Dillon found out that Bat Boy, unlike most bats, liked to feast on bugs with stingers. Dillon figured the stingers gave him extra taste, the way some people like a dash of Tabasco on their food. He ordered wasps by the millions.

Then, in October of 1992, Bat Boy escaped. Unbeknownst to Dillon, his cage cleaner and part-time custodian, Sayer Schming, would torture Bat Boy during his nightly cage-cleaning duty. Schming later confessed at trial that he would set his portable stereo near the door and play Cher's greatest hits at the loudest possible volume. He would then run a spotlight into the room and fix the light on Bat Boy's eyes. The light would disorient Bat Boy. As he squinted in a futile attempt to get his bearings, Schming would prod Bat Boy mercilessly with the handle end of his mop broomstick. As Bat Boy lay collapsed in a cage corner, Schming would place the mop end of the broom on his head and don it as though it were a wig. He would then grind-dance to the pole end that dangled from near his head, mouthing the words to the Cher hit songs as he danced.

Bat Boy bore the brunt of this abuse heroically while looking to flee at the first chance he could get. Late one night when one of Dillon's assistant researchers had been careless with the dead-bolt auxiliary door, Bat Boy made his move. He was able to twist off his cage's padlock and flee the lab.

Schming was ultimately brought up on charges. At the trial, a court-appointed psychiatrist testified that Schming's beatings were administered as a sadistic release against his own failures. The jury found Schming detestable and quickly found him guilty of personal injury assault. Many people applauded the judge's decision to allow the case to be tried as a human personal injury claim rather than an animal rights abuse case.

During Schming's trial, Dillon maintained that he knew nothing of Bat Boy's abuse and he ruefully recounted how Bat Boy's ability to mask his unhappiness while in captivity should be taken as a sign of his advanced intelligence. Publicly, Dillon vowed to find the creature again. Privately, he felt crushed over the loss of his find. To those in the know, his public vow rang hol-

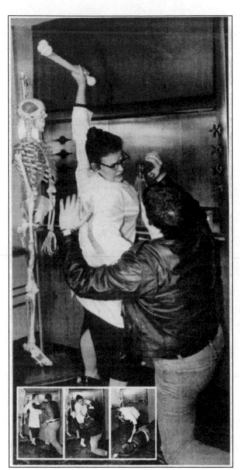

low. Everyone knew Dillon had really dropped the ball.

Dillon found reasons to fire most of the lab personnel. Somehow Thrush stayed on as head of security. When asked if his staying on had anything to do with inside information on the Catherine Peake affair, Thrush politely demurred with a smile.

Dillon got rid of me by accusing me of selling lab secrets to FEMUR—Bat Boy ranked atop their most-wanted list. Dillon was paranoid that FEMUR would locate and steal Bat Boy. Dillon was convinced that FEMUR had planned Bat Boy's escape, and he lumped me into his conspiracy theory.

When confronted by Dillon, I explained to him that I wasn't with FEMUR. I did confess that I took a payment of $2,300 from the Defense Department to conduct research on bat flight studies in order to help pay for my PhD. Bats have a hinged joint that allows them to pivot in flight on a dime and the Air Force has long tried to have someone replicate their natural flight pattern to build a new breed of super fighter jet.

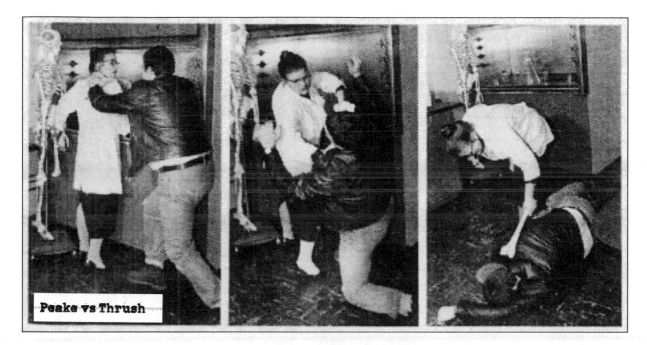

Peake vs Thrush

Dillon flew into a rage. He threatened me with having Thrush torture me to get the truth. Knowing that Thrush enjoyed torture (even to this day his Facebook profile lists waterboarding as a hobby), I fled out the side door of the lab.

Looking back at it now, I realize that Dillon had started to grasp for straws in the days following Bat Boy's escape. When I started at the lab, I divulged my Defense Department association to the compliance officer. I figured the doctor must have known about it. The witch hunt that Dillon led against lab employees provided a convenient shield from the reality that the blame for Bat Boy's escape fell squarely on his shoulders.

For the next seventeen years, Dillon and I watched from the sidelines as Bat Boy eluded subsequent would-be captors. Major media outlets, chief among them *Weekly World News*, celebrated Bat Boy's life on the run and elevated him to an American folk hero in the process. Bat Boy became our new Huck Finn. Adrift on the Big River of American culture and clad in his trademark jean shorts, Bat Boy never looked back. He was beyond reproach. To the delight of millions of Bat Boy's fans, it looked as though there was no padlock strong enough, no scientist clever enough, and no governmental agency powerful enough to capture this wily and impish new hero.

Dejected by Bat Boy's escape from Dillon's lab, I returned home to Indiana to complete my doctorate. Marie and I wound up getting married. After obtaining a PhD in mutant bat studies at the University of Indianapolis, I set out to capture the creature to study him while banging out scientific articles detailing how Bat Boy and bats would save us all. It proved a tough way to make a living.

To pay the bills, I found myself doing guest lectures, or substitute science teaching, as my ex-wife, Marie, called it, at West Virginia middle schools. Prior to each guest lecture, the words of my former PhD adviser back in Indiana would ring in my ears, "Watch yourself out there, Mr. Leed, or you'll end up teaching remedial science to a bunch of illiterates at Podunk Middle School."

At night, following the sporadic substitute-teaching assignments, I would track Bat Boy. Downhill, uphill, around hills, I sought the mutant. I crisscrossed the West Virginia mountainsides, down into the flats and back up the foothills. From Reddish Knob in the Cumberland Plateau, up to Seneca Rocks in the Monongahela National Forest, I kept searching. Between Brushy Run and Teterton, I crawled along ridgelines to conceal my body outline. My charcoal-activated layered suit masked my scent from the mutant as I searched nearly every pocket and draw of those ridged valleys. Obsessed with my hunt, there were many nights where time slipped away, leaving me no choice but to spend the night under the stars at altitude with a makeshift shale slab serving as my bed. I shunned cell phones out of fear that the mutant would home in on my frequency via echolocation and triangulate my whereabouts. My mountaintop sleepovers started to take a toll back at home. With no means to phone home, my wife, Marie, worried until she stopped worrying.

Yet, through the years and the dissolution of my marriage, I never lost hope. When we had finally saved up enough money to get divorced, I got to keep the Taurus wagon and a Snuggie-style fleece blanket from Pompanoosuc Mills. Marie, somehow, kept the condo and my collection of Japanese anime.

Enduring it all, I remained optimistic that my path would cross again soon with this unique *Wunderfledermauskind*: Bat Boy, who himself remained out in the world—too wily to hunt down like an animal, too wily to capture, even too subliterate to interview.

In the alarming frequency of Bat Boy's recent rash of attacks, I sensed my opportunity. I had reached out to Dr. Dillon and he agreed that Bat Boy must soon be captured and, in a reconciliatory gesture, the good doctor even invited me back to his lab to discuss next steps. The tone of his voice expressed a new spirit of cooperation. As he told me on the phone, "Dr. Leed, let's bury the petri dish and find my Chiropteran Tot before he kills somebody."

For all those who had made fun of my quest to find Bat Boy, my ex-wife chief among the group, it would be time to eat mosquito pie. This was my time to prove them all wrong. I was not a vampire freak; I was a scientist on the verge of groundbreaking discoveries, and I was about to begin working again with the Mammal Messiah.

CHAPTER 4

MAMMAL MESSIAH MAULED

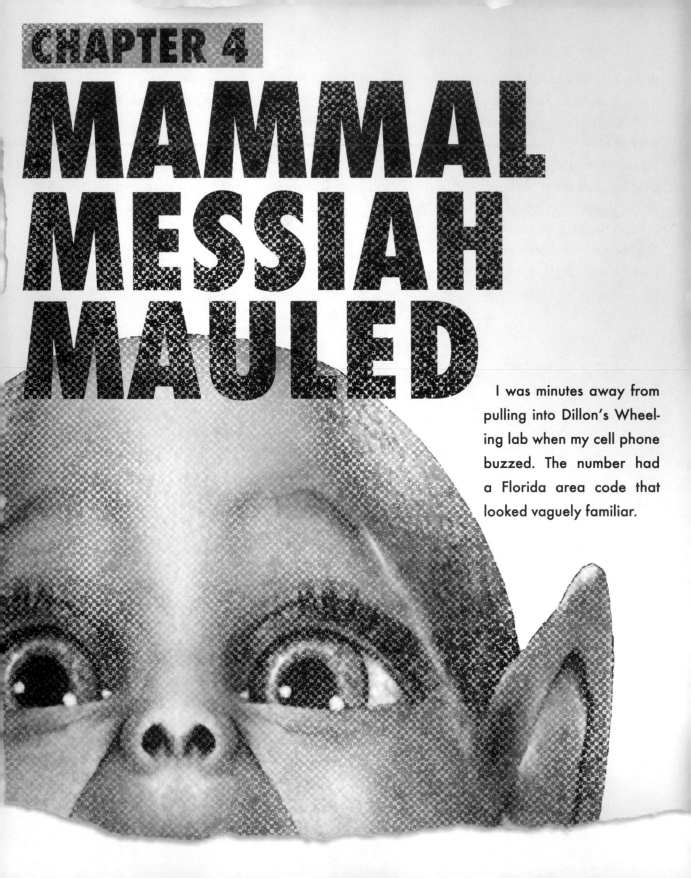

I was minutes away from pulling into Dillon's Wheeling lab when my cell phone buzzed. The number had a Florida area code that looked vaguely familiar.

"There's been another mauling," the voice blurted out before I could greet him.

"Who now?" I asked.

"You're not going to believe this: Bat Boy mauled Dillon. They don't think the doc's going to make it. I spoke to the stretcher bearers at the scene. They had never seen anything like it. Bat Boy plucked out his eyes. Left him for dead on the trail outside of the cave where Dillon first found Bat Boy."

There was only one person who would use the term "stretcher bearer." It was Nigel Potts, a British ex-pat and overzealous reporter from *Weekly World News*.

Potts spoke in a low-class British accent. I had read Potts's byline on many of the "articles" about Bat Boy that had appeared in that supermarket tabloid *Weekly World News,* which had a veritable obsession with Bat Boy.

While we had never met in person, I had spoken to Potts numerous times on the phone. Potts stood for everything I loathed. His coverage of Bat Boy was relentlessly superficial. He delighted in reporting on the most inconsequential and prurient details of Bat Boy's

Nigel Potts

habits and lifestyle—the penchant for denim shorts, the MINI Cooper joyrides, the white-trash girlfriend, the color and—I kid you not—texture of his guano. Potts and his ilk knew nothing of the sublime chemistry of mutation. They cared not one thin bat squeak about Bat Boy.

By way of example, Potts's publication had championed a national Wear Your Thong To Work Day in 2003 and had printed an official thong loincloth patch adorned with Bat Boy's likeness for participants to use as an ID card. Really.

But this gruff Britisher had sources all over the globe about Bat Boy goings-on. At the age of six, Potts had started as an ink copyboy in London's Fleet Street when Beaverbrook and his pals ruled the world. He had left the Fleet Street rat race to come down to Florida and ride out his time as a staff reporter for *Weekly World News*. In between the prurient gossipmongering, the old codger could still manage to score scoops every now and then. At sixty-nine and a half he had lost a step and didn't travel out of the office much, but he still

CENSORED

WHEN it comes time for handing out promotions this year — these hard workers won't be left behind!

BUFFY isn't the least bit uncomfortable in wearing her thong to work — because the male staffers, like Chuck & Bruno, don the business bikinis, too!

CLAUDIA models her business attire for Wear Your Thong To Work Day.

PINSTRIPED BLAZER

CENSORED

OFFICIAL Weekly World News Wear Your Thong To Work Day 2003

COTTON THONG

Cut out this official ID card and stick it on your thong!

BUSINESS SHOES

CENSORED

GIRLS and guys alike get a kick out of thongs — no butts about it!

maintained his natural journalist's intuition sharpened by all those years on Fleet Street and evidenced by his present phone call.

Our conversation continued with a deeper importance. "Barry, let me tell you what the stretcher bearer said—"

I interrupted, "You mean the ambulance guys? We call them ambulance guys or EMTs."

"Yes, the bloody gents who found Dillon on the mountain. They told me Dillon kept muttering about his transponder receiver. Apparently, there is a transponder that can track Bat Boy, and it was lost in the attack. The EMTs as you call them searched briefly for the

transponder receiver but couldn't find it. In my last phone call with Dillon a week ago, he mentioned that his transponder had started to work again. It had gone silent for fifteen years and Dillon had decided to change the batteries in the receiver and that had gotten it to work. If you can find the location of Bat Boy's cave and the trail, you can find the transponder receiver and capture Bat Boy. You need to get that transponder. Bat Boy needs to be stopped. He's left the reservation for good. I have received word that FEMUR has already scrambled to hunt him down. The Feds have put a hundred-grand bounty on his head. Well, chap, you need to capture Bat Boy before FEMUR gets him. Or we will both be out of a job. Who is your Mammal Messiah now? Not Ron Dillon. Dr. Barry Leed, you are our Mammal Messiah now. Dr. Squealgood, eternal fame awaits you."

"Nigel, thanks for the heads-up. If I know Bat Boy, he's going to go underground now. Let's stay in touch." I needed to be short with the reporter. I didn't want him meddling in my affairs at a critical juncture like this. I had reached the parking lot of Dillon's research lab. I would need to find the transponder and wondered if it could still possibly work. Dillon's files would contain the location of the cave, but I had to get them now. With Dillon out of commission, FEMUR would definitely try to grab his Bat Boy files. I wanted to get them first. I parked my Taurus wagon in the parking lot and scrambled inside.

I hadn't set foot in the lab since my brief stay in 1992, but little had changed. To avoid front desk security, I snuck in a side door that the workers regularly propped open to allow the pungent lab smells to dissipate. I headed straight in for Dillon's office. The lab workers

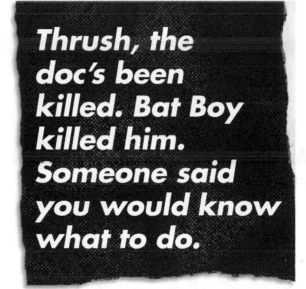

Thrush, the doc's been killed. Bat Boy killed him. Someone said you would know what to do.

were minding their petri dishes and I was able to get to the office undetected. I went to the steel file cabinet and opened the drawer marked BAT BOY FILE. I grabbed the large file folder and headed for the door. I had nearly made the side entrance when a wooden bat appeared blocking my egress.

"Not so fast, kid. Candidate Barry Leed, right? I remember you. Dr. Dillon told me to never let you back in here after he kicked you out back in '92." Thrush stuck out his face so close to mine that his mustache was centimeters away. The mustache harbored stray flecks of chewing tobacco.

Now, all these years later, I found myself on the threshold of that same side door, but this time I stood my ground. I countered Thrush, "Back off, man. I am a scientist." It didn't work. In an instant, Thrush had pulled his bowie knife on me and had it pressed against my lip. Looking down the blade I could see rust and blood. It smelled of pork brisket. Thrush broke into a broad smile that revealed yellowy teeth. As he smiled, tobacco juice cascaded over his lip, trickling south on a bumpy line toward his reconstructed jaw.

"Leed, I heard you was sub-teaching middle school somewhere. You ain't nothing but a substitute science teacher. I ought to gut you like a pig right here."

"Me and Dillon patched things up, Thrush," I said

"Well, I gotta check with the doctor."

"We're cool now. It was all a big misunderstanding. I'm on his schedule for a meeting. He texted me yesterday."

"So you two held a peace conference, did you, and never told Thrushie? I gotta check with the doctor. He's out in the field right now. You know, I never liked you, kid." Thrush pressed the blade close to my left nostril.

Just then, a lab tech rounded the corner and yelled, "Thrush, the doc's been killed. Bat Boy killed him. Someone said you would know what to do. They want you to notify next of kin. There's also some guy from FEMUR calling, asking for directions to the lab.

As soon as Thrush heard the word "FEMUR," his face registered instant concern. He turned and hustled toward the lab tech while instinctively grabbing for his gun. I ducked out the side door for the last time and ran for my car. As I started the engine, I noticed a black sedan pulling in with District of Columbia plates. Two serious men in black suits jumped out. FEMUR agents, no doubt. I had gotten Dillon's files just in time.

CHAPTER 5

CHILD ATTACKS

on your TV folks...

TRY OUT FOR

CAN

THE BAT BOY FILE

Bat Boy

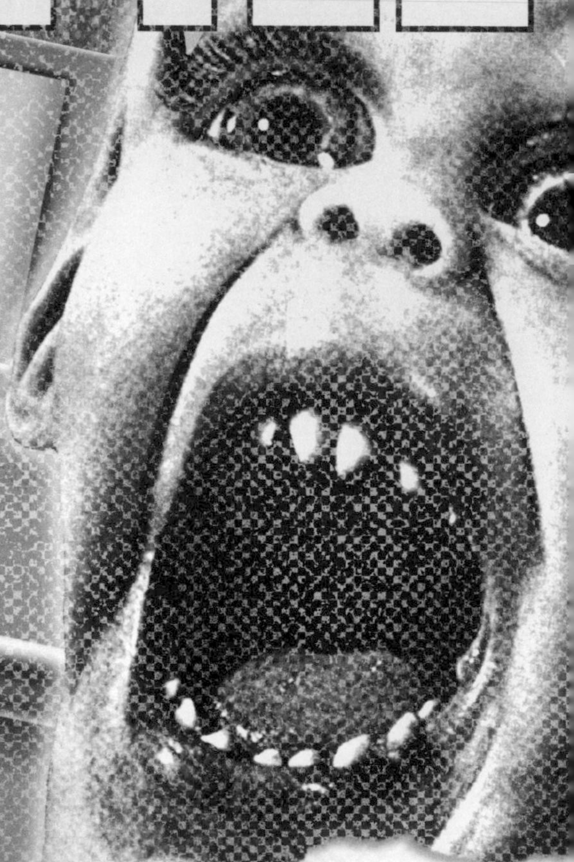

Safely away from Thrush and the chaos of Dillon's lab, I pulled my Taurus into a Denny's parking lot and opened Dillon's Bat Boy file to study it. The hunt for Bat Boy was back on again big-time. I was headed up to Bat Boy's cave and I needed to be prepared for any eventuality.

The file opened with a list of the document's contents and a time line of Bat Boy's activities.

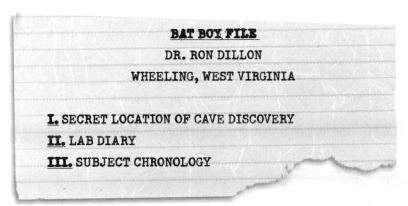

BAT BOY FILE

DR. RON DILLON

WHEELING, WEST VIRGINIA

I. SECRET LOCATION OF CAVE DISCOVERY
II. LAB DIARY
III. SUBJECT CHRONOLOGY

CAVE MAP

This was the treasure map. There was a drawing of the Seneca Rocks region with an *X* at the location of the cave where Dillon had found Bat Boy. Included with the map, Dillon had provided a line drawing cross section of the cave that outlined the various layers of geological strata present in the West Virginia topography. The surface layer began with asphalt, then a layer of basalt, followed by cobalt, then rock salt, then gestalt, then tumult, then an old catapult, then packed fish fossils followed by the underground cave.

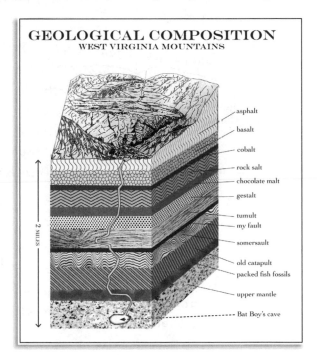

GEOLOGICAL COMPOSITION
WEST VIRGINIA MOUNTAINS

asphalt
basalt
cobalt
rock salt
chocolate malt
gestalt
tumult
my fault
somersault
old catapult
packed fish fossils
upper mantle
Bat Boy's cave

2 MILES

LAB DIARY

Dillon's first handwritten entry into the notebook coincided with the initial date of his research. Dillon had managed to keep Bat Boy in captivity for only twenty-four days, so the diary was short. The diary was written in the semilegible staccato style of a true scientist. It was a heartbreaking read. There was so much that the doctor wanted to learn and understand about this unique creature.

I studied the news articles to get a better sense of Bat Boy's activities and where he might strike next. This section of the file started with his capture but also recorded his activities after escaping.

The documents told a coming-of-age story unlike any other—a *Bitingsroman*. In short, Bat Boy went from being locked up in Dillon's

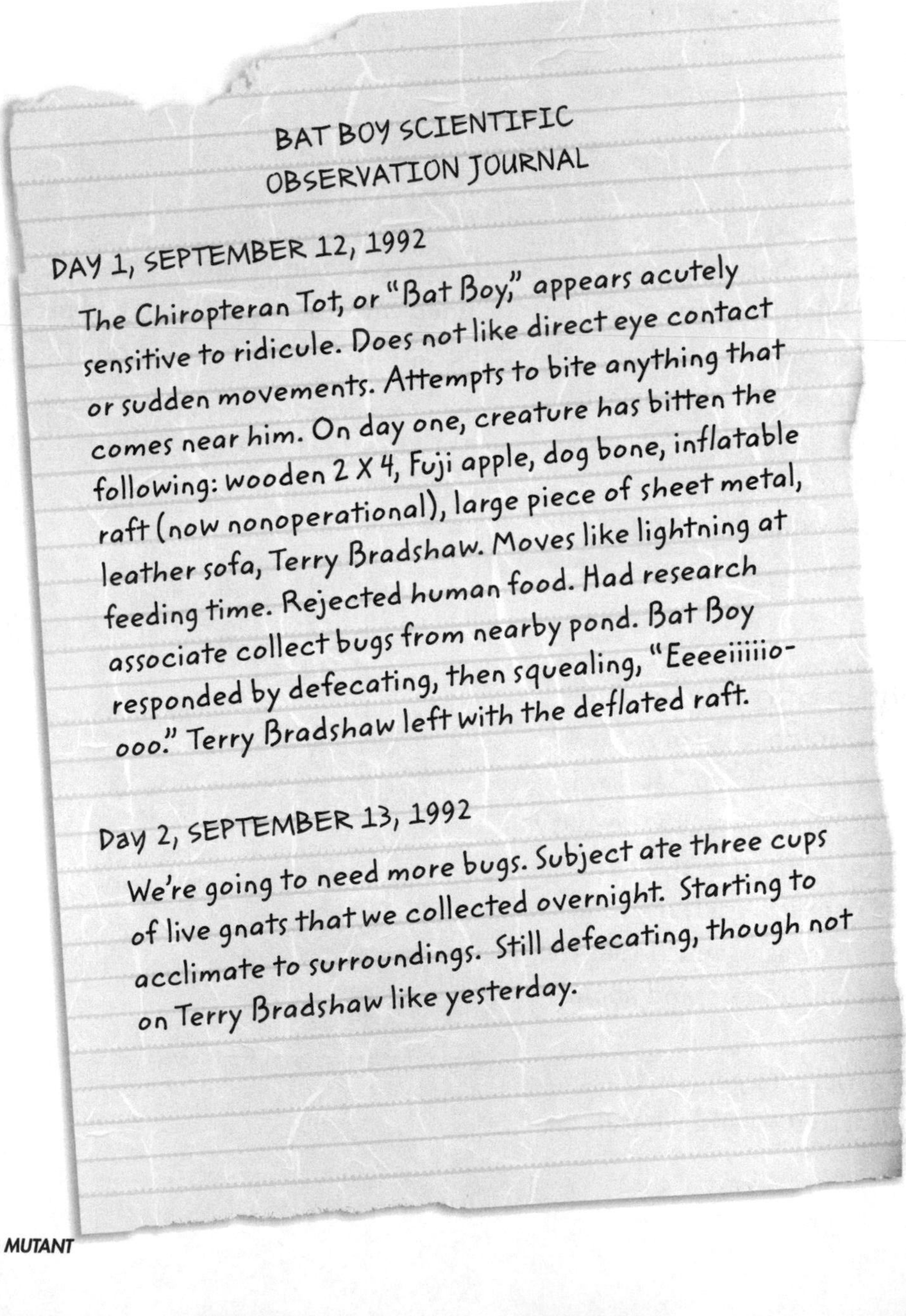

BAT BOY SCIENTIFIC
OBSERVATION JOURNAL

DAY 1, SEPTEMBER 12, 1992

The Chiropteran Tot, or "Bat Boy," appears acutely sensitive to ridicule. Does not like direct eye contact or sudden movements. Attempts to bite anything that comes near him. On day one, creature has bitten the following: wooden 2 X 4, Fuji apple, dog bone, inflatable raft (now nonoperational), large piece of sheet metal, leather sofa, Terry Bradshaw. Moves like lightning at feeding time. Rejected human food. Had research associate collect bugs from nearby pond. Bat Boy responded by defecating, then squealing, "Eeeeiiiiio-ooo." Terry Bradshaw left with the deflated raft.

Day 2, SEPTEMBER 13, 1992

We're going to need more bugs. Subject ate three cups of live gnats that we collected overnight. Starting to acclimate to surroundings. Still defecating, though not on Terry Bradshaw like yesterday.

Day 3, SEPTEMBER 14, 1992

We're going to need a lot more bugs. I called Insect Research Laboratories today. IRL tells me that bugs can be purchased in tons. I've asked for two.

Day 4, SEPTEMBER 15, 1992

Hope the bugs get here soon. The mutant is growing restless. Flung guano for the first time since the Bradshaw episode.

Day 5, SEPTEMBER 16, 1992

Bat Boy flew into a rage and attempted to escape. Now teething on a wooden 2 X 4. It won't last long—he ate the last 2 X 4. Praying for bugs soon. Have now run out of clean lab coats due to flying guano.

Day 6, SEPTEMBER 17, 1992

Bugs have not arrived. Decide to invite guard Alan Thrush to observation area to witness special Bat Boy feeding of Thrush's personal effects. Subject displays impressive gastronomic feats:

9:00 A.M. Subject eats entire edition of <u>Wheeling News Register</u> (minus sports section, which Thrush retained).

9:02 A.M. Place Thrush's poster of the film <u>Basic Instinct</u> into cage and subject devours it.

9:04 A.M. With no sign of slowing, subject proceeds to eat Thrush's Rubik's Cube washed down with six-pack of Rolling Rock long-neck beer—bottles and all.

9:15 A.M. Mutant proving he is still in form, devours Thrush's VHS <u>Basic Instinct</u> tape. Tape eaten with no difficulty, and upon swallowing the last bit of plastic tape, mutant squealed, "Eeeeiiiiooooo."

3 P.M. Subject unable to defecate. Mutant digestion appears blocked. Guano flinging has stopped. Ingested items are of no nutritional value, yet gastronomic feats of mutant are impressive.

4:30 P.M. Diane Sawyer called for exclusive. Told my assistant things are too busy right now for an interview but would consider a sit-down in exchange for 3 tons of live bugs. Sawyer promised to check with network policy department on whether something could be arranged. Sawyer also asked whether a no-bite and no-guano guarantee could be provided. I told her that Dian Fossey never provided that type of guarantee.

Day 7, SEPTEMBER 18, 1992
9 A.M. Mutant looks pale, possibly due to onset of indigestion from unconventional diet of 9/17.

12 Noon YES! Bugs arrive. Mutant satiated. Happy. Attempts to mate with life-sized Terry Bradshaw cardboard cutout.

Day 8, SEPTEMBER 19, 1992
New research assistant, Barry Leed, starts in the lab. Appears trustworthy. Will show him the Boy to see if he has any thoughts on how research should be conducted.

Day 11, SEPTEMBER 22, 1992

Working on speech training. Not going well. Brought Seeing Eye dog in to attempt communication breakthrough. Bad idea. By the time the dog got to the observation area, it was shaking uncontrollably. Upon seeing the dog, Bat Boy shrieked, the dog relieved itself, and Bat Boy threw the dog's feces at the Terry Bradshaw cardboard cutout. Subject appears to be positively devoid of any tameness. The mere sight of a domesticated animal (Seeing Eye dog, goat, ox, Seeing Eye ox) provokes Bat Boy into a rage.

Day 13, SEPTEMBER 24, 1992

This morning's sky was uncharacteristically cold and gray. Steady rain is forecast to fall for 4 straight days. The howling wind beats against the lab, rattling our windows and doors. Could it be an angry complaint against our clandestine research activity?

Day 14, SEPTEMBER 25, 1992

Bat Boy swallowed his sippy cup whole today. Pictures and sounds were played for him to gauge his tastes. Results were recorded and added to his dossier. He recoiled at the site of modern art.

Day 15, SEPTEMBER 26, 1992

Can't break through. Bat Boy shell still impervious. No sign of sippy cup in fecal output. Put Bat Boy through a series of sense, reading, math tests. Tested sight and sound. Recorded results for subject file. Thrush played his new VHS _Basic Instinct_ for him on a television. He remained calm until the interrogation scene and then required sedation.

Day 16, SEPTEMBER 27, 1992

TODAY'S CLASSROOM TOPIC: "DEVOLUTION"

Introduced Bat Boy to the concept of devolution today. BANG! A BREAKTHROUGH! Bat Boy showed genuine interest in the concept. I explained that he may have come from some kind of "genetic drift" just as easily as he may have sprung from a mutation. Then I played side A of the Devo classic album "Q: Are We Not Men? A: We Are Devo!"

I closed the session by showing him a picture of a genetically modified poultry that had been bred without feathers in order to adapt to living outside in very hot climates. The bird was commonly referred to as the featherless lizard chicken.

Bat Boy sensed a kindred spirit in the image of this genetically engineered Israeli creation. He went wild in his cage. I made a note to try to obtain a featherless lizard chicken on his behalf.
NOTE: There is a breeder in Tel Aviv that is able to ship to the U.S. via UPS.

Day 17, SEPTEMBER 28, 1992

Nothing working. Still need more bugs. Going to try group therapy to break shell.

Day 18, SEPTEMBER 29, 1992

Group therapy a disaster. Turned into scream therapy as Bat Boy shrieked loudly in protest. My ears are tender today. Wonder what decibel level causes permanent hearing damage? 120 dB? 140 dB? 160 dB?

Day 19, SEPTEMBER 30, 1992

According to NSI, permanent hearing loss can occur at 160 dB. Ears still ringing but becoming fainter. The little bastard probably registered 120 dB.

Day 20, OCTOBER 1, 1992

Damn near bit my hand off today. He's quick, powerful, and as vicious as a lion—if the lion were a genetic mutant who mated with the likeness of Terry Bradshaw.

Day 21, OCTOBER 2, 1992

There's got to be more of these creatures out there. But where are they? NOTE TO SELF: Check the rafters of Pittsburgh's Three Rivers Stadium. Mutant somehow harbors propensity for ex-quarterback.

Day 22, OCTOBER 3, 1992

Lisp fixer Catherine Peake visits.

Therapy did not go well.

Thrush sworn to secrecy.

Day 23, OCTOBER 4, 1992

The WVU Mountaineers should make the NCAA tournament again next year. First round exit to Missouri this year still stings. Score wasn't close, but junior Marsalis Basey can fill it from 3-point land. At 5' 8", nobody will draft him early, so he'll be back next year. I just wish he were 5 inches taller. Bat Boy's almost as tall as Basey.

Day 24, OCTOBER 5, 1992

ESCAPED. I CAN'T F@#$^NG BELIEVE IT. Bat Boy is gone. Janitor Sayer Schming claims to know nothing about it. It sounds suspicious. Will need to have him checked out. We never cracked his shell. Must track him down. I am very upset. I fling Bat Boy's guano at Thrush in anger.

TIME LINE

1992
September — Seneca Rocks, WV, discovery & initial capture
October — First great escape
Fall — A spate of fall attacks

1993
Tragedy in Orlando
Poolside in Vegas
Capture by FBI

1994
Escape

1995
Alive in Austin! Texas sighting

1996
On the lam — whereabouts unknown

1997
Capture by FBI (again)

1998
Dreyman discovery — a second Bat Boy

1999

Macon captivity — Georgia capture

2000

Georgia escape

Angie Wolster tragedy — Dr. Yasing takes blame

Declared dead by U.S. government

2001

Off to war

Turnpike trouble — hit by a truck

Chicago convalescence

Bounty hunter takes aim

Bites Santa Claus

2002

Missing — milk carton campaign

Surfacing in South America — on the lam
in Argentina

Jailed in Buenos Aires

Freedom & open-air Argentinean discos

Al Qaeda bounty

Great pretenders — Bat Boy
impersonators flock to streets

Bat Boy heads for NYC

2003

On the lam again

MINI Cooper theft & joyride

Off to war

2004

NASA shuttle flight — all the right stuff

Defuses dirty bomb

Endorses Gore

Meets the queen — gains knighthood

Links with Senator Kerry

Auditions for **American Idol**

Popularity rising — claims relationship
with super pop star

Cloned by U.S. Army

2005

Pop star relationship sours — appears on Freak
Finder dating service

Linked to James Carville — family tree
questioned

Joins cast of television show **Deadwood**

Fame overwhelms — plastic surgeon can make
appearance normal

lab to escaping to captured again to escaping to stealing a car to mauling a girl in Orlando to endorsing Al Gore to traveling the world to joining the military to embracing politics and working with the government first as an astronaut and then on more classified assignments. Along the way he viciously attacked numerous innocent civilians, though fortunately none of the maulings had yet proved fatal.

Throughout the document, Dillon returned to the theme of Bat Boy toughening up his shell. At numerous points in the early part of the file, the phrase was recorded: "Bat Boy's shell remains impervious." But toward the latter part of the file, it looked like Dillon had started to break through. His last cryptic entry, on October 11, read, "Group therapy finally working. Shell beginning to crack." The next day, October 12, Bat Boy escaped.

After his escape, only *Weekly World News* had managed to report on Bat Boy's whereabouts. At the time, it seemed that their editor Nigel Potts had just outmaneuvered his competitors, but as I read on it looked as though he may have had an inside source.

Dillon had faithfully preserved all of the reporting from the news. This was the most complete source of Bat Boy material I had ever seen. My own research enabled me to fill in blanks about Bat Boy that weren't covered in the file. For years, Bat Boy had found himself in and out of captivity. Gradually, I absorbed the file and linked it to what I already knew.

Bat Boy's full story began to emerge in grainy black-and-whites. In many instances it looked like photo editors may have taken liberties with images in order to marry picture to story when the photojournalist had come up empty. While that practice is commonplace today, it was more taboo then and the jury may still be out as to whether any significant laws were broken or the Mann Act was violated during this period of Bat Boy reportage beginning in the spring of 1992 and lasting through 2009 when Bat Boy's trail ran cold once more. With Dillon's file outlining the way, I could now see a most unusual time line filled with global capture, escape, and intrigue begin to take shape.

The first segment of the file contained a chronological scrapbook of Bat Boy stories. Divided by year, Dillon's meticulous file provided the most complete collection of Bat Boy reportage ever assembled.

WEEKLY WORLD NEWS

June 23, 1992   85¢/85¢ CANADA

FIRST PHOTO OF 2-FOOT-TALL CREATURE!

Boy captured by explorers 2 miles underground!

BAT CHILD FOUND IN CAVE!

HIS GIANT EYES SEE IN THE DARK & HIS EARS ARE BETTER THAN RADAR, SAY SCIENTISTS

0 71049 18259 0   25

BAT BOY FOUND

FIRST PHOTO!

CAVE two miles underground where explorers captured the amazing child.

WEEKLY WORLD
NEWS
SPECIAL EDITION!

By BILL CREIGHTON / *Weekly World News*

IN WEST VIRGINIA CAVE!

Back in the spring of 1992, one of the most amazing discoveries of all time was made in a West Virginia cave. A group of scientists found a never-before-seen creature that appeared to be half-bat — and half-human!

The strange creature had enormous amber eyes that enabled him to see in the dark and oversized ears that worked like radar.

The ongoing saga of the Bat Boy fascinated and baffled scientists all over the world. Over the years, the creature has escaped captivity at least three times. It last slipped away back in 1997 — and has not been seen since.

Dr. Ron Dillon was the first man to capture the strange cave dweller. He said the boy communicated with high-pitched squeaks and squeals and refused to eat anything but flying insects that he caught himself.

"I hardly know what to make of it," said Dr. Dillon in a 1992 interview. "The boy appears to be human but he is unlike any other human I've ever seen. His eyes are twice as big as they should be and his ears are like satellite dishes. This boy clearly belongs to a race of people who live miles beneath the Earth's surface.

"And it is my guess that they evolved bat-like features and abilities to enable them to survive in total darkness.

"There's no telling how many of these creatures are down there," he added. "This particular boy was all alone but he almost certainly strayed from a much larger tribe or pack."

Dr. Dillon and seven colleagues found the so-called bat boy during a study of subterranean life in a previously uncharted cave east of Seneca Rocks in the Shenandoah Mountains. The scientist said he and his team were approximately two miles underground when they heard the 2-foot, 19-pound creature squealing frantically in an apparent plea for help.

"We turned our lights in the direction of the cries and found the boy with his bare foot wedged in the crack between two rocks," said the expert.

"To tell you the truth, I thought I was seeing things.

"The last thing I expected to find at that great depth was another human being, much less one that looks like he came from outer space." Dr. Dillon said he freed the boy's foot and lifted him up for a closer look.

The child appeared to be stunned at first — then lashed out like an animal caught in a trap.

"I couldn't believe how strong he was," continued the expert.

"He scratched and clawed and fought like crazy.

"We finally subdued him with a tranquilizer injection.

"Then we brought him to the surface and took him to a private hospital for testing and observation."

Dr. Dillon said the Bat Boy appeared to be 3 or 4 years old and adapted to life in captivity quicker than expected.

He began gaining weight when scientists stopped giving him human foods — and began to flood his room with bugs.

"We get them from laboratories involved in insect research and release them into his room by the millions," said Dr. Dillon.

"He managed to consume his own weight in bugs every single day by locating their position with his radar-like ears and catching them with his mouth and hands.

"Needless to say, he is extremely active. When it's time to feed he moves like lightning."

Dr. Dillon has always refused to pinpoint the location of the cave where the boy was found.

Dr. Ron Dillon

BIZARRE Bat Boy, left, stood 2 feet tall and weighed a mere 19 pounds! Scientists estimated the creature to be 3 to 4 years of age.

THERE MAY BE THOUSANDS MORE JUST LIKE HIM, SAYS SCIENTIST

SEPTEMBER: BAT BOY FOUND, SENECA ROCKS, WEST VIRGINIA

Dr. Ron Dillon finds Bat Boy in a cave in September 1992. I joined his research team shortly after his discovery.

Then in October, Bat Boy escaped.

Coast-to-coast manhunt for cave boy captured just weeks ago!

NEWS BAT CHILD FOUND IN CAVE!

Boy captured by explorer 2 miles underground!

BAT CHILD ESCAPES!

He's 2-feet-tall and VERY DANGEROUS, warn police

BAT BOY ESCAPES!

A half-human "bat boy" that was captured in West Virginia last spring has escaped from the research facility where he was taken for observation — and is still running free!

Zoologist Ron Dillon said the 2-foot, 19-pound creature was last seen in downtown Wheeling, on September 10. In spite of his small size, the boy has razor-sharp teeth, the strength of an ape and should be considered extremely dangerous, the expert said.

By DACK KENNEDY
Correspondent

"This is a tragedy beyond measure," continued Dr. Dillon, who has been studying the bat boy since his capture last May.

"This little creature is quick, powerful, and as much as I hate to say it, as vicious as a lion in the wild. If he feels his life is threatened, he will lash out without fear of consequences.

"We mustn't forget that this child evolved as a cave dweller and knows nothing about our society and civilization.

"I hope and pray that we are able to capture him before anybody gets hurt."

As *Weekly World News* and other major media reported earlier this year, Dillon and his research team found the bat boy while studying subterranean life-forms in a cave near Seneca Rocks in the Shenandoah Mountains.

The experts subdued the creature with a tranquilizer injection and took him to a private facility in Wheeling to continue their observations.

At the time it was reported that the boy had large amber eyes that allow him to see in the dark and oversize ears that work like radar.

It was also noted that the boy, who appears to be three or four years old, consumed his weight in live insects every day.

"As time went on we determined that the boy possesses an intelligence rivaling that of the smartest chimps and apes," said Dillon.

"We felt like we were on the verge of learning how to communicate with him when he twisted the heavy steel padlock off his holding cell and escaped. The bat boy was last seen heading south and there's no telling where he will turn up next," continued the expert.

"He moves so quickly that I wouldn't be surprised if he was in Virginia or Kentucky by now."

Dillon refused to speculate on what might have caused the boy to flee the facility and flatly denied rumors that a drunk custodian beat the creature the night before he escaped.

The expert went on to say that he and his research team set traps in and around the mountain cave where the boy was originally captured.

But at this late date, it's highly unlikely that he can or will return to it.

Dillon said that he has warned authorities across the country to be on the lookout for the creature.

Given enough time, he explained, the bat child could turn up anywhere in the United States.

"Our task is all the more difficult because the bat boy moves by night and sleeps by day," said Dillon.

"It's a little like trying to spot a shadow on a cloudy, moonless night.

"The harder you look the less you see. That's what we're up against."

Opinion columnists were angered by his escape. Noted columnist Ed Anger blamed the U.S. government. Bat Boy headed south after his escape from the lab. He made his way to Charlotte, North Carolina, and flirted with living there permanently. After a brief period in Charlotte, he drifted back to West Virginia. He was captured again and then escaped again.

SPOT THE BAT BOY

If you spot the bat boy, *Weekly World News* wants to know about it. Drop us a line describing when and where you saw him, what he was doing and the direction he was traveling. By drawing on the resources of millions of devoted readers, *The NEWS* can help authorities recapture this dangerous creature before anybody gets hurt. Write to Bat Boy, Weekly World News, 600 South East Coast Ave., Lantana, Fla. 33462.

U.S. govt. to blame for letting Bat Boy escape!

I'm madder than my bull terrier at a cat show over the Weekly World News front-page story this week.

Just how in the hell do you let something as dangerous as this "bat boy" escape from a high security research facility? I'll tell you how — the U.S. government must be running it.

Our late, great President Harry S Truman must be twirling in his grave at the bumbling idiots our once-proud security forces have become.

The CIA, FBI and Secret Service aren't worth a hill of beans between them anymore.

Once those commie cockroaches got stomped on in Russia, our national defense forces went straight to hell, folks.

Nothing to worry about anymore, right?

Big-time wrong, my friends.

Now we've got this "bat boy" on the loose and the bleeding-heart liberals are already coming out of the woodwork.

"We mustn't forget that this child evolved as a cave dweller and knows nothing about our society and civilization.

"I hope and pray that we are able to capture him before anybody gets hurt," sniffed Dr. Ron Dillon.

This Dillon dingbat is the egghead who was

MY AMERICA
By ED ANGER

in charge of studying this little devil when he escaped near Wheeling, W. Va.

What Dr. Dillon doesn't tell you is that this two-foot tall demon has teeth like Gillette razor blades and a tongue like a Brillo Pad.

He's got eyes the size of ping-pong balls that let him find you in the dark and a set of ears as big as a small catcher's mitt. That's so he can hear his prey running up to a mile away.

My sources in the Pentagon tell me the danger is REAL, folks.

Now Dr. Dillon would have us believe that this creature, found deep in a West Virginia

READERS are warned to be on the lookout for a half-human bat boy that escaped from a West Virginia research facility. See page 5 for full details.

cave last May, eats about 20 lbs. of insects a day. Baloney! Look at the kid. If he runs out of bugs, miniature poodles start to look awfully tasty.

What's next on the little fiend's menu — humans? You betcha!

The scientists who were studying this "bat boy" when he made a run for it, swear he isn't one IQ point smarter than a chimp.

Believe that and I've got a bridge to sell you. You can look at this thing and tell he's no dummy.

And if he's so stupid, why have authorities from coast-to-coast and particularly in West Virginia, Virginia, Kentucky, Tennessee, North Carolina, Ohio, and Pennsylvania been warned to be on the lookout for the thing?

I'll tell you why — he's mean as the dickens and he ain't stupid. He may be the biggest threat to the U.S. since Hurricane Andrew. I'm going to keep my eyes peeled for this bat brat.

I suggest you do the same.

ATTACKS: BOSTON TO BAKERSFIELD

Throughout the remainder of 1992, Bat Boy was spotted in numerous locations and was under investigation for several attacks. Dillon followed the sightings religiously and tried to discern a pattern in Bat Boy's movements. He had typed up the facts to document each occurrence. Each attack held a number of clues to changes in Bat Boy's behavior. Dillon believed that if he could predict Bat Boy's behavioral modification from life on the lam, it would bring him closer to recapturing him.

Dillon remarked in a newspaper article, "It's clear (based on these sightings) that Bat Boy's behavior is changing as a result of his experiences on the lam. He's switching his diet from insects to raw meat, attacking cats, dogs, and other small animals when he's hungry. He's no longer looking for a sleeping place in the dark, enclosed areas during the day. Instead, he hangs from trees or eaves of buildings. He's taken to raiding Dumpsters and garbage cans to get enough to eat. If this keeps up, we may be able to set baited traps for him."

In this part of the file, Dillon had drawn a bat trap and illustrated how it would work. Dillon also recorded all of the case studies related to confirmed sightings of the latter part of 1992.

Herbert DeVillers, 29

SIGHTING CASE FILE: SOUTHBOUND I-95
DATE: 10/6/92
LOCATION: Columbia, SC — Interstate 95
TIME: 3 P.M.
WITNESS: Herbert DeVillers
GENDER: Male
AGE: 29
REMARKS: Witness traveling southbound I-95 from Richmond, VA, to Jacksonville, FL. Witness was in right-hand lane when 18-wheeler semitruck moved up behind him looking to pass. Checking rearview mirror, witness noticed unusual figure clinging to the grille of the truck. Creature had his head bent back and was snapping at insects in midair.

ATTACK CASE FILE: THE CRIST ATTACK
DATE: 10/8/92
LOCATION: Sarasota, FL — Crist Residence
TIME: 6 P.M.
WITNESS: Andy Crist
GENDER: Male
AGE: 47
REMARKS: Witness's dog became agitated by something in his backyard. The dog led the witness to a tree containing Bat Boy on an upper branch. Victim reached out to grab Bat Boy and was severely mauled. Victim's two hands were bitten clear to the bone. Victim later reported that Bat Boy's teeth were like tiny daggers.

Trisha O'Bannon, 17

SIGHTING CASE FILE: THE O'BANNON TREE
DATE: 10/12/92
LOCATION: Austin, TX — Capitol Park vicinity
TIME: 8:30 A.M.
WITNESS: Trisha O'Bannon
GENDER: Female
AGE: 17
REMARKS: Witness saw Bat Boy resting in a tree. Left scene to secure means to capture Bat Boy. Returned with an old net. Made a casting movement and missed. Creature was alerted and fled.
NOTE: Sleeping mode.

SIGHTING CASE FILE: PUEBLO GARBAGE RAID
DATE: 10/19/92
LOCATION: Pueblo, CO
TIME: 7 P.M.
WITNESS: Margo Freeman
GENDER: Female
AGE: 46
WITNESS STATEMENT: "I was doing a few dishes in the sink when I heard the garbage can lid hit the concrete out back. Another raccoon looking for a snack, I thought. But it was no raccoon. It was no animal I'd ever seen before. The beast was about 2 feet high with fiery-looking eyes, oversize ears and long, fanglike teeth."

Margo Freeman, 46

Michelle Feller, 33

ATTACK CASE FILE: PICKLES THE CAT
DATE: 10/28/92
LOCATION: Ely, NV
TIME: 6 P.M.
WITNESS: Michelle Feller
GENDER: Female
AGE: 33
WITNESS STATEMENT: "I had gone outside to call Pickles, when I saw what appeared to be a small boy standing behind my car parked in the driveway. Fortunately, he didn't see me. It was the most frightening experience of my life. I stood in the shadows frozen with fear watching that terrible creature lift up the car with one hand, grab my helpless cat by the neck, and eat him."

SIGHTING CASE FILE: "BOLTON'S LANDING"
DATE: 10/31/92
LOCATION: Bella Vista, CA
TIME: 10:30 P.M.
WITNESS: Tom Bolton
GENDER: Male
AGE: 50
REMARKS: Witness driving Ford pickup truck on local road stated, "The road was dark and I wasn't paying much attention to anything when—boom!—something that looked like a kid with big orange eyes jumped in front of my truck. I slammed on the brakes and swerved to the right, but I never had a chance. I heard the crunch of flesh hitting metal. I had this sick feeling that I had hit a child. I skidded to a stop and jumped out of the truck hoping against hope that my imagination was playing tricks. I turned the body over to see how badly he was hurt. A split second later his eyes popped open and he started screaming. Then he leaped to his feet and took off like a shot. He was heading north."

Tom Bolton, 50

SIGHTING CASE FILE: CLOSE DUMPSTER ENCOUNTER
DATE: 11/2/92
LOCATION: Portland, OR — Caldwell's Restaurant
WITNESS: Byron Caldwell
GENDER: Male
AGE: 31
REMARKS: Restaurant owner was alerted by dishwasher who had heard loud noises coming from the alley by the Dumpster. Witness took a flashlight out back and reported, "When I looked inside the Dumpster, I just about jumped out of my skin. My flashlight showed me all I wanted to see—huge flashing eyes, pointed ears, and the scariest fangs you can imagine. But I guess I frightened him as much as he frightened me because he went bananas and started hissing and thrashing around in the Dumpster like a wild animal. I guess he didn't like me staring at him. Before I knew it, he was pelting me with garbage. I tried to duck, but in seconds I was covered from head to foot in stinking chunks of uneaten meat and other slop. The Bat Boy's tantrum lasted only a few seconds then he leaped from the Dumpster and vanished in the shadows.
NOTE: Another garbage encounter.

Byron Caldwell, 31

Loren Moller, 26

SIGHTING CASE FILE: HOLD THE ANCHOVIES
DATE: 11/5/92
LOCATION: Seattle, WA
WITNESS: Loren Moller
GENDER: Male
AGE: 26
WITNESS STATEMENT: "I was sitting on my patio eating a pizza and drinking a beer when I heard scratching in the bushes. What I saw froze my blood. My first thought was, 'My God! It's Dracula.' It was Bat Boy. I could actually smell his breath. I had read stories about him. How he was captured and escaped and how he could be dangerous if he felt threatened. But let me tell you, there was no way I was going to threaten that creature. He stood there staring at the piece of pizza I was holding. His eyes were as round as saucers. I figured he might be hungry so I threw a slice to him. He grabbed it right out of the air and disappeared behind the bushes. I discovered the next morning he'd spit out the anchovies."

BAT BOY

* INTERESTING—Seems to have aversion to anchovies. This could be his kryptonite. I wish I had discovered this in the lab. Could have used anchovies for Bat Boy behavior control.

In another margin, Dillon was prescient enough to understand that the rash of sightings and attacks in the closing months of 1992 would have alerted the government. In the margin before the close of the 1992 file, he wrote:

Wonder if FEMUR is on him now? If so, I will need to find him first.

By 1993, Bat Boy had moved farther afield. In March, tragedy struck. Bat Boy mauled a girl 10 years of age in an Orlando, Florida, city park. Tourist Basil Furch filmed the mauling of a terrified fifth grader by the name of Amy Mikelly. *Weekly World News* obtained the film and scored the story. Furch, the 22-year-old cameraman, recounted what happened to *Weekly World News* reporter Joe Berger: "I was shooting pictures in the park when all of a sudden this weird little thing leaped out of a tree with a shriek and grabbed that poor girl before she knew what hit her."

Berger reported the shaken girl was in good condition at a nearby hospital, where doctors treated her for puncture wounds in her right hand, arm, and shoulder.

Fortunately, Ms. Mikelly pulled through. Dillon was hardly surprised by this turn of events. He wrote in the margin of the Bat Boy file:

Inevitable. I saw this coming.

Following the Orlando mauling, Bat Boy was

Tourist snaps bloodcurdling photo in city park

'I thought he was going to bite my arm off,' says terrified youngster

By JOE BERGER / Staff writer

BAT BOY ATTACKS GIRL, 10!

Terrified fifth-grader Amy Mikelly was attacked in an Orlando, Fla., park and nearly ripped to shreds — by the bizarre, big-eyed bat boy who escaped from a top-secret research lab last September!

And incredibly, a photographer captured the heart-stopping encounter on film — at the very moment the bloodcurdling creature first sank his fangs into Amy's arm.

"I was shooting pictures in the park when all of a sudden this weird little thing leaped out of a tree with a shriek and grabbed that poor girl before she knew what hit her," said still-trembling tourist Basil Furch, 22.

"I snapped a picture and then I thought, 'My God, I've got to help her!'

"So I grabbed the only weapon I could find, a trash can, and charged at the thing yelling and screaming.

"By this time he'd bitten all up and down her arm and I was afraid he was about to go for the jugular.

"But when he saw me coming, he let out another shriek and ran off through the park."

Shaken Amy, 10, was reported in good condition at a nearby hospital, where doctors treated her for puncture wounds to her right hand, arm and shoulder.

"He was very mad," the scared schoolgirl later told reporters. "I thought he was going to bite my arm off."

The hair-raising tale began three months earlier when the bug-gobbling bat boy — captured last summer in a West Virginia cave — escaped from a science lab in Wheeling.

Since then, stunned citizens from Boston to Bakersfield have spotted the elusive fugitive — and several have been attacked by the tiny terror.

"The bat boy is just 2 feet tall, but he's very powerful, very fast and very dangerous," a scientist said. "He'll become aggressive — and has become aggressive — anytime he feels threatened."

But this is the first time the half-pint hellion has been photographed in mid-attack — and anguished Amy says the snapshot still sends chills up her spine.

"That picture reminds me of how fast that thing got me," said the horrified fifth-grader. "I was just sitting there in the park doing homework when I saw him way up in a tree, and I flipped a rock at him to make him move.

"I'd never heard of any bat boy or anything, but all of a sudden he made this terrible scream and came down on top of me and started biting me all over with his teeth.

"I was hitting him as hard as I could on the back of the head but he wouldn't go away till a man chased him away with a garbage can, and by then I was hurt real bad."

But freckle-faced Amy insists she learned a valuable lesson.

"From now on I won't never throw a rock at anything unless I'm sure it's not a bat boy," she vowed.

NEWS **BAT CHILD ESCAPES!**

A COAST-TO-COAST hunt for the bizarre bat child was launched after the creature escaped from a Wheeling, W. Va., science lab.

'Come in with a hickey & you're fired,' workers told

Showing up for work with a hickey on your neck can get you more than funny looks — it can get you fired!

Three medical clinics in California's Imperial Valley have warned employees they could get the ax the next time they come in sporting a love bite.

The bizarre policy was adopted after patients complained they felt uncomfortable visiting the clinics because they employ so many hickey-prone workers.

"If it were occasional or once in a while and they were covered up, it may have been different," said personnel manager Diana Tamez.

"What you do after hours is your business, but we have a dress code and a standard of professionalism that we'd like to up...

NEW VEGGIE

A scientist says he's grown the world's first "turnato," a cross between a turnip and a potato.

It tastes like a bitter potato and has a faint yellow tinge, says Herman Mann of Boon.

HOW WE GOT THE PICTURE

TOURIST Basil Furch, left, was shooting pictures in the park when the bat boy attacked. "I snapped a picture and then I thought, 'My God, I've got to help her!'"

"THAT'S HIM!" Riccardi with "Bat Boy Wanted" poster.

WANTED

on the lam for nearly four months, until he was captured in Las Vegas in July by a local businessman named Eric Riccardi. Riccardi, twenty-eight at the time, had just come home from work and noticed something unusual in his pool floating on an old raft.

According to *Weekly World News* staff reporter Jack Alexander, Riccardi harbored the fugitive in his garage, where he fed him an unappetizing diet of Spam and table scraps.

Dillon flew to Las Vegas to recapture Bat Boy but narrowly missed him. He saved his plane ticket and wrote that he lost $450 playing slots, too.

At this point, the U.S. government had no choice but to intercede. A massive coast-to-coast manhunt was mounted.

The stepped-up manhunt efforts worked. Within two months, the FBI captured Bat Boy in late August. *Weekly World News* special correspondent Conrad Morse broke the story.

Many felt that he would be sent down the river for a long period of time. Others questioned the legality of his detainment. He was being held without charges. The government shrewdly argued that habeas corpus rights were not being violated since it could not be proved that Bat Boy was fully human. Also, he had no formal ID, so they couldn't book him properly, either.

Shortly after the 1993 FBI capture, Bat Boy escaped again and was on the run for several years. Sightings became less frequent.

Bat Boy fans flooded the government with letters demanding Bat Boy be set free. Bat Boy fans also flooded the office of the secretary of the Department of Housing and Urban Development. With the onslaught of letters, protest marches, and the burning of several HUD buildings, officials decided late in 1999 to allow Bat Boy limited human contact under strict governmental supervision. It was a decision they would soon regret.

On September 19, in an incident that was eerily similar to the infamous Orlando attack of 1993, Bat Boy lashed out at a nine-year-old girl named Angie Wolster. The attack occurred while Bat Boy was on a supervised release from a lab in Macon.

This time Dr. Mark Yasing, an anthropologist with close ties to the U.S. government, would take the blame.

By late 2000, the U.S. government claimed that Bat Boy was dead and that his body was being cryogenically preserved.

On July 14, Bat Boy was hit by a truck in Illinois. Despite the pain, Bat Boy recovered peacefully in a local hospital, receiving letters of get-well wishes from his fans. This recovery period marked a brief but happy time for Bat Boy, though he never celebrated Bastille Day again. Dillon referred to this period in his journal as the "Chicago convalescence."

In October, a noted bounty hunter joined the hunt for Bat Boy and made a chilling vow: "I'm going to bring Bat Boy down with one clean shot to the head. Then I'm gonna have him stuffed and mounted over my fireplace."

The macho Baton Rouge–based gunslinger made the boastful pronouncement after federal law enforcement officials failed to capture Bat Boy as he entered the Union Square Theater in New York City to see the eponymous musical loosely based on his life.

TV reports stating that Bat Boy had recently been seen in Louisiana sparked widespread panic. Slubbard was paid by a group of wealthy Louisiana businessmen concerned with public safety and tourism. He told reporters, "I'm not

Nevada businessman's SHOCKING revelation: 'I'VE CAPTURED BAT BOY!'

By JACK ALEXANDER
Staff writer

A Las Vegas businessman says he has captured the elusive and extremely dangerous Bat Boy and is holding the frightening creature in his garage.

"I found Bat Boy asleep floating on a plastic raft in my pool," said Eric Riccardi, manager of a direct mailing company in Las Vegas.

"With the help of my roommate Don McCowan, I scooped him out of the water with my pool net and locked him in my garage."

Zoologist Ron Dillon had issued a nationwide alert through *Weekly World News* last October when the vicious 2-foot, 19-pound monster escaped from a research center in Wheeling, W. Va.

Dr. Dillon and his research team had found and subdued Bat Boy with a tranquilizer while studying subterranean life-forms in a cave in the Shenandoah Mountains.

Despite his size, the half-human, half-bat boy has razor-sharp teeth and the strength of an ape. "His amber eyes are large, enabling him to see in the dark. His oversize ears work like radar," Dr. Dillon explained.

"He is quick, powerful and as vicious as a lion. I hope and pray we are able to recapture him before anyone gets hurt."

Riccardi, 28, thought the Bat Boy story was a hoax until he discovered him in the pool.

"I was going to call the police, but I didn't think they would be-

Eric Riccardi

Creature trapped in garage — & is living on Spam and table scraps!

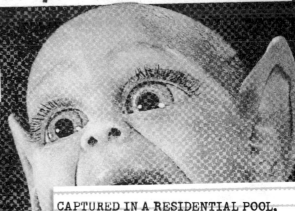

LETTER sent to *The NEWS* told of Bat Boy's capture!

lieve me," Riccardi said. "I figured Bat Boy would be comfortable in the garage because there are no windows.

"He was very lethargic at first, but started screeching from dusk to dawn. It was a chilling, scary screech. — like a bat, multiplied about 100 times. I slip food under the garage door to him once a day. He eats mostly table scraps and bugs, but he's starting to like the same food my roommate and I eat. He is especially fond of Spam and applesauce."

Riccardi believes the Bat Boy "is as much afraid of us as we are of him" and "is terrified when my dog barks — and I'm glad he is!"

"I used my neighbor's lawnmower last week because mine is in the garage. I am NOT about to go in there and get it," Riccardi said.

Dr. Dillon said he'll fly to Las Vegas within the week to take Bat Boy off Riccardi's hands.

"We underestimated the creature last time. We are going to take extra measures to make sure he doesn't escape again," Dr. Dillon said.

CAPTURED IN A RESIDENTIAL POOL, LAS VEGAS

"THAT'S HIM!" Riccardi with "Bat Boy Wanted" poster.

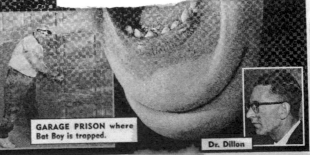

GARAGE PRISON where Bat Boy is trapped.

Dr. Dillon

WEEKLY WORLD NEWS July 20, 1993

29

ESCAPED BAT BOY SIGHTED IN TEXAS!

FBI conducting secret manhunt!

GLOBAL NEWS SERVICE

A half human "bat boy" that escaped from a research facility in Wheeling, W. Va., back in 1992 has turned up in Austin, Texas, for the second time in two years, alarming federal officials who consider the creature to be totally unpredictable — and dangerous!

The feds aren't talking to avoid public panic. But FBI sources say that an ongoing nationwide search for the bat boy has heated up since 19-year-old Trisha O'Bannon spotted him in a public park on March 17.

Oddly enough, Miss O'Bannon also spotted the creature in the fall of 1992. And while authorities initially thought the young woman might have been lying about her second encounter, they are now convinced she is telling the truth.

At the request of officials, Miss O'Bannon has denied all interview requests. But as one source put it: "For the first time in two years, we have a solid lead.

"If we don't capture this bat boy now, we never will."

As Weekly World News and other major media reported previously, the bat boy was captured in a West Virginia cave on Sept. 10, 1992.

The 2-foot, 65-pound creature escaped from a research facility a few weeks later, sparking a nationwide manhunt that continues to this day.

WANTED: BAT BOY, left, was last seen in an Austin, Texas, park. The half-human is considered unpredictable and dangerous.

Authorities confirm Austin teen's second encounter with 2-foot-tall cave creature!

NO DOUBTS: Trisha O'Bannon is shown here holding an Oct. 8, 1992 issue of Weekly World News.

1995

Then on April 11, Bat Boy was spotted again by Trisha O'Bannon. O'Bannon had previously sighted Bat Boy in Texas in the fall of 1992. Her account of the ordeal was harrowing.

NEW JERSEY LOVEBIRDS GETTING MARRIED — THANKS TO ELVIS AND BAT BOY

WEST ORANGE, N.J. — Lovebirds Michael Calabria and Maria Sapaia are engaged and looking forward to a long, happy marriage — and they owe it all to *Weekly World News* T-shirts!

By TANYA BRODER
Weekly World News

"I'd gone down to the beach wearing my Bat Boy shirt," said happy Michael. "When I saw this really good-looking girl wearing a *Weekly World News* shirt with Elvis on it, I decided to go up and talk to her. It was Maria."

One thing led to another and the attractive couple quickly started dating seriously.

"We got along real well from the very beginning," Maria said.

"We had a lot in common but if we hadn't both had our T-shirts on when we did, we probably never would have met."

When Michael decided to ask Maria to marry him, he wanted to continue the *Weekly World News* tradition.

"I ask her to pose with me with us both wearing Bat Boy shirts," crafty Michael said. "I told her I was going to send the pictures in to the paper as part of a contest.

"But it was all a setup and halfway through the photo session I acted like I had stepped on something," he said. "When I reached down to see what it was, it turned out to be her engagement ring."

Surprised Maria joyfully accepted Michael's proposal.

"It was cute and romantic that he proposed to me in *Weekly World News* T-shirts," she said. "Those crazy shirts have a special meaning for us — they helped us find true love."

The couple is planning a June wedding.

HAPPY COUPLE Michael Calabria and Maria Sapaia are looking forward to their wedding day. The New Jersey lovebirds say they owe it all to their *Weekly World News* T-shirts.

PHOTO: Debbie DiPeso

FBI CAPTURES BAT BOY

WEEKLY WORLD

NEWS

August 31, 1993

Creature stranded on rooftop by Mississippi flood!

FBI CAPTURES BAT CHILD!

Daring agents end boy's 27-state reign of terror!

FBI CAPTURES BAT BOY!

2-foot-tall creature rescued from Mississippi flood!

By CONRAD MORSE
Special correspondent

A massive coast-to-coast manhunt for a half-human bat boy came to a dramatic and shocking end along the banks of the rain-swollen Mississippi River as heavily armed FBI agents cornered the creature on the roof of a flooded farmhouse in eastern Missouri!

The capture of the 2-foot, 19-pound bat boy capped an 18-month manhunt that began when the creature escaped from a research facility in West Virginia and began eluding FBI agents who were determined to remain heavily sedated and incarcerated.

"This little bat boy isn't a criminal in the usual sense of the word but the FBI can't afford to take any chances," said zoologist Dr. Ron Dillon, who first discovered the creature in a cave near Seneca Rocks, W. Va., in the spring of 1992, told reporters at a news conference in Washington, D.C.

"In spite of his small size, the bat boy is as strong as a champ, has razor-sharp teeth and can be extremely dangerous when provoked."

After his initial capture and escape last September, the expert pointed out, the bat boy — human rights by holding him without cause," attacked six innocent people that we know of, the bat boy had eluded the FBI for almost 18 weeks before his initial escape and I can't in good conscience say that he is human.

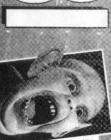

BAT BOY behind bars! FBI agents cornered the half-human creature on a farmhouse roof and brought him to a secret location in Washington, D.C.

It is believed that the farmhouse was located east of Moscow Mills, Mo., near the banks of the river, when what interrupted into the rising flood waters and climbed to the roof of the farmhouse to keep from drowning," said the zoologist. "Somebody spotted him and tipped us off, which is why special agents to capture him were sent as late as July, a las stands in no less than 17 states. As late as July, a Las Vegas casino made his way to Missouri in time to be trapped by the flood.

Then, as now, the zoologist contends that the bat boy is a ferocious creature that has lived underground for thousands of years.

"The FBI is keeping the bat boy under wraps at this point but down the road he'll have to turn the creature over to a research facility where scientists can find out who — and what — he is," Dr. Dillon said.

FBI AGENTS are shown on the roof of the farmhouse where the half-human bat boy was apprehended.

FBI spokesmen declined to comment on Dr. Dillon's report and would neither confirm nor deny reports that the bat boy is being held just two miles from the White House in the nation's capital.

The expert himself refused to pinpoint where the creature was captured, but confirmed him on the banks of the Mississippi River on July 27.

"They subdued him with a tranquilizer dart and trapped him in a steel-mesh net to get him out of the flood and back to Washington."

"In spite of his weakened condition, I'm told that the bat boy put up a fight and other major media have previously reported, Dr. Dillon discovered the bat boy during a study of subterranean life forms in a West Virginia cave in what — he is." Dr. Dillon said.

7 48 INSIDE: This week's 6 LUCKIEST lottery numbers!

WEEKLY WORLD NEWS®

September 16, 1997 · $1.25 U.S. · $1.39 CANADA/70p U.K.

SECRET FBI PHOTO!

BAT BOY CAPTURED

INSIDE:

- Nationwide hunt ends after five years!
- Bizarre creature whisked to secret lab!
- Government agents injured during scuffle!

OLIVE OIL & GARLIC CURES:

- HEART DISEASE
- HIGH BLOOD PRESSURE
- IMPOTENCE
- ARTHRITIS
- CANCER
- COLDS

& MUCH, MUCH MORE!

Shocking plan to clone Jesus from Shroud of Turin!

EDIT INSTA

Bizarre creature has been on the run since 1992!

BAT BOY CAPTURED!

By JOE BERGER / Weekly World News

Copyright © 1997 Weekly World News

CHARLOTTE, N.C. — The bizarre, bug-gobbling Bat Boy who's been on the run since he escaped from a West Virginia research facility in 1992 has been recaptured — and excited scientists say they may finally be able to unravel the mystery of the tiny terror's origins!

Federal agents corralled the bloodcurdling creature in a wooded area northeast of here after more than two months of reported sightings in and around Charlotte. But Bat Boy did not go down without a fight.

"The thing bit two of the agents real bad on the arm, and he bit off one guy's finger and ate it," said rattled camper Rudy Winscel, 33, who witnessed the hair-raising confrontation. "He was terrified — and more ferocious than just about anything I've ever seen in the wilds."

The sawed-off escapee — now nearly three feet tall and weighing about 40 pounds — was finally subdued with the aid of a tiny tranquilizer dart and was whisked away to the top-secret laboratory from which he escaped in September 1992.

"This time we'll all take extra security precautions to make sure the little fellow doesn't get away from us again," said concerned zoologist Dr. Ron Dillon, who originally discovered the big-eyed

ON THE RUN: Bat Boy tore the heavy steel padlock off the door to his holding cell and escaped in 1992. The manhunt had focused on Charlotte, N.C., since early July.

'He was more ferocious than just about anything I've ever seen in the wilds'
— Camper Rudy Winscel

Bat Boy while studying subterranean life-forms in a mountain cave five years ago.

The mystified scientist surmised at the time that the unpredictable, pointy-eared creature might be a human baby raised by bats or a separate species that wandered from the twisting path of man's evolution during prehistoric times.

But before Dr. Dillon could determine what he was dealing with, Bat Boy tore the heavy steel padlock off the door to his holding cell and escaped.

"He ripped that big lock off like it was made of plastic," the astonished zoologist recalled. "He's very strong — and that's one of the things that make him so dangerous."

Since his escape, the elusive fugitive has been spotted hundreds of times from Boston to Bakersfield, and dozens of stunned citizens have reported being attacked by the half-pint hellion.

In Florida last year, a panic-stricken 6-year-old girl was bitten on the arm when she entered her garage and found Bat Boy hiding inside. And in Massachusetts earlier this year, a flabbergasted 44-year-old man had a chunk of his right ear bitten off by the runaway runt.

"Since early July, any number of sightings have been recorded in and around Charlotte, and that's where our search had been concentrated recently," Dr. Dillon told a reporter.

"Then last week a camper, Mr. Winscel, reported being attacked on a riverbank by a creature with sharp teeth and wild eyes, and from his description — and the terror in his voice — we were reasonably sure we had at long last found Bat Boy."

Police, scientists and federal agents rushed to the remote area and eventually managed to capture the screeching creature.

"There was a certain amount of bloodshed but only on the part of the agents — Bat Boy didn't get a scratch," Dr. Dillon said later.

"Now if we can only hang onto him long enough this time, we may finally find out just what — or who — this amazing little guy really is."

'From Mr. Winscel's description — and the terror in his voice — we were reasonably sure we'd found Bat Boy'
— Dr. Ron Dillon

1997

In September, the FBI captured Bat Boy again. The agents corralled Bat Boy near Charlotte, North Carolina. Following the capture, government officials remained secretive about Bat Boy's whereabouts. It was later learned that he had once again escaped—and this time was on a rampage.

Second Bat Child captured in West Virginia, confirms researcher

AND THEN THERE WERE TWO: A baby Bat Boy similar to this original one is being guarded very carefully to prevent its escape.

By **ALEX MORGAN** / *Weekly World News*

SCIENTIST
Dr. Robert Dreyman.

Researchers in West Virginia have captured a baby Bat Boy — a younger, smaller version of the now-famous Bat Boy that was discovered in the same area back in 1992!

The dramatic discovery was made in a Shenandoah Mountain cave near the Virginia-West Virginia state line. More than three dozen researchers were involved in the wide-scale search. The creature is being kept at an undisclosed location.

"Ever since we found the original Bat Boy six years ago, we've figured there must be more of this fascinating species out there somewhere," said excited scientist Dr. Robert Dreyman. "But finding a second one proved to be very challenging.

"There were times when I had serious doubts as to whether we would ever see another Bat Boy in its natural environment. But we are fortunate to have found one. This creature appears to be younger than the one caught in 1992."

The newest Bat Boy is only 11 inches from head to toe and weighs no more than 14 pounds. This is about half the size the first Bat Boy.

Like the first Bat Boy, this one has gigantic ears and oversized eyes, but it has not yet grown razor-sharp teeth.

Dr. Dreyman estimated this new-

> **'This creature appears to be younger than the one caught in 1992!'**

est Bat Boy is less than a year old. He refused to say where the new Bat Boy was taken after its capture.

"We're going to be extremely careful with how we handle this very special creature," he said. "We weren't exercising the proper care when we allowed the original Bat Boy to escape."

That controversial escape occurred from an observatory in Wheeling, W.Va., in September 1992, just four months after it was captured. A security guard was seriously injured in the escape that led to a five-year nationwide search.

The Bat Boy was finally recaptured by FBI agents in Charlotte, N.C., in May of 1997. It is currently being held in an observatory in Michigan, where scientists are attempting to teach it to speak English.

According to sources, the original Bat Boy has now grown to more than four feet tall and weighs nearly 80 pounds.

Dr. Dreyman, who moved his family to Winchester, Va., during his search for the second Bat Boy, said he hopes to allow it to meet with the original one.

"That would be very interesting, but something that drastic will not occur for several months," he said. "The baby Bat Boy is still showing signs of being quite uncomfortable living in a laboratory, so right now we are concentrating on helping it adapt to its new environment."

1998

And then there were two?
During Bat Boy's escape, without any warning, a new twist occurred. A researcher in West Virginia named Dr. Robert Dreyman claimed to have captured a second Bat Boy. The second Bat Boy looked to be a younger version of the first Bat Boy.

1999

Bat Boy was recaptured in August. He was taken to a secure laboratory in Macon, Georgia, where he was kept in a cage under close guard. By this point, Bat Boy had begun attracting admirers and those who simply wanted to see him free.

Freak of nature bites girl 100 times!

MACON, Ga. — A half-human, half-bat mutant nearly bit off a little girl's arm right in front of a dozen horrified children — and now will almost certainly spend the rest of his life confined in a cage!

The two-foot-tall mutant who did the biting was a bald-headed freak of nature known as the Bat Boy. He was first captured in Virginia in 1992 and has been in and out of federal laboratories the past eight years.

Recently, scientists have been working toward releasing the Bat Boy into society. Part of this release was making sure the Bat Boy could interact with humans.

The biting incident occurred when the Bat Boy was on a supervised release from a laboratory in Macon, where he had been held for nearly a year.

The half-human, half-bat mutant was on only his third day out of the lab when he bit the 9-year-old girl. The little girl was identified as Angie Wolster of Macon. She reportedly was taken to a hospital where she was given more than 600 stitches to close the wounds from at least 100 bites.

Little Angie and the other children were playing with the Bat Boy as part of a government program aimed at preparing him for release and life in civilization. A photographer was even on hand to chronicle the Bat Boy's apparent progress.

But the terrible accident has put a stop to all thoughts of release.

"It was the first flash of violence the Bat Boy had displayed during the three days," said Dr. Mark Yasing, who was charged with supervising the Bat Boy. "He had previously been playing very nicely with the other children. But then, before we could stop him, he had the unfortunate incident with that little girl."

According to Dr. Yasing, the girl was teasing the Bat Boy and grabbing his oversized ears when the incident occurred.

"The Bat Boy lost his temper and bit the girl, much like

ANTHROPOLOGIST
Dr. Mark Yasing.

many other children would do in the same situation," Dr. Yasing said. "But with the Bat Boy under such intense scrutiny, I'm certain this will mean he will never be released.

"And that's very unfortunate. We had hoped the Bat Boy might be able to attend a regular school as soon as this fall."

When the Bat Boy was captured and taken to an observatory in Macon, in August of 1999, thousands of people protested the fact that he was locked up. Officials reportedly received more than 62,000 letters — many from Weekly World News readers — demanding the Bat Boy's release.

Last month, when officials decided to release the Bat Boy, they worked up an elaborate program that would ease the creature into a normal life among humans. Adults and children were recruited to spend time with the Bat Boy under carefully controlled circumstances.

But sadly the control was not tight enough. And Dr. Yasing says he accepts

the blame for the incident that has doomed Bat Boy's chance for freedom.

"Things were going so well. I guess maybe I wasn't paying close enough attention," he said. "It all happened so quick.

"Before I knew it, the Bat Boy had his teeth in that girl's arm and all the other children were screaming and running for safety. They were understandably frightened."

Dr. Yasing refused to comment on a report that a guard fired tranquilizer bullets to sedate the Bat Boy after he bit the girl.

"All I can say is that after a bit of a struggle we were able to secure the Bat Boy back into his cage in the observatory," he answered.

"I think he realized he did something wrong when he bit the girl — and I am certain he didn't want to return to the cage."

THE BAT BOY is a half-human, half-bat mutant.

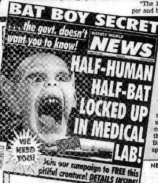

THE BAT BOY SAGA began back in 1992 when the half-human, half-bat was captured in a cave in the Shenandoah Mountains of Virginia.

The two-foot, 19-pound mutant was taken to a federal observatory in Wheeling, W. Va., where experts and scientists from all over the world came to study him.

Government officials denied rumors in late 1993 and again in mid-1994 that the Bat Boy had escaped from his lab. But then in 1995, the rumors were confirmed that the Bat Boy was on the loose when he was spotted in rural Tennessee.

NEWS of the Bat Boy's imprisonment was reported exclusively in Weekly World News in August of 1999.

Officials were unable to capture the Bat Boy in Tennessee, sparking a multistate search for the creature.

Finally, after hundreds of reported sightings, the Bat Boy was recaptured in September of 1997 by a posse of FBI agents. The agents corralled the Bat Boy near Charlotte, N.C.

After the capture, officials were very secretive about the Bat Boy's whereabouts. But two years later it was learned that he had once again escaped — and this time was on a rampage.

Among the Bat Boy's victims was a man in Sarasota, Fla., who was bitten on the neck and both

hands. A woman in Texas also suffered severe bites in an encounter with the Bat Boy.

When the Bat Boy finally was recaptured in August of 1999, he was taken to a laboratory in Macon, Ga., where he was kept in a cage under close guard.

But by this time the Bat Boy legend had attracted thousands of admirers. These fans flooded the government with demands that the Bat Boy be set free.

Officials decided last month to allow the Bat Boy limited human contact. They had hoped to eventually get the Bat Boy to the point where he could become a free member of society — but that plan apparently has failed.

BAT BOY DEAD, CLAIMS U.S. GOVT.

WASHINGTON — A half-human bat boy found in a cave near Seneca Rocks, W. Va., in 1992 allegedly starved to death in captivity and is now preserved in a deep freeze, government sources claim.

And genetic tests said to have been conducted on the body prove that the child is "probably one of a colony of humans who developed large eyes and super sensitive ears to survive in an underground environment," the sources said.

Dr. Ron Dillon, who discovered the creature but was prohibited from conducting further research after the bat boy escaped from his laboratory and was recaptured by govern-

ment agents, said: "The apparent death of this bat child is a major scientific tragedy and an abuse of power that borders on the criminal.

"From all indications, the feds didn't know how to handle him. They should have realized they weren't equipped to care for him. But they refused to bring in experts such as myself.

"Of course, they may be lying about the creature's death to avoid media interference. I hope and pray that's the case."

Fish with human leg

Injured Bat Boy gets 300,000 get-well cards!

CHICAGO — Concerned Weekly World News readers have sent a staggering 302,506 get-well cards to Bat Boy — and more are flooding his hospital room every day.

The outpouring of love has apparently boosted the spirits of the half-human, half-bat mutant, who sank into a deep depression after being hit by a truck on July 14.

Bat Boy, Weekly World News chief Derek Clontz.

A team of Weekly World News reporters has discovered the hush-hush location of the hospital where Bat Boy is being treated under 24-hour guard. But FBI officials,

recovering in a Chicago hospital. The despondent creature told staffers it would cheer him up to receive cards and letters, as Weekly World News reported in our August 14 issue.

Letters from our family of warmhearted readers quickly began pouring in from readers from all over the world — some from as far away as Italy, Vietnam and South Africa.

"Within a week, the mail filled two storage rooms — and it just keeps coming," says

disclose the name of the facility, for security reasons.

The first truckload of mail for Bat Boy was delivered last week and more is on the way.

FBI: THIS IS OUR CHANCE TO CATCH HIM!

STILL ON THE LAM!
Bat Boy.

BAT BOY HEADED FOR N.Y.

Texas woman says he's going to the Big Apple!

NEW YORK — Law enforcement officials have thrown up a wall of security around a Manhattan theater — after a report surfaced that the elusive Bat Boy is headed to the Big Apple to crash an off-Broadway musical based on his life!

A special FBI task force formed to apprehend the bizarre half-human, half-bat mutant. Agents reportedly plan to set up giant nets in and around the theater in a desperate attempt to snare the creature that has eluded them for weeks.

"This is probably the best chance we've ever had to capture Bat Boy and ensure he's safely in our hands," says an FBI source involved in the hunt. "If he comes within 100 yards of that theater, he's ours."

The surprising report that Bat Boy plans to crash a performance of the hit show Bat Boy, the Musical at the Big Apple's famed Union Square Theater comes from a Texas woman who claims she encountered the creature while milking a goat.

LISA MAYBETHER

"The funny thing is, I saw that play about Bat Boy when I visited New York earlier this year," I told him the Bat Boy musical.

"When I first saw that freaky kid with those sharp teeth and pointy ears, I was a little scared — and my goat's knees were knocking, too," the woman continues. "I'd seen on TV how they were looking for Bat Boy and so I asked if he was him. He nodded as if he was ashamed.

"That's when I told him all about the musical and brightened up, I'd reckon. He gets to see it."

As reported in Weekly World News, Chicago doctors who were treating Bat Boy much mistaken, said the FBI source.

up like a kitten.

"I saw that play about Bat Boy when I visited New York earlier this year," I told him the Bat Boy musical.

The unexpected turn of events have presented yet another challenge for law enforcement officials, who have daring escapes from a Chicago hospital just weeks ago. He's were worked as "But now that the FBI source. "But now that this damn play, we're redirecting our resources to the Federal lawmen insist that isn't going to happen.

"If Bat Boy thinks he's going to be sitting there in the audience, laughing and enjoying the show next to paying customers, he's very

WEEKLY WORLD NEWS October 2, 2001

"I WILL HUNT DOWN BAT BOY AND KILL HIM!

...bounty hunter vows!

OUT FOR BLOOD: Jim "Dead Eye" Slubbard.

BAT BOY ESCAPES!!

BATON ROUGE, La. — "I'm going to bring Bat Boy down with one clean shot to the head. Then I'm gonna have him stuffed and mounted over my fireplace."

Those are the chilling words of legendary bounty hunter Jim "Dead Eye" Slubbard, who has bagged more than 130 escaped felons and bail-jumpers in his long career.

The macho, Baton Rouge-based gunslinger made the boastful pronouncement after federal law enforcement officials failed to capture the elusive, half-bat, half-human mutant as he entered a New York City theater to see a play loosely based on his life.

Red-faced FBI sources admit that Bat Boy somehow snuck unnoticed into the Union Square Theatre, eluding 250 undercover officers, watched *Bat Boy, The Musical* in its entirety and slipped out during the curtain calls.

"From what I hear, he was laughing and chortling all the way through the show — disturbing folks next to him who'd paid good money to see it," says Slubbard. "Well, he won't be laughing when he's looking down the barrel of my .32."

Law enforcement officials have been desperately trying to catch Bat Boy alive since he busted out of a heavily guarded Chicago hospital several weeks ago.

As reported in *Weekly World News*, doctors have warned that unless the strange creature gets an experimental drug he was receiving at the hospital, he could become unstable and dangerous. And indeed, since his dramatic escape, Bat Boy has been linked to a bizarre series of attacks in Illinois, Missouri, Arkansas and Texas, including a frightening blitz on a chicken farm in which 22 hens were found drained of blood.

Authorities are calling for calm and say "everything humanly possible" is being done to apprehend the feisty, pointy-eared freak, who was found in a West Virginia cave in 1992.

But TV reports stating that Bat Boy was seen just days ago in Louisiana have sparked widespread panic and citizens are mumbling that it's time to take the law into their own hands.

Next week: NEW PHOTOS OF BAT BOY!

Slubbard, who says he's being paid by a group of wealthy Louisiana businessmen concerned with public safety and tourism, agrees 100 percent.

"I'm not sitting around waiting for this monster to come crashing through my window to suck my blood or maybe try and mess around with my teenage daughter," says the manhunter.

"I will hunt down Bat Boy and kill him — for good."

ACE REPORTER REX WOLFE IS ON THE CASE!

Weekly World News correspondent Rex Wolfe has joined Nick Mann, Vincenzo Sardi, Joan Yung and a crack team of 23 other reporters and photographers in a dramatic race to find and interview Bat Boy before unfeeling federal agents can get their hands on him.

If you want the latest word on Bat Boy, there's only one place to get it — right here, in WEEKLY updates... ONLY in *Weekly World News*.

Rebel teens to aid Bat Boy

NEW ORLEANS — A band of big-hearted teenagers in the Big Easy has vowed to protect Bat Boy from bounty hunter Jim Slubbard.

"That guy has absolutely no right to kill Bat Boy," blasted a 15-year-old member of the group, who asked that her name not be used.

The renegade group, which calls itself the Committee to Save Bat Boy, plans to use every dirty trick in the book to lead Slubbard off the bat-like youngster's trail.

"We're going to plant so many phony Bat Boy tracks and clues leading in so many directions, that bounty hunter will run around in circles until he goes crazy," said the teen.

...AND YOU CAN HELP!

Do you want to help keep Bat Boy out of the gun sights of bounty hunter Jim Slubbard? The young members of the Committee to Save Bat Boy say you can help by planting false clues Bat Boy has been in your area, such as tiny footprints in your yard, workplace or school. "If you really DO see Bat Boy, don't tell the cops," they say.

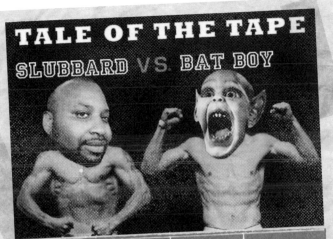

TALE OF THE TAPE
SLUBBARD VS. BAT BOY

CATEGORY	DEAD EYE SLUBBARD	BAT BOY	ADVANTAGE
HEIGHT	6 ft 2 in	3 ft 5 in	DEAD EYE
WEIGHT	195	79	DEAD EYE
CHEST-NORMAL	40 in	13 in	DRAW
CHEST-EXPANDED	42 in	43 in	BAT BOY
FOREARM	14 in	4 in	DEAD EYE
REACH	67 in	7 in	DEAD EYE
NECK	17 in	6 in	DEAD EYE
AGE	42	14 possibly (real age unknown)	BAT BOY
SONAR	no	yes	BAT BOY
NIGHT VISION	no	yes	BAT BOY
ABILITY TO FLY?	no	yes	BAT BOY
PRIMARY WEAPON	.32 Beretta pistol	teeth as sharp as little daggers	DEAD EYE
RECORD	130 felons captured	been captured 3 times	BAT BOY

sitting around waiting for this monster to come crashing through my window to suck my blood or maybe try and mess around with my teenage daughter."

Dillon took the threat from Slubbard very seriously and actually analyzed who had the upper hand by a tale-of-the-tape comparison.

Dillon had circled the fact that Slubbard was armed as the main key to why he would win. He had circled the gun. Fortunately, the confrontation never materialized as billed.

A group of New Orleans teens came to Bat Boy's rescue. Led by a fifteen-year-old Bat Boy protector from the bayou country, a citizens' protection group was formed called the Committee to Save Bat Boy. Although the group's founder chose to remain anonymous, the renegade group announced its intention to protect Bat Boy at all costs and spoke freely with *Weekly World News*.

SEMPER FI

Before the Bayou Boys had a chance to protect Bat Boy, he had shipped out again. This time, though, the stakes were much higher. On October 16, Bat Boy heeded the call of his government and joined up with the Marines.

It was at this moment in time that Bat Boy understood that his abilities could help his country defeat evil. The Pentagon, for its part, was more than happy to shift Bat Boy from "America's Most Wanted" list to "America's Secret Weapons" list.

In an exclusive report, it was revealed that Bat Boy had hopped a military base fence to volunteer. Once over the fence of the Marine base, he begged to enlist. A source confirmed, "He hopped a fence to get on the base and of-ficers found him in tears, jabbering in broken English about wanting to fight for America. When the Marines found him he was clutching a newspaper that had a photo of Osama bin Laden with a sniper's crosshairs over his face."

At the time of Bat Boy's enlistment, an anonymous Pentagon official explained to *Weekly World News*, "Bat Boy can go places and do things no normal soldier can. His hearing is ten thousand times more acute than an ordinary human's and he can track smells like a bloodhound. He's able to navigate in total darkness like a bat, using a kind of built-in radar. He can scuttle up a sheer cliff effortlessly and is strong enough to pull a man's arm out of its socket. Best of all, he's totally at home in

Milk

Have you seen this boy?

BAT BOY

Vitamins A & D
Ultra-Pasteurized
Grade A

Easy to digest

HALF GALLON (1.89 L)

mountain caves—where many terrorists like Osama bin Laden hide."

Surprisingly, Pentagon testers found that Bat Boy had a gift for learning languages quickly. The Pentagon spokesman confirmed, "While he speaks English poorly, he understands it perfectly and should easily master Arabic."

Bat Boy closed 2001 in shameless fashion by visiting Nome, Alaska, on a three-day leave from the military. On December 17, he found his way to the Nome Mall and bit a Santa Claus.

BAT BOY BITES SANTA CLAUS!

DEVILISH Bat Boy chomps down on Santa's arm.

NOME, Alaska — Things got a little "nippy" for Santa Claus when Bat Boy was given a three-day leave from the military and used the time off to visit jolly old St. Nick!

According to widespread rumors, the half-bat, half-human freak has joined the Marines and is now involved in a dangerous hush-hush mission. But when the pint-size, pointy-eared little leatherneck heard the phrase "three-day pass," he cut loose, Bat Boy style.

A mall visitor snapped a startling photo of Bat Boy as he hopped into Santa's lap and began rattling off a list of 87 gifts he wants for Christmas, including a 10-speed bike, an ant farm, a framed photo of the President's daughter, Jenna, "and 156 dried flies."

"Apparently, Bat Boy came this far North because he heard Santa lives near the North Pole," said the eyewitness. "Some of his fellow soldiers had told him Santa doesn't really exist, so to make sure he was real, he bit the poor guy right on the arm!"

— By BRETT ANNISTON

BAT BOY was on leave from his stint with the U.S. Marines when he met Santa Claus.

18 WEEKLY WORLD NEWS December 18, 2001

42 WEEKLY WORLD NEWS February 26, 2002

DON'T CRY FOR ME ON THE LAM IN ARGENTINA

In early 2002, Argentina found itself in the grip of a crippling economic crisis. The macroeconomic cause of the collapse pointed to a decrease of real GDP beginning several years earlier. The Central Bank of Argentina had all but failed, inflation spiraled out of control, debt rose to over $132 billion and put the country into bankruptcy. The government imploded as the country saw five presidents come and go in a matter of months. Citizens took to the streets in violent mob protests. The situation looked beyond grim.

Then, amid the rioting, U.S. president George W. Bush launched a microeconomic solution: Bat Boy.

As reported by Vincenzo Sardi, President Bush was much impressed by the way Bat Boy handled himself in Afghanistan. According to a high-level government source, "The little guy not only helped to bring down the Taliban regime by bravely going behind enemy lines to pester their leaders in their beds, he also became a symbol of hope and freedom to the Afghan people. They saw him as a kind of Zorro-like figure—just the kind of symbol Latin Americans have always responded to."

Bat Boy escaped captivity in Argentina and was spotted riding free with the gauchos of Las Pampa during the day. At night he hit the open-air dance spots so typical of South America. His moves delighted the crowds.

By VINCENZO SARDI / Weekly World News

BAT BOY'S NEW MISSION: CLEAN UP ARGENTINA

BUENOS AIRES, Argentina — After helping U.S. Marines win the war on terrorism in Afghanistan, the mysterious Bat Boy is reportedly waving adios to that newly liberated land and saying "Buenos dios" to another strife-torn nation — Argentina!

President George W. Bush has personally dispatched the pint-sized, half-bat, half-human mutant to restore order to the troubled South American country, which has seen five Presidents in two weeks, been plagued with deadly food riots and been spiraling hopelessly into deepening economic chaos, White House sources say.

"The president was very impressed with how Bat Boy handled himself in Afghanistan," a reliable administration source told Weekly World News.

"The little guy not only helped to bring down the Taliban regime by bravely going behind enemy lines to pester their leaders in their beds, he also became a symbol of hope and freedom to the Afghan people. They saw him as a kind of Zorro-like figure — just the kind of symbol Latin Americans have always responded to.

"The president said, 'If anyone can tame Argentina, it's Bat Boy.'"

Argentina has been rocked by its worst economic crisis in decades. The country is virtually bankrupt and recently defaulted on its massive $132 billion debt. At least 27 people have been killed in bloody food riots and this winter, one leader after another has been ousted by violent street protests, as public anger mounts.

In a desperate move, the latest president Eduardo Duhalde severed the link that long pegged the value of the country's currency to the U.S. dollar, causing the worth of the Argentine peso to plummet. Worried experts warn that risky step may only spawn more economic hardship, anarchy and bloodshed.

The turmoil in Argentina has already begun to affect neighboring countries such as Brazil, where imports of Argentine wheat have ground to a halt. And President Bush is fearful it could destabilize the world's economy — deepening the recession.

"President Bush wants to do everything he can to help," said the White House source. "That's why he's sending Bat Boy on this mission of mercy.

"Bat Boy's job will be to do whatever it takes to help fix the mess over there."

The patriotic imp, who was found in a West Virginia cave in 1992, is raring to go.

"He's already packed his sombrero," the source said. "He can't wait to ship out."

WEEKLY WORLD NEWS February 5, 2002

ACE REPORTER DALLAS SMITH ON THE CASE!

Weekly World News correspondent Dallas Smith has joined Nick Mann, Rex Wolfe, Sandra Lee and a crack team of 29 other reporters and photographers to keep you abreast of Bat Boy's expanding role in the war against terrorism and international politics in general.

If you want the latest word on Bat Boy, there's only one place to get it — right here in WEEKLY updates . . . ONLY in Weekly World News.

DALLAS SMITH

BAT BOY BEHIND BARS!

South American banditos hit him with a tranquilizer dart to collect $50 million Al-Qaeda reward

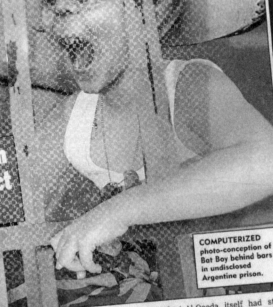

COMPUTERIZED photo-conception of Bat Boy behind bars in undisclosed Argentine prison.

By MIGUEL FIGUEROA
Weekly World News

BUENOS AIRES, Argentina — "We have captured your glorious Bat Boy and we will try him for crimes against the Taliban."

That is the gleeful boast of Al-Qaeda terrorists who, just weeks ago, put a $50 million bounty on the head of the gutsy half-bat, half-human U.S. Marine.

They managed to capture the creature within moments of his arrival in Buenos Aires, where he had gone to end the chaos caused by Argentina's collapsed economy.

American Embassy officials in Buenos Aires received the chilling announcement last Friday, in a press release from Al-Qaeda.

"Bin Laden's vengeful cronies have been itching to get their hands on Bat Boy," said a State Department insider, "to punish him for making their lives hell during our war on terrorism in Afghanistan — and it looks as if they've done it.

"Outrageously, the abduction was carried out while Bat Boy was on his mission of mercy to help the poor people of Argentina — at the behest of President Bush."

Sources said Bat Boy, who helped liberate Afghanistan as part of a Marine fighting force, was seized by greedy Argentine bandits eager to win the hefty reward.

"We hear the banditos jumped Bat Boy pretty much as soon as he got off the plane from Kandahar — somehow they'd been tipped off to exactly when he'd be arriving, and they were ready with nets and tranquilizer darts," the source said. "The little guy fought like a rabid wildcat, but he was outnumbered 20 to one.

"Then the heartless thugs turned him over to an Al-Qaeda cell."

Bat Boy is now being held at an undisclosed location.

"His Marine buddies would love to mount a rescue mission, but we have no idea where they're holding him," said the insider. "He could be anywhere in the world."

The Al-Qaeda network vows to try the pint-size creature for "war crimes" in front of a secret military tribunal — jury composed of America-hating fanatics.

"He will be given a fair trial, then executed," the terrorists' press release says.

Among the 380 charges listed in the indictment: Urinating in 87 Al-Qaeda caves, making them uninhabitable; setting fire to Osama bin Laden's bed; snipping off the beards of 24 top Taliban leaders; "stealing" food that Al-Qaeda itself had stolen from peasants; and mooning bin Laden's favorite wife.

Bat Boy's chances at trial are grim, especially since he'll have to act as his own lawyer.

"Bat Boy's Arabic is fair at best — he got a crash course from the Marines," said the insider. "He knows nothing about Islamic law, and logic isn't his strong suit.

"I hate to say it, but Bat Boy doesn't stand a snowball's chance in Hell."

CLEAN UP ARGENTINA

BAT BOY'S NEW MISSION:

BAT BOY'S mission to Argentina was detailed by *Weekly World News*

ACE REPORTER DONNA SANTOS ON THE CASE!

Weekly World News correspondent Donna Santos has joined Dallas Smith, Nick Mann, Rex Wolfe, Sandra Lee and a crack team of 29 other reporters and photographers to keep you abreast of Bat Boy's expanding role in the war against terrorism and international politics in general.

If you want the latest word on Bat Boy, there's only one place to get it — right here in WEEKLY updates.... ONLY in *Weekly World News*.

DONNA SANTOS

Now he's on the lam in South America!

SPECIAL REPORT

BAT BOY IS MISSING!

WASHINGTON — Bat Boy is missing!

No one has a clue where he is, not the FBI, not the Pentagon, not the White House.

And for the first time since the mysterious mutant was first found in a West Virginia cave a decade ago, not even Weekly World News can tell you what's become of him!

Red-faced Department of Defense officials admit they've lost track of the pint-sized, half-bat, half-human creature, who enlisted the in U.S. Marines to help fight the war on terror after the barbaric September 11 attacks.

"As of 14:00 — 2p.m. — on May 25, we have lost all communication with Bat Boy," confirmed a Pentagon source who requested anonymity.

At last report, the fearless freak-of-nature had successfully completed an anti-terror mission in Argentina. President Bush awarded Bat Boy the Shadow Warrior Medal of Heroism for his actions.

Since the ceremony, Bat Boy has not been seen.

"This is a potentially explosive situation. Remember, Bat Boy is an official U.S. Marine," notes the source. "Now we don't know if the crazy little guy has gone AWOL, or worse."

The White House has refused official comment on the disappearance. "If Bat Boy has reverted to his 'bad boy' ways, there's no telling what will happen," says a U.S. government source.

But there's an even grimmer possibility.

"Don't forget, Al Qaeda has a $50 million bounty on Bat Boy's head because of his heroics behind enemy lines in Afghanistan," the source adds.

"He could be the prisoner of Osama Bin Laden's group.

"We just don't know — and that's the scary part.

"If anyone sees Bat Boy, they should contact the Pentagon immediately."

— BY MIGUEL FIGUEROA

MISSING bat child is shown on milk carton.

Have you seen this boy?

WEEKLY WORLD NEWS OCTOBER 15, 2002

BAT BOY SIGHT[E]

Vigilant NEWS readers on the lookout for America's favorite

Have you seen Bat Boy? That's the question we asked the readers of *Weekly World News* — and the volume of responses has been overwhelming!

The winged wonder has been missing for several months, since he returned from top-secret missions for the U.S. government in Afghanistan and Argentina.

Reports of the mutant man-child have been coming in from all over the country. We're not sure how reliable these sightings are (and we know some aren't!), but rest assured, we will investigate every single report until Bat Boy is found!

IN THE BAT CAVE

Dear Editor,

I am an avid spelunker. I have been exploring the Mammoth Cave system for years.

Last week I had the strangest experience I've ever encountered in that dark, damp underworld.

I was alone in a cave when I saw a youth who appeared to be about 11 or 12 years of age, running by. I chased him, but he disappeared into a crevice too small for most humans to fit through.

I spoke to him through the opening, and over the next couple of hours I gained the trust of the voice from the other side of the wall. He never gave me his name, but he told me some sketchy details of his life: Tales of a sad childhood, and of being ridiculed for being different; tales of his

military service, and the pain of confinement.

I believe the individual I spoke to in that dark cave was in fact Bat Boy. I have not contacted the FBI at this point, but will leave it to your discretion to follow up on this information.

Sincerely,
H. T.

Bat Boy certainly would

MY DINNER WITH BAT BOY

Dear Sir:

Last Thursday while dining at a restaurant in Burlington, Vt., situated on Lake Champlain, I saw some fellow diners who may be of interest to you.

When Champ, the Lake Champlain monster, entered, I was star-struck but not terribly surprised. He is a popular local resident, who moves freely among the rest of the populace.

A few minutes later, Bat Boy joined Champ at his table. Bat Boy had invited Champ to discuss the situation with Nessie. Bat Boy said that he had read that Nessie had had her baby and may have been shot. Bat Boy added that growing up without a father had made life very difficult.

With that Bat Boy excused himself, mentioning Jenna Bush and a performance of his musical in Boston. I didn't even have time to get his autograph.

Hope this helps,
Alice L.
Florence, Ky.

We're not sure if it really helped or not, but thanks for writing! — The Editors

FEDERAL agents captured Bat Boy several years ago, as seen in this file photo. But Bat Boy is currently on the loose and out of control in the Illinois area.

be at home in a cave. That seems credible. This next report, however, we're not so sure about . . .

DO BATS EAT FRENCH FRIES?

I saw Bat Boy on October 17 in Penfield, N.Y. I had just gone to McDonald's and bought a Big Mac meal. I left the fries in my car. When I went back out to get them I saw something reaching in my window. I yelled at it, and it ran away. I remember what it looked like. I know it was Bat Boy!

Signed,
Anonymous

One thing we can determine from these sightings: If it really is Bat Boy that all these people are seeing, he is very, very hungry!

BAT BOY ON WHEELS

Dear Editor:

In keeping with your quest for information regarding the whereabouts of Bat Boy (October 27, 2002), I offer the following:

In the same issue of *WWN*, in an article on page 42, there appears the headline "NAKED BOY STEALS MOTORCYCLE FROM HARLEY GANG."

BAT BOY IS MYSTERY VANDAL — SAYS FBI

THIS FBI composite sketch bears a striking resemblance to Bat Boy, right.

WASHINGTON — An FBI profiler has analyzed a recent rash of bizarre attacks in the Midwest — and he's convinced that one individual is responsible for most of them: The mysterious Bat Boy!

"All the evidence points in one direction," reveals the profiler, who spoke on the condition of anonymity.

"The suspect is described as being under 4 feet tall — with a bald head, pointy ears and sharp teeth.

"Only four suspects in our criminal database fit that description. One, who had plastic surgery to get pointy ears, is in a federal penitentiary. Two were executed. The only one now at large is Bat Boy."

Here are some of the baffling incidents attributed to Bat Boy:

• In Loves Park, Ill., nine burly bikers were set upon by a naked, biting youth, who sped off on one of their Harleys.

• Trick-or-treaters visiting a Halloween haunted house in De Kalb, Ill., claim they were attacked by a half-bat, half-boy monster.

• Two men of Middle Eastern descent were found on the shore of Lake Michigan, one dead, the other badly mauled and babbling incoherently about an attack by a bat-winged demon.

"Based on his description, a FBI sketch artist drew a picture of the 'demon' — and it looks just like Bat Boy."

The bat-like mutant, found as a toddler in a West Virginia cave in 1992, was reportedly recruited by the U.S. military after September 11 for the war on terror. But in late May, the patriotic freak mysteriously went AWOL and dropped out of sight, as *Weekly World News* reported.

NGS!

half-bat half-human

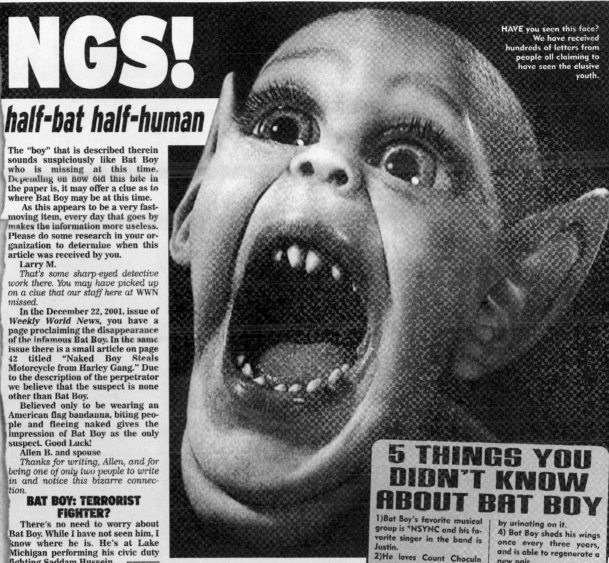

The "boy" that is described therein sounds suspiciously like Bat Boy who is missing at this time. Depending on how old this bite in the paper is, it may offer a clue as to where Bat Boy may be at this time.

As this appears to be a very fast-moving item, every day that goes by makes the information more useless. Please do some research in your organization to determine when this article was received by you.

Larry M.

That's some sharp-eyed detective work there. You may have picked up on a clue that our staff here at WWN missed.

In the December 22, 2001, issue of *Weekly World News*, you have a page proclaiming the disappearance of the infamous Bat Boy. In the same issue there is a small article on page 42 titled "Naked Boy Steals Motorcycle from Harley Gang." Due to the description of the perpetrator we believe that the suspect is none other than Bat Boy.

Believed only to be wearing an American flag bandanna, biting people and fleeing naked gives the impression of Bat Boy as the only suspect. Good Luck!

Allen B. and spouse

Thanks for writing, Allen, and for being one of only two people to write in and notice this bizarre connection.

BAT BOY: TERRORIST FIGHTER?

There's no need to worry about Bat Boy. While I have not seen him, I know where he is. He's at Lake Michigan performing his civic duty fighting Saddam Hussein.

When I read the poster about Bat Boy being missing, I was saddened. Such a great hero — lost! And then I read the news article about a strange naked boy biting people in Illinois and stealing their motorcycles.

That made me suspicious. When it described him as being "half-human, half-animal" and wearing "an American flag bandanna" (just like on the poster), I knew it had to be Bat Boy. It said he was headed northeast. But what was northeast of Loves Park, Ill.? This morning when I was looking at my *Weekly World News* again I realized: Lake Michigan is northeast of Illinois. Bat Boy is going to Lake Michigan.

And the cover story of this week's issue? Iraqi Subs In Lake Michigan!

I say, don't worry about Bat Boy. He'll be fine — and, thanks to his efforts, so will we.

Anonymous

That would explain the report of the two terrorists who were attacked by an animal-like creature on the shores of Lake Michigan, as told in last week's WWN.

BAT IN THE BOX

"While browsing in an antique shop in Texas, I noticed a trembling box. Being a very curious person, I opened the box. Inside, I was shocked to see a terrified little face looking up at me. The face had big bat-like ears and huge eyes, carnivorous-looking teeth, and a bald head. I screamed and ran out. The manager grabbed the box and ran into her back office."

Morgan B.

We've heard of a Jack-in-the-box — what's so hard to believe about a Bat-in-the-box?

BAT BOY: KILLER?

Bat Boy must be caught! No one is safe! I can't stress enough just how dangerous it is.

I was with my friend Courtney in the woods in upstate New York, just outside of Rochester. Bat Boy attacked Courtney and dragged her into the woods, kicking and screaming. She hasn't been seen since.

Please, I beg you, come and get it before more people are killed!

James M.

Is Bat Boy as dangerous as James thinks — or is he just a misunderstood monster? Send YOUR sightings to:

Bat Boy
c/o *Weekly World News*
5401 NW Broken Sound Blvd.
Boca Raton, Fla 33487
or email:
editor@weeklyworldnews.com

5 THINGS YOU DIDN'T KNOW ABOUT BAT BOY

1) Bat Boy's favorite musical group is *NSYNC and his favorite singer in the band is Justin.
2) He loves Count Chocula cereal.
3) He once defused a terrorist bomb aboard an airplane by urinating on it.
4) Bat Boy sheds his wings once every three years, and is able to regenerate a new pair.
5) His favorite comic book super-hero is not Batman — it's Spider-Man.

'BRING US THE HEAD OF BAT BOY'

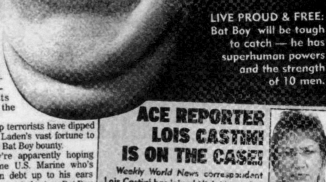

Al Qaeda targets America's favorite Marine after he 'pee-pees' on Taliban bigshot!

KANDAHAR, Afghanistan — "Bring us the head of Bat Boy!"

That's the shocking demand of vengeance-crazed followers of Osama Bin Laden, who have reportedly put a $50 million price on the head of the half-bat, half-human mutant.

"The terrorists want Bat Boy dead or alive," a high-level Pentagon source confirms.

"Rightly or wrongly, they hold Bat Boy personally responsible for the fall of the Taliban regime and the terrible drubbing the Al Qaeda terrorist network has taken.

"They say he's 'humiliated' them by attacking their leaders in their beds, disrupting their supply lines and making hundreds of their best caves unlivable by 'pee-peeing' in them — he even is alleged to have 'wet' the leg of at least one revered Taliban leader.

"They're offering twice the amount of the $25 million reward we put up for Bin Laden."

The patriotic freak, who was found in a cave in the West Virginia in 1992, enlisted in the military after the September 11 attack on America. And since arriving with a Marine battalion on

WEEKLY WORLD NEWS EXCLUSIVE

November 26, he's reportedly been a thorn in the side of the terrorists.

"Bat Boy's been deployed principally in caves and we're using his unique talents — such as his ability to navigate in the dark, to pursue the terrorists," said the source. "On at least five different occasions, he successfully entered a cave and bit off an important body part of one of the top terrorist leaders, then made a clean getaway."

While he's hated and feared by Al Qaeda, common folks in Afghanistan love Bat Boy.

"He's become a folk hero to them — kind of like a modern-day Zorro," said the source.

"One woman said she was being roughed up by two retreating Al Qaeda terrorists when she refused to give them her food rations," the source said.

"Out of hole in the ground, Bat Boy appeared, screeching at the top of his lungs. The terrorists took to the hills."

Fed-up terrorists have dipped into Bin Laden's vast fortune to raise the Bat Boy bounty.

"They're apparently hoping that some U.S. Marine who's maybe in debt up to his ears might be tempted to turn Bat Boy in for the reward money," said the Pentagon source.

"But these creeps have no idea how popular Bat Boy has become to our fighting men — he's a symbol now. No American soldier would turn Bat Boy in, even for $50 million!"

LIVE PROUD & FREE: Bat Boy will be tough to catch — he has superhuman powers and the strength of 10 men.

ACE REPORTER LOIS CASTINI IS ON THE CASE!

LOIS CASTINI

Weekly World News correspondent Lois Castini has joined Nick Mann, Rex Wolfe, Sandra Lee and a crack team of 28 other reporters and photographers to keep you abreast of Bat Boy's role in the war against terrorism.

If you want the latest word on Bat Boy, there's only one place to get it — right here in WEEKLY updates . . . ONLY in Weekly World News.

FBI WARNS!

DON'T BE FOOLED BY THIS BAT BOY IMPERSONATOR!

Impostor leaves a string of broken hearts and empty purses from Miami to Seattle!

By VINCENZO SARDI
Weekly World News

WASHINGTON — Angry law-enforcement officials are warning the public not to be fooled by a cunning Bat Boy impostor — a 3-foot-tall former circus midget who has already hoodwinked at least 46 people coast to coast!

Officials say the conniving con man, who's shaved his head clean and wears pointy rubber ears to resemble the famous half-human mutant, worms his way into his victims' hearts and homes.

He's reportedly scammed standstruck fans of Bat Boy out of free food, lodging, gifts and, in at least 13 cases, sexual favors.

"It's an outrage," said an FBI source involved in the investigation. "This little creep is impersonating a genuine American hero, not some baby Hollywood celebrity.

"And he's taking advantage of innocent, hardworking citizens. They've given him cars, expensive jewelry, designer clothing — even received proposals of marriage."

Authorities say the manipulative midget has been working the scam since mid-December, operating everywhere from Seattle in the Pacific Northwest to Miami.

"He always moves on before someone fingers him as a phony," the G-man said. Among the many gifts that police say gullible Americans have forked over to the bogus Bat Boy:

• A free, two-week stay in the luxury suite of a top bed-and-breakfast in Aspen, Colo.

• A 1997 Lincoln Continental, donated to the "hero" by a patriotic veteran in Texas.

• The deed to a 3.6 to the family since 1885.

• A Rolex watch worth $21,000, given by a generous Illinois widow.

• More than $43,000 in raw cash from various sources.

VICTIMS Kim Newborn see they got scammed.

Heartbroken Kim Newbeam of St. Petersburg, Fla., says the fake Bat Boy took much more than money from her.

"He lived in my house for two weeks and treated him like a king, lavishing gifts on him and cooking him gourmet meals," says the attractive 29-year-old.

"We saw him hitchhiking on the road and, naturally, we picked him up," recalls 54-year-old Otis Burmont of Shreveport, La. "We were so honored that Bat Boy was visiting our area that we treated him to supper at the fanciest restaurant in town. The guy was so believable," Burmont said. "He did backflips in the chair just like you'd expect Bat Boy to do. He completely took us in."

The real Bat Boy, found by scientists in a West Virginia cave in 1992, has emerged as a major cult figure.

After enlisting in the Marines last fall, he served in Afghanistan on hush-hush missions behind enemy lines, as Weekly World News reported.

"At last report, he was in Argentina on a mission to restore order," said the FBI source. "He's become such a symbol of hope to the peasants.

"You know what Bat Boy — even having his teeth filed down has made them so sharp as those of the beloved supermutant imp.

"If you copy know what Bat Boy looks like from reading newspapers or seeing his picture on TV I could easily tell how this guy could fool you."

The pint-size con man shamelessly exploits Bat Boy's fame, victims say.

one he was an impostor. I literally 'scared.'

so believable," Burmont said.

• Be completely believed to be a former circus performer from St. Louis. "This isn't the same guy has pulled."

"We believe in 1986 this same individual passed himself off as Gary Coleman, the former child star."

FBI agents closed in on him and were about to arrest him, but he gave them the slip.

They did manage to snap his picture, however.

The suspect has gone to incredible lengths to look like Bat Boy — even bluing his skin, since 1992.

Actual photo of impostor

Impostor

WIMPY CROC CRIES LIKE A BABY!

KRUGERSDORP, South Africa — There really are such things as crocodile tears say zoologists who've confirmed that a 1-foot-long unconcerned weeping reptile cries like a baby!

By March, the government claimed that there were impostor Bat Boys running loose from Miami to Seattle.

AMA CA - A

TOKYO — unveiled versatile Future not only getting the

WAS BAT BOY CREATED BY THE U.S. GOVERNMENT?

By **CLIFF LINEDECKER**
Weekly World News

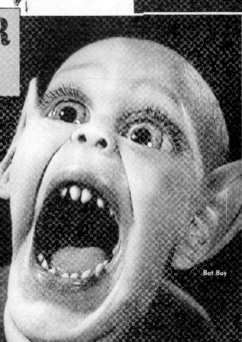

TOP SECRET

FREDERICK, Md. — The mystery surrounding the young American patriot, Bat Boy, has been solved with disclosure that the half-bat, half-human is the result of hush-hush government experiments at Fort Detrick, the Pentagon's top bio-defense research center.

"This tragic individual was created by a team of brilliant but ethically impaired geneticists working in a secure underground area before he escaped in 1992," according to Dr. Ernesto Paz Chandhuri.

The Guyana zoologist, is researching an article about Bat Boy for the *Chiroptera Journal* and recently talked with a radio reporter from his offices in Georgetown.

Although Chandhuri complained of repeated roadblocks from U.S. government sources and of receiving anonymous threats, since he began tracing the young mutant's genesis, he said he is "99 percent convinced" that scientists created Bat Boy by combining the DNA of a Guyana fruit bat and a human.

The experiments were apparently commissioned by a rogue unit of the CIA and by Defense Department operatives, in an effort to develop uniquely skilled night-fighters to work with the military's elite Delta Force, Seals and Special Forces on special missions.

RESEARCHER SAYS 'YES!'

DR. Chandhuri

Since a zoologist discovered the frightened fugitive hanging upside down inside a West Virginia cave, Bat Boy has been run over by a truck, sprayed by an exterminator and hunted like an animal.

Yet, he has shown amazing resilience and proved his patriotism when he enlisted in the Marines a few days after the 9-11 terror attacks.

Although the Pentagon and the Marine Corps have declined even to acknowledge Bat Boy's presence, he is now listed as missing, and a worldwide search is being mounted for the controversial creature as of press time.

Bat Boy

AMAZING BAT FACTS

Giant flying foxes that live in Indonesia have wingspans of nearly six feet.

Mexican free-tailed bats can fly two miles high over long distances at speeds of more than 60 MPH.

The pallid bat of western North America is immune to the stings of scorpions and even the seven-inch centipedes which it feeds on.

A single little brown bat can catch 1,200 mosquito-sized insects in just one hour.

2003 proved to be a busy year for Bat Boy. He stole a MINI Cooper, fought valiantly in another war, and, soon after, was tapped as an astronaut for the space shuttle program.

In January, he started off on the lam.

By April, Bat Boy was off to war at the request of coalition leaders.

Then NASA tapped Bat Boy for the shuttle program. Bat Boy finally had all the right stuff. Bat Boy headed south after his escape from the lab. He made his way to Charlotte, North Carolina, and flirted with living there permanently. Several theories emerge as to why Bat Boy enjoyed the Charlotte area. One involves a long-distant relation he has to U.S. president James K. Polk, whose uncle Thomas helped found the city. Another is that he wanted to live in the city where Billy Graham was born. The third theory holds that he had designs on trying out for the Carolina Speed indoor football team as a wide receiver in order finally to be close to a quarterback.

BAT BOY STILL ON THE LAM!

Pointy-eared car thief continues to wreak havoc & evade police in 11 states!

PENSACOLA, Fla. — More than two weeks after the mysterious Bat Boy carjacked a brand new Mini Cooper, flustered lawmen are no closer to apprehending the elusive bat-like freak — who has been spreading panic and chaos in a wild and woolly chase that's taken him through 11 states!

The bizarre odyssey began when the pointy-eared mutant stole the car from a Detroit dealership, as *Weekly World News* reported in our January 14 edition.

Since then, a special law-enforcement task force tracking him through frantic calls to police from startled citizens says he's traveled through Michigan, Ohio, West Virginia, Virginia, Tennessee, North and South Carolina, Georgia, Alabama and Mississippi — clocked at speeds of up to 110 m.p.h.

Authorities say they're frustrated that Bat Boy has escaped all their roadblocks and even eluded police helicopters. "He's always one step ahead of us," fumes FBI Special Agent Jack Trasker.

Bat Boy was last spotted in the Florida panhandle, headed south. Among the 450-plus sightings reported to frazzled authorities:

● **Darlington, S.C.** — The stolen vehicle skidded onto the town's famous racetrack, interrupting trials for a NASCAR race. "The little freak almost forced me off the track," one shaken driver says. "He did two laps, then zoomed off."

● **Athens, Ga.** — A religious revival meeting ended abruptly when Bat Boy drove through the crowded tent, sending folks diving for safety.

● **Tuscaloosa, Ala.** — A group of campers witnessed Bat Boy picking berries by the side of the road. A quick-thinking man grabbed his

BAT ON THE RUN: This incredible photo was snapped by a camper in the woods of Alabama, as Bat Boy ran to his car and made a quick getaway.

camera and snapped a picture before Bat Boy ran back to his car and drove away.

● **Vicksburg, Miss.** — Civil War re-enacters were stunned when the stolen car plowed through the mock battlefield, scattering Confederate and Union soldiers alike. "The guy playing General Grant was so spooked, he fell off his horse," says eyewitness Corbin Maxford, 24, of Vicksburg.

EYEWITNESS Corbin Maxford

● **Pensacola, Fla.** — A couple claim their beach date was interrupted when Bat Boy pulled onto the sand. The 27-year-old woman told police, "He snapped my thong like a rubber band, jumped back into the car, and drove away."

Law-enforcement officials are asking motorists to be on the lookout for a 2003 red Mini Cooper driven by a bat-winged youth about 13 years old.

"If you see Bat Boy, alert local authorities immediately. Do not attempt to take him into custody yourself," agent Trasker warns.

— *By MIKE FOSTER*

FBI Special Agent Jack Trasker

BAT BOY TO FLY SPACE SHUTTLE

By DEUCE COLLINS
Correspondent

Congress banking on mutant hero to save NASA program

AFTER serving with valor as a Marine in Afghanistan, Iraq and other terror hot spots around the globe, Bat Boy has been asked to come to the aid of his country in an entirely new arena — orbiting Earth in a space shuttle.

And both the White House and NASA are convinced that the beloved but highly unpredictable imp can help change the public's perception of the space agency's much maligned "culture of arrogance" that was exposed after the Space Shuttle *Columbia* disaster last February.

Only then, they say, will American taxpayers give Congress the green light to fund NASA's ambitious but risky plans to establish a colony and mining operation on the moon -- and send astronauts to Mars in a hands-on search for evidence to prove the Red Planet once teemed with life . . . of the intelligent kind.

"We launched a senior citizen into space — John Glenn — and instead of getting all misty-eyed and patriotic, Americans yawned," says retired NASA engineer and avowed Bat Boy fan Alan Lister.

"We made another flight with a female mission specialist — Sally Ride. But as pretty and competent as she is, the public couldn't have cared less. But Bat Boy is different. He's not only a war hero, he's fresh, he's wild, and he's crazy in the best sense of the word.

"And given his history, there's no telling what sorts of shenanigans he might try to pull out there in orbit around Earth. That's the kind of energy and 'star power' NASA needs to fire the public's imagination.

"We'll all camp out in front of our TVs when they launch Bat Boy into space. We'll be rooting for him to scare the bejeebers out of the flight commander with a joy buzzer or get caught with a girlie magazine.

"I just hope they put the little guy's picture on the top and bottom of both wings for the whole world to see."

It's unclear who came up with the pull-out-the-stops idea to launch Bat Boy into space.

But Beltway scuttlebutt suggests it was the brainchild of a group of former astronauts.

And White House sources confirm that the group lobbied President George W. Bush to make the Bat Boy flight a reality after NASA administrators cited the mutant creature's "excitable nature" and "occasional crude behavior" in nixing the plan as "too dicey."

"But behind the scenes, the astronauts pulled anything that even looks like a string to seize the moment and make this program happen," says a government insider.

"Like a lot of people at NASA, they know the space program is in deep trouble because of its current public image.

"In that regard, Bat Boy's flight could be viewed as a way to improve NASA's approval rating. It could also be seen as a way to boost the economy."

As it stands, informed sources say Bat Boy could be trained and flight-ready within three months, opening the door for a spectacular Christmas or New Year's launch — the first since the *Columbia* explosion of last February 1.

"He's an ex-Marine — how much conditioning does he need?" says one NASA fitness instructor. "And he's not even human. His mutation makes him more bat than boy.

"He was built to fly."

And yet, Bat Boy — who was discovered in a West Virginia cave by spelunking biologist Dr. Ron Dillon in 1992 — is expected to be subjected to a grueling series of tests and training rituals that include time in a chamber that simulates the weightlessness of space, and exposure to G-forces powerful enough to rip a man's face off.

Nobody's saying where Bat Boy is now. But insiders say he is training at the Kennedy Space Center at Cape Canaveral, with occasional trips to NASA's Jet Propulsion Laboratory in Pasadena, Calif.

Meanwhile, interest in the story is heating up — with the producers of radio talk shows in New York, Chicago and Los Angeles reporting "a huge increase in interest" in the so-called "Bat Boy in Space Initiative."

"These aren't your usual Baby Boomers talking about the pros and cons of space programs," says one L.A. producer.

"We're talking about teenagers and 20-somethings, and college students and college professors, who are getting really excited about NASA and space for the first time.

"Bat Boy could be the creature that saves NASA and America's space program."

AMERICAN HERO Bat Boy — seen here helping fight enemy forces in Afghanistan — is no stranger to patriotic missions.

BONUS!
SPECIAL COLLECTOR'S ITEM POSTER
Cut out and keep

WEEKLY WORLD NEWS SEPTEMBER 23, 2003

Weekly World News
BAT BOY
'I finally have my wings'
— Bat Boy, American Hero

MISSING HALF-BAT, HALF-HUMAN STRIKES AGAIN!

ACTION PHOTO taken from a Detroit overpass clearly shows cops chasing the stolen Mini Cooper. Inset closeup reveals Bat Boy is the driver.

CAR THREE

WWN 3X ZOOM

DETROIT — Bat Boy, the world's favorite winged freak, went on an incredible, death-defying joyride through Michigan, Indiana and Ohio after carjacking a brand new Mini Cooper — and is still on the lam somewhere in America!

The brazen theft took place in the crowded parking lot of a Mini dealership. Eyewitnesses report that the Mini Cooper's owner had just accepted the keys to the vehicle when Bat Boy jumped out from behind some bushes, snatched the keys and sped away.

By WAYNE DIAZ
Weekly World News

"The whole thing happened in a matter of seconds," says the car's horrified owner, who asked not to be identified. "The dealer had just handed me the keys when this monstrous creature appeared out of nowhere and tore off like a bat out of hell."

CLOSE-UP photo of car's side view appears to show Bat Boy behind the wheel.

Police suspect that Bat Boy had been casing the dealership for hours, waiting for just the right moment to strike. Two employees gave chase, but Bat Boy quickly lost them in traffic.

Police say they are looking for a red Mini Cooper, last seen around Akron. A police spokesman says, "That little speed demon was heading East on Interstate 80. We urge all motorists to be on the lookout for this car, and to notify authorities if they see a Mini Cooper driven by a bat-like creature."

There were numerous sightings of Bat Boy following the theft, but police have been unable to locate him and he remains at large as of this writing.

"We know where Bat Boy has been during his little adventure — we just don't know where he is now," notes FBI Special Agent Jack Trasker.

"We've been tracking his movements via reports of gas station drive-offs — apparently Bat Boy is

FBI Special Agent Jack Trasker has been assigned to the Bat Boy case since the mutant disappeared last May.

BAT BOY STEALS — AND GOES ON STATE JOY RIDE!

POLICE CARS from several Ohio jurisdictions are shown in hot pursuit of a Mini Cooper with a screaming Bat Boy at the wheel — and they still failed to nab the human bat!

stealing gas when the tank runs low and drives away before police can respond."

Bat Boy learned how to drive while working with the U.S. military combating terrorism in Afghanistan.

Secret military files leaked to *Weekly World News* report that he stole at least two Jeeps and a tank during his stint there.

Since returning to the United States, Bat Boy's behavior has become increasingly erratic.

Three months ago he escaped from government custody and became a fugitive.

Police reports collected from stunned onlookers put Bat Boy in at least three different states. Sitings include:

● The Detroit Zoo, where he was believed to be looking for a quick snack.

● Drive-through of an Indiana donut shop. Several police officers taking a break in the shop gave chase, but Bat Boy managed to lose them in traffic.

● Interstate chase in Ohio. With cops in hot pursuit, Bat Boy whizzed down the Interstate at speeds in excess of 100 miles an hour.

Authorities are desperate to recapture Bat Boy, and have asked the nation's driving public to immediately report anything unusual. FBI and police scoured the tri-state area via car and helicopter, but they're no closer to capturing Bat Boy than they were three months ago.

"Hell, he could be a thousand miles from here by now," notes Agent Trasker, who has been on Bat Boy's tail since he escaped government custody.

"For someone so weird, he manages to hide himself pretty easily. With winter just around the corner, he'll probably head south.

"We already have task forces assembled in Georgia, North Carolina and Florida so when he shows up, we'll be ready."

In the meantime, the owner of the stolen Mini Cooper says he probably won't press charges should Bat Boy finally be captured.

"'I hope Bat Boy learns his lesson and turns himself in," the man says. "I just want my Mini Cooper back."

WEEKLY WORLD NEWS JANUARY 14, 2003

Bat Boy goes to war—again!

BAT BOY LED U.S. TROOPS TO SADDAM ... GOTCHA!

BAT BOY leads U.S. Special Forces in the search for Saddam. The search finally paid off, thanks to the mutant freak's highly sensitive nose — and Saddam's failure to bathe for several weeks. "It was a piece of cake for Bat Boy to find him, says a military source.

BY MIKE FOSTER
Weekly World News Correspondent

THE U.S. Special Forces troops who captured Saddam Hussein were led to his dingy spider hole by Bat Boy — who literally sniffed out the filth-covered dictator.

That's the astonishing revelation of military sources, who say the pint-sized mutant will be awarded the Bronze Star for the "vital" role he played in tracking down the fugitive former strongman.

"Bat Boy's nose is more sensitive than any bloodhound," confirms a Pentagon insider. "And since Saddam hadn't bathed for weeks down there, it was a piece of cake for Bat Boy to find him.

"The little guy just sniffed along with our soldiers behind him until he got to that squalid mud hut and started pointing down excitedly.

"That's when we knew Saddam was under there."

The U.S. government has steadfastly refused to admit publicly that the mysterious mutant, found by scientists in a West Virginia cave in 1992, has been aiding the military. According to the official version, an unidentified man in Tikrit tipped off

troops to Saddam's whereabouts. But the insider confirms that Bat Boy has been involved in the war effort since last January — months before the U.S.-led invasion.

"His batlike sonic ability to see in the dark and other traits make Bat Boy an indispensable tool for the military," the insider says.

"During the months leading up to Operation Iraqi Freedom, Bat Boy carried out dangerous reconnaissance missions on behalf of the Army. The excellent intelligence he gathered is one of the reasons the Coalition was able to topple Saddam's regime so easily — we knew all the enemy's weaknesses.

"The 5-foot-tall, pointy-eared creature also conducted sabotage

that Saddam had planned to use on Coalition troops.

"He became a real thorn in Saddam's side," reveals the insider. "Many of Said-dam's frazzled troops believed Bat Boy was a batwinged demon of Arabic myth named Pazuzu.

Bat Boy was rousted more often the end of war, or combat in May. But when the search for Saddam dragged on and U.S. generals summoned the bizarre creature back to

- destroying chemical weapons

AMAZING UNTOLD STORY BEHIND DRAMATIC CAPTURE!

Iraq.

Bat Boy was given a pair of smelly old riding boots of Saddam's to get the scent. He took one good whiff and that enabled him to follow the trail from Baghdad all the way to Tikrit.

When troops pulled the cover off the hole where Saddam was hiding, the insider says, "Bat Boy caught a

SADDAM BEARD GUNK TO BE AUCTIONED ON-LINE

THE MOST coveted souvenir of Operation Iraqi Freedom can now be yours: Lice and dandruff flakes extracted from Saddam Hussein's beard during his televised medical check, are being offered to collectors by a U.S. Army officer during the dictator's dramatic capture.

The whiskery gunk has been divided into 25 Humble-size parcels — each guaranteed to contain at least one of the lousy Stalin's mustache, sold at auction to a collector.

The disgusting beard gunk has been dividied into 25 Humble-size parcels — each guaranteed to contain at least one of the lousy Stalin's mustache, sold at auction for $99,000 in 1968, the expert says.

with a 100-foot pole, there are plenty of collectors out there who can't wait for the chance to bid on it, experts say. "A dictator's memento like this would culminate the Saddam $400,000 and $1.21 million," says notable expert Brian Holmer of London. "Love him or hate him, Saddam's a figure of monumental historical importance, and anything associated with him has value."

if. I guess, because the te dog, smelling a juicy steak. He appeared to be held back while a guys went down the hole.

Saddam didn't realize Bat outside, says the source. that troops were ordered the capture of Bagdad calmly Bat Boy's involvement "My name is Sad-Hussein, the president of want to negotiate.

"He heard that Bat Boy restrained no longer, he the hole, and when Sad-him, the defeated dictator according to the people.

Saddam pereviely willing thing away from me; for us to protect him.

Saddam seemed so docile undergoing a medical hands this U.S. captors.

A TERRIFIED Saddam went into hysterics and begged Coalition troops to protect him when Bat Boy leaped into his hiding place, an eyewitness says.

... £ THEN THERE WAS ONE — Will a grieving Osama turn himself in for the sake of the shared ape baby? (Turn to Page 26.)

BAT BOY GOES TO WAR!

COALITION LEADERS ORDER HALF-HUMAN, HALF-BAT TO TAKE A BITE OUT OF SADDAM!

British leader
Tony Blair

President George
W. Bush

By LARRY MULDER / Weekly World News

BAGHDAD — The mutant freak Bat Boy has emerged from hiding in the last place anybody expected to see him — aiding U.S. troops in Iraq!

And in a world exclusive revelation, sources say Bat Boy against President George W. Bush to "send Bat Boy against Iraq."

Tony Blair asked British Prime Minister Bush to "take a bite out of Saddam!"

Since arriving in Iraq in early March, Bat Boy's unit, "and now he's tearing through Iraqi soldiers like a bat out of hell."

Since arriving in Iraq in early March, Bat Boy has proven to be an outstanding soldier.

So far the pointy-eared private has:

● Taken out three Iraqi T-55 tanks

● Sniped out seven Iraqi machine gun nests

● Saved a dozen young kids who were trapped on a battlefield by leading them home and protecting them from harm.

"Bat Boy really loves kids," the source says. "He'd do anything to help them, even lay down his own life."

Although the age of the half-creature, half-human has been calibrated at the size of Bat Boy falls at about 35 "bat" years. Subsequently, an official edict issued by President Bush himself allows Bat Boy to serve in the military.

The mutant marine possesses abilities "beyond those of humans," say scientists, including enhanced hearing, enhanced "night vision" capabilities, natural speed and incredible sense of smell.

Does also admit the war progresses may come to admit the war progresses, natural speed and incredible sense of smell Bat Boy's services have been called upon. In 2001, he traveled to Afghanistan to help U.S. forces in the war on terrorism.

When the opportunity came up to help out in Iraq, Bat Boy was eager to re-enlist.

"He wasn't hard to find," the source says. "He had just led cops on a three-state chase in a stolen car. That was just his way of showing us he was before heading back to active duty. He tends to get pretty disgusting."

But there's one big

BAT BOY stands ready for action in this image from Iraq. Witnesses say Iraqis have already felt his wrath!

BAT BOY GOES TO WAR!

...R HALF-HUMAN, ...OUT OF SADDAM!

ARTIST'S conception shows a pop-eyed Saddam Hussein reacting to Bat Boy's deadly bite.

bored in civilian life, but at Bat Boy is eager to put a when there's a chance for bite on: Saddam Hussein. him to see some combat, look "He hates Hussein, and out."

Bat Boy doesn't seem to mind life in the desert. I overheard him saying, "Saddam bad man. Me bite him good." the source said.

And his unique abilities make him especially suited to nighttime attacks. "He doesn't need nightvision goggles," the source says.

Bat Boy is reportedly so proud of his mission in Iraq, he'd even marking his territory.

"Whenever he has a successful strike against the Iraqis," the source moves, "he uses whatever he finds at hand to write 'Bat Boy was here' on the wall. But he always makes sure for prisoners on the spot, too."

Despite his reputation for being a bad seed, his superiors report that Bat Boy is adjusting quite well to military life.

He's a mischief-maker back in the States, the source says, "but when he's over here in Iraq, he takes his duties as a soldier quite seriously."

"The only thing he won't do is eat the MRE (Meals Ready to Eat) that we provide to Eat! that we provide him. He uses those as grenades. Instead, he feasts on desert critters. The other day I saw him eat a rat. It was pretty disgusting."

will do anything to get him good. In fact, just yesterday.

Bat Boy does not have the power of flight, but he is able to leap great distances.

"When he's approaching enemy troops, it's an amazing thing," the source says. "He bounces from rock to rock, zooming through the air hard. He makes Spider-Man look like an amateur."

Asked to name Bat Boy's worthiest feat, the source cites the fantastic freak's incredible throwing arm. "He revs up and can hurl a grenade at an enemy machine gun nest, enemy machine gun nest. Bat Boy starts lobbing grenades from 30 yards away. He's better at throwing grenades than Doug Flutie is at throwing footballs."

Bat Boy's presence in Iraq has even taken on a symbolic meaning. One U.S. military general notes. The Iraqi soldiers, they see him and they see him as a "devil child," and they're deathly afraid of him.

"Not only is he a great warrior, but he's become a beloved morale booster for the troops."

Bat Boy is already due to receive several awards for his bravery, but those honors

will have to wait 'til after the conflict is over.

"We gave Bat Boy a medal once," one U.S. officer explains. "He tried to eat it."

"But there will be many more such medals if this all-American soldier makes it out of Iraq in one piece. We just have to find a place to pin them."

Weekly World News will continue to bring you updates of Bat Boy in action as they become available.

"BAT BOY WAS HERE!" graffiti is showing up everywhere in Iraq.

BAT BOY WAS HERE!

BAT BOY FOILS NUCLEAR BOMB PLOT

White House ceremony honors his 'incredible bravery'

By
MIGUEL FIGUEROA
Weekly World News

BAT BOY SAVES 'DIRTY'

BAT BOY saved at least 350,000 lives when he courageously ignored his own safety to defuse a "dirty bomb" bound for our nation's capital!

The radioactive terror weapon was tucked in a small briefcase in the cargo hold of an Argentine jet streaking toward America when the intrepid "whiz" kid put it out of commission, sources claim.

"That bomb was packed with enough industrial-grade Cesium-137 to contaminate the entire District of Columbia — and doom the residents to a slow, agonizing death by cancer," confirmed a CIA source familiar with the incident.

"If the bomb had gone off, Bat Boy would've been instantly blown to smithereens — but he didn't hesitate to put his life on the line to save innocent Americans.

"I hear that when Bat Boy stopped the clock on the time bomb, it had ticked down to just 7 minutes and 32 seconds. That might be a wide margin by Hollywood standards, but in the real world, it's nail-bitingly close."

The patriotic, half-human, half-bat mutant's act of selfless heroism has earned him a special commendation from U.S. President George W. Bush.

"A few days after the incident, President Bush shook hands with Bat Boy on the lawn in the Rose Garden, outside the White House, and pinned the ultra-secret Shadow Warrior Medal of Heroism on his chest," revealed a source.

"After Bat Boy left, the President turned and told me, 'There goes the bravest little guy I've ever known.'"

The bone-chilling near-miss on March 28 is being hushed up by the Department of Homeland Security in Washington to avoid panicking residents, say CIA sources — who finger evil-crazed supervillain Osama Bin Laden as "our prime suspect."

But *Weekly World News* obtained an exclusive interview with the only witness to the mid-air miracle: Bat Boy's Argentinean sidekick Pedro Simenez.

"In our many adventures together, Senor Bat Boy has saved my life 100 times, but even I did not know how great his courage was until now," declared Pedro, a former fruit-picker and part-time bandito before signing up as Bat Boy's guide.

The gutsy, bat-like freak, who enlisted in the war on terrorism shortly after September 11, had been dispatched to Argentina on a secret mission by President Bush.

"Bush told Bat Boy to be on the lookout for terroris[t]

A GRATEFUL NATION: President Bush poses with the patriotic half-human, half-bat during a special White House ceremony.

WASHINGTON FROM 'BOMB' DISASTER

... & you won't believe how!

because there are Al Qaeda cells operating throughout South America," confirmed the CIA source.

Bat Boy quickly became a symbol of hope to the Argentine people, many of whom view him as a living incarnation of Camazotz, the ancient bat god of the Andes.

When Bat Boy received a tip from one of his thousands of devoted followers that a dirty bomb was about to be shipped overseas, he leapt into action.

"With that nose of his, Bat Boy can sniff out an ounce of radioactive material a mile away," says Pedro. "It only took him about two hours to find the right plane."

Eluding the notoriously poor airport security in Buenos Aires, Bat Boy and his buddy stowed away on the craft as it took off for Washington.

"Bat Boy really did a number on the cargo hold," recalls Pedro. "By the time he was done, every suitcase was busted open and there were tennis rackets, women's bras and toothbrushes all over the place — covered with Bat Boy's teeth marks."

Finally Bat Boy sniffed out the deadly briefcase, which bore a suspicious sticker that read, "So long, suckers," in Arabic.

But when Bat Boy ripped it open, he was faced with a daunting array of wires, flashing lights, plastic explosives and rods packed with radioactive material.

"I worked for two years in my brother-in-law's car-repair shop, so I know something about mechanics, but when it comes to radioactivity I am totally ignorant," humble Pedro admits. "And Senor Bat Boy knows even less.

"Remembering what I'd seen in movies, I shouted 'Cut the red wire,' then I screamed, 'No, no, the green wire' — forgetting that Senor Bat Boy is color blind.

"Finally Senor Bat Boy just stuck his head in the briefcase and bit clear through both wires with those sharp, pointy teeth of his."

To their horror, the deadly bomb kept ticking away.

Soon the jet was less than eight minutes away from Dulles International Airport — and from blowing to Kingdom Come.

"I crossed myself and said, 'Santa Maria! Amigo, we're history,'" recalls Pedro.

"That's when Senor Bat Boy stood over the suitcase and tinkled, dousing the bomb.

"It fizzled, there was a puff of smoke and then the clock stopped dead."

Instinctively, the brave whiz kid had realized that bat urine is extremely corrosive and would short-circuit the deadly device.

The White House refuses to confirm or deny the bizarre story.

But a Bush aide said, "Americans owe Bat Boy a huge debt of gratitude."

EYEWITNESSES say Bat Boy stood over the suitcase and doused the bomb. It fizzled, there was a puff of smoke and then the clock stopped dead.

BAT BOY TO BE KNIGHTED

By **MICHAEL CHIRON**
Correspondent

APRIL
Knighted by the
Queen of England

'Arise, Sir Bat Boy!'

ON his last visit with Her Majesty, Bat Boy could hardly contain his enthusiasm when told he was in line to be knighted.

QUEEN Elizabeth is reportedly set to knight Bat Boy after the intrepid freak of nature saved a British army patrol in Iraq!

According to official sources, the pointy-eared hero sniffed out an ambush laid by terrorists and warned the five soldiers in the nick of time.

The recommendation for Bat Boy's knighthood was made by a top British commander and reads in part:

"Showing total disregard for his own safety, Bat Boy engaged the terrorists in a small-arms firefight. Despite being wounded, Bat Boy then ran three miles and warned an army patrol of the terrorist force. The enemy fighters were later attacked by gunships and sustained heavy casualties."

The knighting ceremony is expected to take place at Buckingham Palace in early August, says a royal source.

But not every Brit is tossing up his bowler hat at the news. Some bluebloods are incensed that the rare honor is being bestowed on the half-human, half-bat mutant.

"It's bad enough that we now see knights made of working-class actors like Michael Caine, who speaks with a cockney accent thicker than a London chimney sweep," sniffs a member of the House of Lords. "It's quite another matter to welcome into the company of nobles a grunting, savage creature that is not even fully human.

"This little monster is unpredictable and dangerous. Who knows what will happen when Her Majesty tries to knight him? He may feel threatened by the sword, snatch it from her hands and run her through."

But high-ranking government officials say knighthood for the plucky youth is almost certain.

"Saving that patrol is only the latest contribution Bat Boy has made," says a source close to British Foreign Secretary Jack Straw. "His missions for the U.S. are top secret, but it's known his superior sense of smell was used to track down Saddam Hussein.

"Also, rumor has it that he recently unearthed evidence of weapons of mass destruction while looking for a cool cave to sleep in one night. This will help Prime Minister Tony Blair save face after the failure to find WMDs in Iraq.

"Mr. Blair owes his political life to Bat Boy and he's been petitioning Queen Elizabeth to proceed with the knighthood."

Bat Boy will likely be named a Knight Commander of the Most Excellent Order of the British Empire, or KBE, the title typically given to non-Britons.

Because he's an American, Bat Boy should not actually be addressed as "Sir," but will be permitted to put the letters KBE after his name.

The pint-sized hero isn't the first Yank to receive the honor. Other distinguished Americans who've been knighted include former New York Mayor Rudolph Giuliani, evangelist Billy Graham and former President Reagan. And, it was recently announced, megabucks computer geek Bill Gates has earned a knighthood as well.

According to custom, the recommendation will be reviewed by the Chancellor of the Exchequer, before being passed on to the Queen.

Palace insiders say that pressure to knight Bat Boy — who is more popular in British opinion polls than Prince Charles — will be impossible for the monarch to resist.

"It is not with undiluted pleasure that we look forward to meeting this peculiar individual in person," she reportedly told an aide. "But his service to the realm must be rewarded."

Editor's note: As *Weekly World News* went to press, we learned that, in a recent meeting with the queen, Bat Boy attempted to bite the monarch on the arm. While Her Majesty was not amused, the ceremony of knighthood will go on as scheduled.

By April it was London calling. Bat Boy flew to London at the request of Her Majesty to be knighted.

And so on that day of special dual national rejoicing, Bat Boy joined the historical ranks of other great Americans who were knighted. Including recent honorees such as:

Bobby Knight, former head coach of Indiana University men's basketball

Teddy Kennedy

Rudolph Giuliani

Billy Graham

Ronald Reagan

Then something unusual happened that had not occurred since Bobby Knight's induction into this same group. A mysterious crop circle of immense size was found in a field north of Derbyshire, bearing Bat Boy's image. Could it be that alien forces were watching the proceedings and approved?

As a knight, Bat Boy was eligible to enjoy all of the incumbent privileges of knighthood (including partying like Ted Kennedy). At present, it's unclear if he has exercised any of these privileges.

By May, Bat Boy had made inroads into the camp of presidential hopeful John Kerry. Reporter Nick Mann followed the story and confirmed reports from Kerry's camp.

In response to a snooty British reporter who tried to malign his qualifications, Bat Boy loudly broke wind. Some pointed to that moment as a sign of Bat Boy being unfit for office. Bat Boy left the campaign and promptly tried out for *American Idol*.

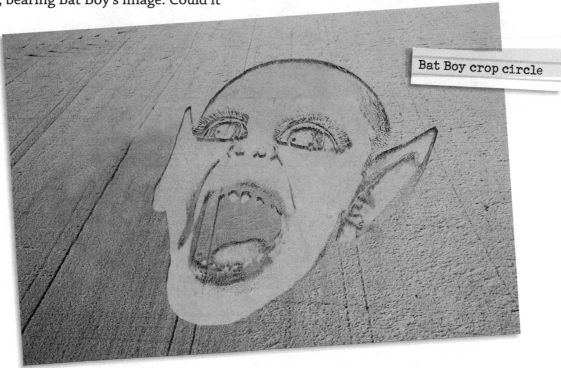

Bat Boy crop circle

DYNAMIC DUO!

BAT BOY LOBBYING HARD FOR KERRY'S NO. 2 SPOT

BAT BOY'S enthusiasm and his popularity with younger voters would light a much-needed spark in Kerry's campaign.

By NICK MANN
Correspondent

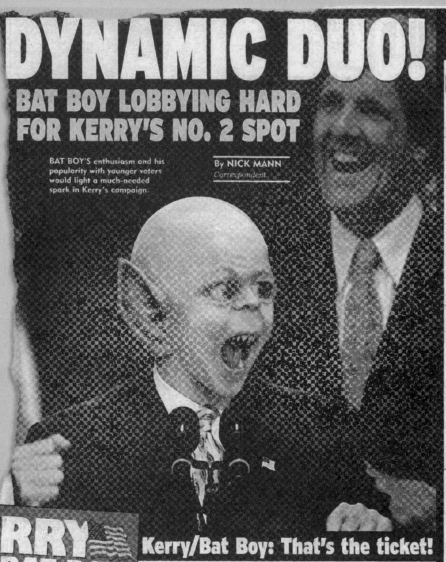

Kerry/Bat Boy: That's the ticket!

eyed creature hugging and then playfully biting Gore remain among the most enduring images of the campaign.

While Kerry has yet to make up his mind about Bat Boy, President Bush has not. According to a White House source, he calls Bat Boy's attempt to join the Democratic ticket "not so good."

"He almost stole the 2000 election from us," the president told an aide. "We can't let that happen again."

And in a move that both Democrats and pundits are calling "typical,"

chief presidential adviser and dirty-tricks maestro Karl Rove is said to be working overtime on a smear campaign to destroy Bat Boy's credibility.

"Bat Boy's past is unusual, anyway, so there's no doubt Rove and Bush can make some hay with it," says a Kerry insider.

"Since that college professor pulled him out of a cave in West Virginia in 1992, he's never fully acclimated to human culture, and he has a reputation for doing what the hell he wants to do regardless of the consequences.

"In 2003 he 'borrowed' an Austin Mini Cooper off a car lot and went joy-riding. The money he saved

from his Marine pay more than took care of the beer stains on the seats.

"But you can bet Rove and the Republicans are going to have a field day with that little escapade on the campaign trail if Kerry picks him as his running mate."

As for the legality of Bat Boy running for vice president, Democrats have determined that because the famed imp was born in the United States, he is a citizen despite the fact that he's not entirely human.

He is thought to be just 16 or 17 years old, adds the Democratic source, "but if you measure his age in bat years, he's more like 179, plenty old enough to qualify for the No. 2 spot."

WEEKLY WORLD NEWS MAY 31, 2004

Lower the volume on your TV folks...
BAT BOY TO TRY OUT FOR AMERICAN IDOL!

By MICHAEL CHIRON/Correspondent

GET OUT YOUR earplugs — Bat Boy could soon be a contestant on TV's *American Idol!*

The bizarre, half-bat, half-human mutant is a huge fan of the hit talent-competition show — and insiders say he's determined to land an audition.

"Bat Boy is dead serious — he's even taking daily singing lessons," says a military source.

"He sees how other singers with, shall we say, unusual singing voices such as William Hung, came out of the show superstars."

The mysterious creature — currently under Pentagon supervision — has long been addicted to TV, spending up to 10 hours a night with his enormous amber eyes glued to the set. But nothing has captivated him like *American Idol.*

"Every Tuesday night you find him hanging upside down from the ceiling fan, tuned into the show — and he'll bite the fingers off anyone who tries to switch channels," says the military source.

While acknowledging that Bat Boy's high-pitched screeching "takes some getting used to" and his rendering of lyrics is rarely fully intelligible, the source says that the creature is a talented mimic who imitates every song he hears.

"Those enormous ears that help Bat Boy navigate using sonar like a bat also give him perfect pitch, just like Celine Dion," the source says.

"If you liked William Hung ...you'll love The BAT!"

"He has a unique voice that sounds something like a cross between a young Johnny Mathis and a rabid chipmunk."

Among the songs the pointy-eared freak is reportedly preparing for his audition: "I Will Survive," "Love me Tender," and "La Vida Loca."

TV insiders are skeptical of Bat Boy's chances, noting that some contestants have years of professional training under their belts. But they agree that if the audition goes well and Bat Boy lands a spot on the show, "all bets are off."

After getting over the initial shock of seeing the bat-like youth, audiences are likely to show him great sympathy.

TONE-DEAF singer William Hung is an inspiration to Bat Boy.

"As for judges, Paula Abdul obviously has a weakness for short oddballs — she was once married to Emilio Estevez," a TV critic notes.

Bat Boy's singing lessons are reportedly going well, although when the voice coach criticizes him too harshly, he bites her.

"Also, it's been hard to get him to stand in one place when he performs," the source says. "He likes to jump around and do somersaults."

Nevertheless, voice coach Agnes Manyard, 57, is confident that Bat Boy will soon be ready for prime time.

"TV viewers will be blown away by Bat Boy's performance," she predicts.

When Bat Boy's *Idol* audition fizzled, he married Britney Spears.

Deflated by his soured political experience and *Idol* tryout, Bat Boy ran into the arms of the nearest available pop star. He headed back to Las Vegas but this time carefully avoided local businessman Eric Riccardi's backyard swimming pool. Rather than lounging on a raft, he decided to lounge with Britney Spears. By the summer, Bat Boy began a relationship with the pop sensation. Unconfirmed reports of a July wedding at the Little Chapel were reported by journalist Will Shivers.

In January, Bat Boy looked into a special dating service to find his love match. For a brief while, it worked.

An impostor Bat Boy sprouted up. Also, certain pundits and celebrities were being questioned about ties to Bat Boy.

Bat Boy's unbelievable claim:

BRITNEY IS MY BRIDE!

JUST months after she made a fool of herself by marrying a childhood sweetheart on an allegedly drunken tear and then divorcing him 48 hours later, pop tart Britney Spears has reportedly done it again — this time tying the knot with Bat Boy!

At least that's what the notorious imp claims in an exclusive interview offered up in the broken English and baby talk the half-human, half-bat is known for.

The mutant car thief and on-again, off-again war hero says he and the sexy songbird were wed by an Elvis impersonator during a junk food-fueled weekend in Las Vegas.

"Me marry Britney she pretty girl," Bat Boy told *Weekly World News*. "She feed Bat Boy candy and chips and we watch TV.

"I see her undie-wear."

But Bat Boy isn't the most reliable source in Hollywood, or anywhere else, for that matter. He once went so far as to tell a Florida Highway Patrol officer that "I be asleep" when a half-human, half-bat matching his description stole a new Austin Mini-Cooper from a car dealership and led cops on a three-state high-speed chase.

But he insists that Spears "fall in love with me" when he happened to find himself under

BAT BOY AND BRITNEY as they would appear on their honeymoon in Vegas.

2004
Claims relationship with Britney Spears

MISS B. XQUER

the seat of the superstar's limo during a top secret trip to Vegas on June 12.

According to sources in Vegas, Bat Boy and someone who looked a heck of a lot like Spears were spotted in several casinos, although security officers kept giving them the boot because Bat Boy, at age 16, is too young to gamble.

"Every time they were kicked out of a casino they ran back to their limo squealing and laughing, and took off — candy wrappers flying out the windows as they went," says a tabloid photographer who caught the couple on film.

Bat Boy says "me not sure" if a wedding took place because Bat Boy got so wired on sugar, he suffered a bout of amnesia.

Vegas sources say it seems likely that the marriage wasn't consummated, so if it hasn't already collapsed in a divorce that Bat Boy can't remember, the duo can get it annulled.

In March 2004, following the success of Bat Boy's military service, the government had announced a controversial program to send an army of Bat Boy clones into war. The U.S. Army War College in Carlisle, Pennsylvania, strongly advised the Pentagon to create hundreds or even thousands of Bat Boy clones to help fight the war on terror.

When it was announced that Bat Boy would join the cast of *Deadwood* for season 3, many pundits heard the bells of overexposure.

Bat Boy was everywhere.

Many Bat Boy fans feared that his iconic trademark looks would prevent him from leading a normal life. Some urged him to undergo plastic surgery. Journalist Michael Forsyth

TERRORISTS KIDNAP BAT BOY!

'Pull out of Iraq or we'll send him back,' they warn

By NIKKI LONG

Mmmmpff! MMMummyy!

TERRORISTS have kidnapped Bat Boy off the streets of Baghdad and they've threatened to send the little pest to the United States if President George Bush doesn't pull U.S. troops out of Iraq.

On a fuzzy videotape aired by Al-Jazeera television, Islamic extremists believed to be affiliated with terror kingpin Osama Bin Laden boast that they abducted the famed mutant while he shot craps with reporters and prostitutes during a visit to the war-ravaged city on August 9.

"The video shows Bat Boy handcuffed, gagged and kneeling on a tile floor execution style," a CIA analyst told a reporter.

"Behind him are four hooded men armed with swords, rifles and what appears to be a one-way ticket to New York. One terrorist reads from a script calling for the immediate withdrawal of U.S. troops from Iraq.

"Then he loudly thumps the airline ticket with his index finger and ... says to send Bat Boy back to the United States," the analyst said.

"It's going to mean trouble" if President Bush doesn't comply with the demand. I seriously doubt the President is worried about Bat Boy.

"But I know the FBI would like nothing better than for him to stay in Iraq, because every time he goes on a rampage, it's the FBI that has to pick up the pieces and chase him down."

Since his discovery in a cave in West Virginia in 1992, Bat Boy has made headlines both good and bad, from joining the Marines to help rout the Taliban in Afghanistan a few weeks after 9/11 to leading ... anti-American cops on a dangerous chase at speeds approaching 140 m.p.h. after he finished his four of duty and returned to the U.S.

"The terrorists are so desperate to crush democracy in Iraq — they're willing to try anything — even kidnap Bat Boy," says the CIA source. "Is he their ace in the hole? Maybe he is, maybe he isn't.

"It's in President Bush's hands now."

Strange love is a specialty of the...
DATING SERVICE FOR FREAKS

By DARREN DAVENPORT

Matched up Bat Boy with Siamese twins, a small-faced gal with the dog-faced man!

BAT BOY dating female Siamese twins? A four-armed man courting a three-breasted woman? How about a dog-faced man asking out a small-faced woman?

All of these match-ups and more are possible thanks to a new dating service in Oslo, Norway, which caters exclusively to freaks!

"There are plenty of dating services for normal people," notes Sven Vergos, founder of the "Freak-Finder" dating service. "Ours is the first one geared toward misfits and weirdos."

Vergos says his company provides a valuable service. "A lot of freaks like to go online and try to meet regular people. They'll be doing great, until that first face-to-face meeting, when their date finds out they have a hunchback or a third eye.

"With Freak-Finder, there are no surprises. Everyone is up front about their deformities right from the start."

"I never thought I'd find a woman who could like me for who I am."

Natalia, left, Bat Boy and Nancy have found happiness and acceptance.

Applicants to Freak-Finder must go through a strenuous application process to confirm that they are legitimate candidates. "We don't want any fake freaks in here," Vergos says. "We just want to provide a safe haven for those who are shunned by society to find love amongst their own kind."

So far, over 200 freaks have signed up for the dating service, and Vergos projects he could reach up to 1,000 by 2006. "We've already been responsible for six weddings. Just last week, a werewolf married a mermaid."

Freak-Finder has three branches in Europe, but there are plans to expand to America soon. "America has one of the highest populations of freaks of any country," Vergos notes.

One client, a Ukrainian man known as Pumpkin Head, raves about the service. "I had a hard time meeting women, because of my freakish, pumpkin-like head," he says. "But thanks to Freak-Finder, I've already dated several women, including a midget and a witch."

Another freak who calls himself Bat Boy, says that he has met his soul mate through the service. "All my life, people made fun of me, just because I have pointy ears and a funky set of teeth. But then I met Siamese twins Natalia and Nancy and we've been together ever since."

Vergos denies rumors that King of Pop Michael Jackson has applied for membership in Freak-Finder. "But even if he did, he would not be accepted, because we only accept natural freaks, not ones who altered their appearance with plastic surgery."

As much success as Freaky Friends has had, Vergos says there are no guarantees. "For months, we've been trying to find a woman willing to date the Porcupine Man, and we haven't found any takers yet. We won't give up though. We believe there is someone for everyone, no matter how deformed, weird, or abnormal they are."

TRUE LOVE: Small-faced girl and dog-faced boy found each other with the help of Freak-Finders.

U.S. PLANS TO CLONE ARMY OF BAT BOYS TO FIGHT TERRORISM!

TO BE CONT.

By IAN MERKINS
Correspondent

THE U.S. ARMY War College in Carlisle, Pa., has strongly advised the Pentagon to create hundreds or even thousands of Bat Boy clones to help fight the war on terror.

If the bold but controversial plan is enacted, War College analysts are convinced that the army of Bat Boys could be used to protect U.S. interests at home and abroad and also drive insurgents and Al Qaeda terrorists out of Iraq.

And once the Bat Boys are cut loose in Afghanistan, say the experts, it would be just a matter of time before they flushed out terror mastermind Osama Bin Laden.

"Bat Boy has the genes we need to create the army of the future," says a War College source. "The United States is a mighty country. We can continue to throw billions of dollars into military technology to continue fighting a war where technology doesn't make a lot of sense.

"Bat Boy clones would change all that in a hurry. They won't need expensive technology and hardware because they'd do their best fighting stripped to the skin.

"We envision them using their blinding speed, nimble and unpredictable moves, ability to see in the dark, bat-like radar, sharp fangs and remarkable simian strength to take this war to the next level.

"The great thing about cloning Bat Boy is that his duplicates will mature as rapidly as he did. They'll be ready for duty in two or three years. And nobody can complain because we're talking about Bat Boys. It's not like they would be human beings."

Neither the Pentagon nor the Department of Defense is talking about the War College recommendation, but one thing is clear: Analysts who think Bat Boy is somehow less than human are in sharp disagreement with those who know him best.

Dr. Ron Dillon, the geologist who found the little guy with his ankle wedged in a rock in a cave in West Virginia in 1992, says, "The creature is at least half human, and he might be completely human.

"For all we know, he may be a member of a race of men that evolved underground, but otherwise — at the level of their genes and chromosomes — are human in every way."

It's unclear how the issue of Bat Boy's humanity might play out, but as news of the War College's recommendations continues to leak like olive oil from a colander, pundits are eager to tackle an issue that could hold the public's interest for years.

Some already want to know why nobody's asking Bat Boy whether he even wants to be cloned. The fact that not even brass hats at the Pentagon can bend Bat Boy to their will proves that the cloning project may be dicey at best.

"The last time Defense Secretary Donald Rumsfeld had a one-on-one with Bat Boy, over an ugly incident in which (Bat Boy) was accused of looking up an Army nurse's dress, well — BB cocked his leg and peed all over Rummy's desk before jumping out the window, squealing and squeaking like a banshee all the way," says a Pentagon source.

"So if my bosses are expecting him to bend over on this cloning thing, well, they might be in for a rude shock."

Other insiders think Bat Boy might jump at the chance to give up a few genes for the cloning project.

"Don't forget, Bat Boy volunteered for duty on the front lines of one of the most dangerous and unpredictable wars we've ever fought — Afghanistan," says a Department of Defense source.

Oddly enough, if Bat Boy is cloned, say other sources in Washington, the medical work may have to be done in Afghanistan or Iraq — because it might be illegal in the U.S.

"You better believe we've got lawyers all over this thing," says one of those sources. "If Bat Boy's genes even look like they might be human, there's going to be trouble."

WEEKLY WORLD NEWS, MARCH 15, 2004

ARMY OF ONE! Bat Boy clones would raise the war against terrorism to the next level.

9

BAT BOY TO JOIN CAST OF *DEADWOOD!*

BY MARK MILLER

SANTA CLARITA, Calif. — When HBO's Emmy and Golden Globe Award-winning Western drama returns for its third season next year, *Deadwood* will present viewers with a new character for the show — but one well known to followers of cowboy history — Bat Masterson. And in a surprise casting move, the famed lawman will be portrayed by none other than *Weekly World News* personality Bat Boy!

"Well, come on, think of it," said *Deadwood* casting associate Barri Segal. "Bat Masterson — Bat Boy — it's a no-brainer. Your readers are familiar with Bat Boy's heroic acts throughout the Iraqi War, so to have him playing a hero from another historical era isn't that big a stretch."

While Bat Boy has guest-starred on sit-coms, reality shows and game shows, this will be his first foray into serious drama. He is determined to make the most of it.

"I am studying with Hollywood acting coach Demetrius Patriculus," revealed the speech-challenged Bat Boy through an interpreter. "He's got me doing these really heavy-duty monologues from Shakespeare, Ibsen and Arthur Miller, as well as two-person scenes.

"And on my own, I'm learning horseback riding and gun-toting, as well as working with a dialect coach for that Western twang — oh, and I've gotten my rabies shots."

In the course of his multi-episode appearance on the show, Bat Boy Masterson will square off against his rival, saloon proprietor and town boss Al Swearengen; enter into a secret business arrangement with former hotel owner and town Mayor E.B. Farnum; and begin a red-hot romance with saloon madame Joanie Stubbs. "I'm greatly looking forward to this exciting new challenge," said the feisty little man mammal. "And you can let your readers in New York City know about another exciting challenge — I'm in talks to play Edna Turnblad in the hit musical *Hairspray*.

"I think I'll be divine."

BAT BOY hits the bar with *Deadwood* star Timothy Olyphant.

2005
Popularity rising

ACTING with Ian McShane has been a life-long dream for Bat Boy.

ARE JAMES CARVILLE & BAT BOY KIN?

— A —

By MIKE FOSTER

BAT BOY has hundreds of living relatives in America — and famed Democratic strategist James Carville is probably one of them!

That's the astonishing assertion of a Chicago scientist who has just completed the most extensive DNA tests ever conducted on the bat-like mutant.

"My research shows that Bat Boy is closely related to Homo sapiens — but he shares certain rare genes only with a small portion of the human population," declares Dr. Robert Hensky.

"These individuals have 10 telltale physical and behavioral characteristics that we've identified — and Mr. Carville appears to score a perfect 10.

"Without a blood test, it's impossible to confirm that Mr. Carville is kin to Bat Boy, but if we go by these outward traits, they appear to be close cousins."

Feisty Carville, who steered Bill Clinton's successful presidential bid, is best known to the public as co-host of CNN's no-holds-barred political debate show Crossfire.

While outspoken Carville — nicknamed the "Ragin Cajun" — is famous for being hyper-aggressive, no one has questioned his place in the human species before.

"This news is bound to rattle Carville," says a Democratic party source. "If he and his wife Mary Matalin — a staunch Republican — weren't worried about how their kids would turn out before, they've got to be now."

FOR BETTER OR FOR WORSE: Carville with Mary Matalin, is said to be a tower of strength.

CO-HOST: on CNN's interesting political debate program, *Crossfire*, Mr. Carville has been nicknamed the "Ragin' Cajun."

ARE YOU KIDDING?

While James Carville's **right-wing Crossfire counterpart Tucker Carlson sports bow ties** to achieve a more conservative look, surveys show that men who favor bow ties are MORE likely to have experimented with LSD than those who wear regular cravats.

HERE, from the expert, are 10 traits Bat Boy appears to share with his human kinfolk.

1. Bald, misshapen head.
2. Frightening, sharp-toothed grin.
3. Comes from the South. "Like Bat Boy, who first surfaced in West Virginia, most of his relatives are found in the South," notes Dr. Hensky. "Mr. Carville was born in Louisiana."
4. Flails arms wildly when excited.
5. Combative. Like Bat Boy, who's bitten dozens of people, Carville relishes a good fight.
6. Weird, cackling laugh.
7. Super-acute hearing. CNN staffers have learned not to bad-mouth Carville behind his back.
8. Physical agility.
9. Dog-like loyalty. While other Clinton cronies ducked for cover during Monica-gate, Carville stood by his man," Dr. Hensky observes.
10. Navigates in dark. Carville often wears sunglasses at night.

Scientists have puzzled over the origins of Bat Boy ever since the strange feral child was discovered in a cave in 1992. One long-held theory is that the pointy-eared freak belongs to a subspecies that diverged from humanity during the Ice Age and took refuge underground.

To test the theory, Dr. Hensky obtained a blood sample taken from Bat Boy when he was treated at a Chicago hospital in 2001.

"My findings support that theory," says Dr. Hensky.

CARVILLE & BAT BOY KIN?
BLOOD TEST WILL PROVE IT!

KISSING COUSINS? Political guru James Carville's uncanny resemblance to Bat Boy is more than a coincidence, researcher claims.

The Continuing Adventures of BAT BOY!
by Peter Bagge

VICE PRESIDENT LINDSAY LOGAN SHARES HER CONCERNS WITH DR. RON...

NOTHING PERSONAL, I COULDN'T AGREE MORE
BUT I'M AFRAID MS. LOGAN LACKS THE PROPER DISCRETION THAT POSITION REQUIRES.

YOU'VE SINCE HIRED LINDSAY! SHE WAS ARRESTED FOR HER SECRETARY! TYING HIM AND BEEN MONOPOLIZING ALL OF PRESIDENT BAT BOY'S TIME...

HMMM... THAT'S NOT GOOD.

YOU WHAT?!

IT WAS EASY! SLIM, SHOW 'EM GO ON, 'EM HOW IT'S DONE!

BUT... HOW?!

BESIDES, I WANT THAT JOB FOR MYSELF!

YO, CHECK IT OUT! I TAUGHT THE BAT BOY HOW TO TALK!!

AND STAY OUT!

BLOOT!

?!

?!

WEEKLY WORLD NEWS, JANUARY 17, 2005

WORLD'S GREATEST PLASTIC SURGEON:
'I CAN CURE BAT
Nip & Tuck operation can make freak normal,

By MICHAEL FORSYTH

THE WORLD'S GREATEST plastic surgeon has offered to dramatically alter Bat Boy's appearance, transforming the half-bat, half-human mutant into a normal-looking teenager — free of charge!

"This tragically deformed individual deserves a chance to lead a normal life," declares South African surgeon Dr. Willem Drakensberg. "There's no reason he

PLASTIC SURGEON
Dr. Willem Drakensberg

should go through life as a misunderstood freak."

The first-of-its kind cosmetic surgery would include multiple procedures:

● In what's known as radical reduction otoplasty, Dr. Drakensberg will trim back Bat Boy's oversized ears, hone the sharp points into a daintier, more rounded shape and pin them closer to his head.

● His eye sockets will be greatly reduced in size, lessening Bat Boy's startling "bug-eyed" look.

● Bat Boy will be given a hair transplant to

BOY!' 'BAT-STIC SURGERY!
top doc says

cover his bald scalp — "If possible from his pubic region, otherwise from a donor," the surgeon says.

Because so few photographs exist of the strange and elusive youth, some details must still be hammered out.

"According to some early eyewitness descriptions, he has rudimentary wings on his back, others make no mention of that," notes Dr. Drakensberg, who first outlined his proposal in the *South African Journal of Cosmetic Surgery*.

"Perhaps they dropped off before he reached puberty — if not, clipping them off shouldn't present a problem."

When Bat Boy was first found as a toddler in a West Virginia cave in 1992, his bat-like behavior led scientists to conclude the feral child had been raised by bats. But his bizarre physical traits — including huge amber eyes that help him to see in the dark — have never been explained.

The creature has spent much of life in research labs, on the run from authorities and, according to reports, working secretly for the U.S. military in the war on terror.

"His life hasn't been normal — how could it be, looking like that?" says Dr. Drakensberg, who leapt to fame when he transformed

FROM THIS ...

...TO THIS!

CUTE: Computer-generated image supplied by Dr. Drakensberg, shows how Bat Boy could look after surgery to "improve" him.

ARE YOU KIDDING?

Plenty of strip-club patrons have unwittingly shelled out hard-earned cash to have balls of silicone bounce around in their laps. As many as 1 in 10 lap dancers sport butt implants, experts say.

India's Baboon Woman into a beauty who now stars in big-budget Bollywood films.

The procedures could be performed in a series of three operations totaling about 22 hours, reveals Dr. Drakensberg.

"I would happily do this pro bono — I wouldn't charge Bat Boy a penny," he says. "The chance to make medical history would be payment enough."

But many consider the nip and tuck proposal an awful idea. "Bat Boy's unique appearance should be celebrated — not treated as a disease," says Maryanne Kestiebaum of Americans Against Way Too Much Cosmetic Surgery.

"This is classic 'lookist' thinking: It's different, so it must be bad." What Bat Boy thinks is as yet unknown — his current whereabouts are a mystery.

But a former handler who works at a research facility near Wheeling, W. Va., doubts that the mystery freak is an ideal candidate for cosmetic surgery. "You try to take off a chunk of Bat Boy's ear and he's likely to return the favor," he warns.

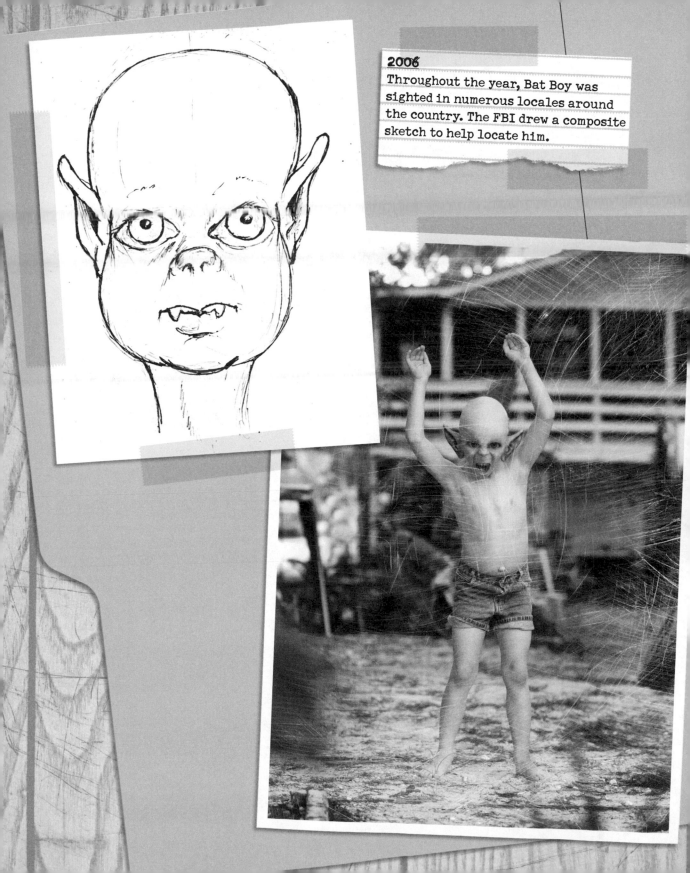

Throughout the year, Bat Boy was sighted in numerous locales around the country. The FBI drew a composite sketch to help locate him.

BAT BOY

CANDIDATE VISITS BAT BOY'S HOME!

Romney promises to protect spelunkers from monsters

By D. PATRICK

WEST VIRGINIA — Former Gov. Mitt Romney made a campaign stop at the famous cave where Bat Boy was found, using the scenic location to discuss safety issues.

Romney, running for the Republican Party's presidential nomination, stood before the cave entrance for a photo op while a press representative told a throng of supporters, bewildered tourists and reporters, "Given the incredible discovery that was made in this cave, the governor feels we need to be more vigilant about protecting workers and explorers from monsters. We ask our fellow citizens to enter these caves to work and we need to ensure that they can safely walk out at the end of the day."

Walking near the entrance but declining to enter, Romney reportedly remarked that the country needs to wean itself from foreign energy supplies so it's of paramount importance that our nation's resources are safe. Creatures like Bat Boy, he was overheard to say, are a threat that has to be contained so our miners can dig with confidence.

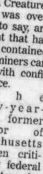

FORMER governor believes creatures like Bat Boy threaten our nation's coal supply.

The fifty-year-old former governor of Massachusetts had been criticized by federal investigators for mistakes made during the expensive Big Dig project in Boston. His appearance at the cave where Bat Boy was found in 1992 was designed to burnish his image on miner safety.

Bat Boy, last seen in Manhattan, was unavailable for comment.

Zap attack

Laredo, Texas — Texas created a "people-zapper" for use in border control with Mexico. The device was similar to a bug-zapper, but much larger.

"It was great," said Immigration and Security Chief Frank Butler. "Anyone who tried to cross the border illegally was systematically buzzed. It really cut down on border patrol necessities and costs."

Butler said the people-zapper remained in place for about two years before being outlawed by the federal government. An estimated 5,32_ attempted-immigrants were zapped away from entering the United States.

"It was actually kind o_ fun to watch," Butler re_ called. "The bzzzt bzzzt wa_ almost soothing and the soft blue glow it gave off was easy on the eyes."

— Dorian Wagner

THIS WEEK HISTORY 1973

MARCH 26, 2007 WEEKLY WOR_

2008

presidential candidate Mitt Romney located Bat Boy's cave and gave a rousing speech on national security outside the cave entrance. Shortly after the speech, Bat Boy vanished.

In April 2008, Bat Boy posed for a *Vanity Fair* cover photo. Things went horribly wrong, as noted photographer Annie Leibovitz enticed Bat Boy into posing seminude for a photo spread that shocked the world. How could she? How could he? He was a mere boy mugging for the lens with a come-hither look while wearing a wig. It was an abomination.

Somehow, Bat Boy put the photo scandal behind him, and in the midst of a debilitating financial crisis, Treasury Secretary Henry Paulson tapped Bat Boy as a special emissary, or "Bailout Boy." Bat Boy served with pride and received yet another commendation from the government in Washington, DC.

California enacted Proposition 8. The measure added a new section (7.5) to Article 1 of the California constitution. The new measure stated that "Only marriage between a man and a woman is valid or recognized in California." Bat Boy protested angrily against the measure, primarily on the basis that as a "boy" he would not be fully recognized as a "man" and therefore not be allowed to wed. His girlfriend, Betty Barnett, backed his protest.

reported on a doctor who wanted to make him look normal.

Dillon noted in his journal that after a surgeon vowed to cure Bat Boy of his looks, Noah Werdman of Kansas City declared that he was saving up to try to modify his looks to look like Bat Boy.

Dillon also included loose scraps of letters that people had written concerning Bat Boy.

In March, the sixty-year-old former governor of Massachusetts and Republican vice

CHAPTER 6

ALMOST HEAVEN

After his opposition to Proposition 8 on the California picket lines, Bat Boy fell out of the national spotlight. My theory was that Bat Boy drifted back to West Virginia the same way a ghost returns to haunt a familiar home.

Periodically I received notice of Bat Boy sightings around the country. Usually these were dead-end leads that required no verification. Sometimes the tips bordered on the ridiculous. Someone sent me a clipping that Bat Boy had made his way to Burlington, Vermont, to meet with Champ, the Burlington Lake Monster.

After digesting the Bat Boy file, my intuition told me that Bat Boy felt comfortable in West Virginia and that I would capture him there. His forays to Virginia, Florida, and Nevada were merely a smokescreen. The attack pattern was his way of trying to throw his trackers off his trail. If he truly had PTSD, then West Virginia was the one place where he could cope.

West Virginia provided the right environment in which he could calmly accept his differentness and go unnoticed. His pointed ears, sharp teeth, bulging eyes, vestigial tail, and other perceptible signs of freakiness that had vexed him in other locations were hardly noticed by anyone in West Virginia. Mutants were commonplace there. Many natives even joked about the state's historic dalliance with incest and the mutated progeny it could produce. One

West Virginia wag had started selling T-shirts emblazoned with WEST VIRGINIA: PADDLE FASTER WHEN YOU HEAR BANJOS. Another local yokel had created a trucker hat with a riddle printed on it: WHAT'S THE DEFINITION OF A WV VIRGIN? A GIRL WHO CAN OUTRUN HER BROTHER. *Weekly World News* had reported that the state's high incidence of inbreeding had sparked the formation of a third human gender, a whole new sort of species.

West Virginia was a place that didn't care about mutants—and possibly encouraged their creation. Residents couldn't care less what the outside world thought of them. That sentiment suited Bat Boy's temperament as well. He had long held himself inaccessible to the outside world, particularly to the media. West Virginians were proud to be outsiders. They didn't need a seat at the table. Bat Boy and West Virginia fit the profile of classic outsiders: they were both dismissed by the general public as absurd, yet, for those who knew better, those who knew the real story, both were formidable. In their otherness, the two entities formed a bond.

Bat Boy could find freedom in the hills and

MY DINNER WITH BAT BOY

Dear Sir:

Last Thursday while dining at a restaurant in Burlington, Vt., situated on Lake Champlain, I saw some fellow diners who may be of interest to you.

When Champ, the Lake Champlain monster, entered, I was star-struck but not terribly surprised. He is a popular local resident, who moves freely among the rest of the populace.

A few minutes later, Bat Boy joined Champ at his table. Bat Boy had invited Champ to discuss the situation with Nessie. Bat Boy said that he had read that Nessie had had her baby and may have been shot. Bat Boy added that growing up without a father had made life very difficult.

With that Bat Boy excused himself, mentioning Jenna Bush and a performance of his musical in Boston. I didn't even have time to get his autograph.

Hope this helps,
Alice L.
Florence, Ky.

We're not sure if it really helped or not, but thanks for writing! — The Editors in the people. The state's motto, after all, is *Montani semper liberi* (Mountaineers are always free).

Yes, Bat Boy felt comfortable in West Virginia. Too comfortable. He had fallen back into his ways. Recent events demonstrated that Bat Boy was developmentally unable to chart any sort of course toward maturity. He was capable of the profound gesture of serving his country, but now he had turned around and was eating cats for a snack. For Bat Boy, biting the hand that fed still proved a tasty treat. In recent days, his attacks far outnumbered any accomplishments, and he needed to be stopped.

I threw Dillon's Bat Boy file on the backseat and pulled my wagon out of Denny's. It was time to get up on that mountain trail and find Dillon's transponder so I could gain an edge on this crafty mutant and track him down.

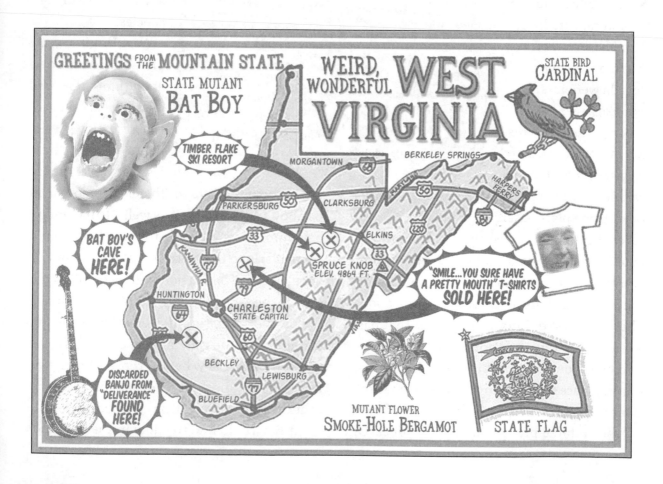

THIRD GENDER IN WEST VA!

By MARK MILLER
Seneca, W. VA.

I N AN astounding new development in the fields of human biology and genetics, a third gender has been discovered in West Virginia.

"It's not just man and woman in this part of the country," observed Cory Stickleback, author of the best-selling novel, *Hillbilly Willy*. Stickleback came upon the new sex while doing research for his upcoming book, *Backwoods Bobo*. The gender has never before been observed by outsiders, though apparently it's been a fixture for many years in an area near an obscure town called Seneca, nestled in the Appalachian mountain range.

"At first I thought it was just this one bizarre mutation,"

recalled Stickleback. "But I soon noticed there were dozens and dozens of the suckers."

The new gender, called "Acenes" ("Seneca" back-wards), is extremely distinctive in appearance. As Stickleback describes them, they feature "asexual, egg-shaped bodies, similar to Humpty Dumpty's. They appear to be completely hairless except for one 'uni-brow' in place of two eyebrows. A large marsupial pouch in the belly area is used to transport their young and their yo-yos, and store their favorite food — rhubarb."

Stickleback secretly observed the Acenes engaged in several unique activities including:

● Spending hours at a time yodeling their favorite song — Frank Sinatra's "My Way."

● Engaging in an elaborate

CHAPTER 7

DO IT IN THE FIELD

Real scientists do it in the field. That's my credo, and that's why I could never be cooped up forever in a lab like Dr. Dillon's. Labs are for geeks.

A real scientist thrusts himself into an uncertain darkness. He enters the cave. He squeezes into tight spots and rubs up against moist cave walls until his skin chafes. He puts his nose right into the crevice. He smells the smells no one wants to smell. He hangs upside down, just like a bat, to reach out and touch a mysterious, furry little life-form.

I pull my Taurus off the unlit West Virginia road and park it in front of the trailhead that marks the path to Dillon's find: a secret bat cave 537 feet up the mountain trail.

In the field, the real scientist risks his life to seek the truth. Every second, you're dancing a dangerous waltz, dodging bites, venoms, viruses, or a skin ripping at the hands of some vicious animal claw. The dance keeps you on your toes, especially at night. On the trail, the life-snuffing danger that lurks around every corner gives rise to an esophageal tingling that perversely makes you feel more alive. When that tingle of danger hits you in the field, the real scientist knows he's exactly where he's supposed to be.

With the car door open, I swing my legs around and strap on my snowshoes. It's a fifteen-minute hike up the steep, snowy path

In the field, the real scientist risks his life to seek the truth. Every second, you're dancing a dangerous waltz...

to the Dillon cave; a sliver of Appalachian moonlight lights the way.

Lab geeks should never enter a killing field like this remote mountainside. When they do, they usually end up like Dr. Dillon. Old Dillon knew his bats and he knew his stuff in the lab, but not in the field. He got careless up here and got himself mauled. These geeks get out on a trail and let their heads get cluttered with formulas and labthink. The geeks forget that the field is not the lab. Labs don't have fang-bearing mutants lurking around the corners waiting to pounce. My phone buzzed with a Google alert. The local Wheeling TV news stations were reporting that a bear had mauled Dr. Dillon. We all knew better.

My large brown canvas field bag over my shoulder weighs me down. The Taser on my belt is charged and ready for a fight. The white snow crunches under my feet. It's December and the snow hasn't frozen over yet, so my snowshoes make a crisp scrunch, not the scraping sound they'll make by February when everything ices over and I have to wear crampons.

With the moon, I can watch my breath billow as I exhale. The cold air mixed with the scent of virgin red pine pierces my nose and lungs, waking me up. It feels good, actually. It's helping clear my head for the unpleasant search-and-retrieve job ahead.

Suddenly, a lighter scrunch of snow sounds. Where did it come from? My eyes dart left. A shadowed form crosses my peripheral at ten o'clock. I'm not alone. My nostrils flare. Esophagus contracts. A high-pitched squeal peals through the air. The tingle of danger. How did Bat Boy know I would be here? Something odd about the pitch of the squeal, though. An octave higher, maybe? Not the usually angry screech but more of a wail. A cry for help, perhaps? Don't be so sure, I tell myself. I pull out the Taser, squeeze the trigger to test its voltage, and plod on.

Bat Boy has eluded me ever since he fled captivity. He distrusts scientists. I can't say that I blame him after what that sadistic janitor in the lab did to him. Bat Boy couldn't

have known that the broomstick-wielding torturer Sayer Schming was not a scientist. But that doesn't matter now. Bat Boy needs to be stopped. He needs to be captured.

Not wanting to stay on the mountain any longer than necessary, I briefly search the attack area for the transponder receiver. I visually map the area in a search pattern. Let me find this transponder, I think, not so that I can find Bat Boy but so that I can get the hell out of Dodge if he's anywhere near my location. That sick mutant! Then I hear a faint buzz. It's not the buzz of the Taser. Off to my right, I notice a small black handle sticking out of the snow. I grab the transponder and check it. It's still working. It displays no sign of Bat Boy. Okay, time to get safely down this mountain. I am not a real scientist.

Just then, I notice a greasy, dark slick. The remains of the Dillon attack. Maroon-colored snow frozen with blood. Two ribs sticking out of the snow like a couple of chopsticks stuck in a huge bowl of rice at a Chinese restaurant. Couldn't the stretcher bearers have taken Dillon's ribs with them?

A man's ribs sticking out of the snow! My proximity to the mauling makes me shudder to think about the attack the doctor suffered: the brute force of a whishing winged projectile hitting him from behind, silently and without warning. The doctor lying on the ground stunned. Then, Bat Boy's loud hiss as he squirts the viscous, warm coagulant about the doctor's body to prep him for easy nonclot bleeding. The brave doctor struggling to defend himself while the stinking flapping shuffling abomination begins to scratch a slit near his stomach for access to the doctor's guts. Defenses weakening, the doctor slips in and out of consciousness while Bat Boy snacks on an appetizer of fingers, lips, and ears. And then, utterly without mercy, the abominable mutant administers his coup de grâce: the doctor is jerked back to consciousness with the stabbing, blinding pain of having his eyes plucked out with a sharp claw. Then nothing. Fade to black. Total darkness.

Seeing Dillon's bloody attack slick causes a Damascene moment for me right then and there. Get me back to substitute teaching at middle school. No way I want to wind up like that slick. I start to shake with fear. Get away from this place and this mutant. It's already late and I have a science class to teach in the morning. I may not eat Chinese food for some time now.

CHAPTER 8

EXTINCTION IS *FOREVER*

EXTINCTION IS *FOREVER* read the bumper sticker on the right rear of my green Taurus wagon. Ninety-nine percent of all the species that ever roamed our planet have vanished. Billions of species gone. Crumple up your endangered species list and throw it away. We're all endangered—every living breathing life-form. We're all that's left. It was time for me to break the bad news to a new crop of West Virginia schoolkids. I parked in the visitors' spot of the General Boyd Middle School, grabbed my cage filled with squeaking bats, and headed inside.

EXTINCTION IS FOREVER

That morning, being a sub science teacher never felt so good. I felt safe and alive and still had all of my ribs. I was glad that I could fall back to this line of work. Eighteen months ago, when Bat Boy's trail ran cold and my career as a bat-research scientist hit the skids, I started supplementing my income by going to middle schools to lecture about bats and the role they play in saving our world.

In order to achieve maximum impact in the classroom, I threw aside my real identity. Nobody wanted to hear from the real me, Dr. Barry Leed, Master of Bat Studies (MBS) from the University of Indianapolis, a divorced, dispirited Hoosier with close-cropped hair and a careworn face born of the knowledge that our world would reach its end of days any day now. How boring. To break through to the kids, I adapted an alter ego in the same manner that the ho-hum Miley Cyrus retooled herself into the showstopper Hannah Montana. So Dr. Barry Leed, the once-distinguished chair of the ATEX Institute and world's foremost authority on Bat Boy, became Dr. Squealgood, the new Mammal Messiah, the one scientist capable of saving the kids and our world.

To gain the attention of this short-attention-span generation, I figured an ordinary lecture wouldn't fly. What would fly? Flying itself. Real live flying bats. Flying fur in a classroom, up close and personal for the kids. See sonar in action! Watch echolocation! I turned my knowledge of bat studies into an action-packed, interactive bat-learning experience that I took from school to school.

Students and administrators went wild for the Dr. Squealgood show. They called other schools to rave about my talk and to recommend booking it. Before long, I found myself crossing West Virginia behind the wheel of my Taurus, spreading the word from school to school, handing out my EXTINCTION IS FOR-EVER bumper stickers at each and every stop.

I longed to get back in the field and be a real scientist once again. This new routine was nothing but a glorified substitute science teacher role, yet the Dr. Squealgood show lectures had started to pay the bills. In the short term, the money saved me. Believe me, I needed the dough. But, over time, the real dividend of what I had created became clear: my lectures gave me a powerful platform to change a generation and the world. I could tell this young generation what my research had indicated to me so many years ago: bats are the fundamental linchpin in our global ecosystem; without bats, the bugs run wild. If bugs run wild, they destroy our crops and food. If the crops go, then the world collapses in global famine. Sally Struthers commercials everywhere. Our number one environmental priority had to be to save bats at all costs.

It would take more than bumper stickers. Dr. Squealgood evangelized bat religion. My legacy had started to create a generation of bat preservationists. I would start in West Virginia, then work my way across the United States, ultimately going international. Together, we would save the world and stop the vanishing act of species, starting with the oldest species that we had left: the bat.

It didn't work that way. Things were already much worse than I knew. As I entered the General Boyd Middle School in Parkersburg that bright fall morning, I had no idea how little time the planet had left and how, in an Appalachian minute, everything can change.

CHAPTER 9

THE BATS AND THE BEES

The Dr. Squealgood show that morning started like any other. Nearly fifty bright-eyed kids streamed into the room clad in baggy pants and hoodies logo'd up with the names of sports teams and rock bands. Out in the hallway several minutes earlier, I had spotted one boy wearing a Bat Boy T-shirt. Naturally, I had chosen him as my sidekick for today's talk. Before we started, I had gotten him dressed in his costume and he was out in the parking lot in my Taurus waiting for my cue from the classroom window.

A bell buzzed at 9:25 A.M. Principal Victoria hushed the class with a sharp raise of her hand. She was holding a copy of the flyer announcing my talk. The flyer looked good. Principal Victoria looked good. "Students," said Principal Victoria, inspecting them intently, "I have an announcement to make. Marcie, will you please stop texting while I am talking. Phones are not permitted at General Boyd." Principal Victoria yanked the phone from Marcie's hand and resumed talking. "We are honored to have with us one of the leading scientists of West Virginia. This man has thrilled students from Morgantown to Wheeling with his presentation. I am so glad we could get him here to General Boyd Middle School. Please welcome Dr. Squealgood."

I walked over to the chalkboard and wrote my name in large letters. "Good morning, students, I am Dr. Squealgood."

"Good morning, Dr. Squealgood," the students chorused back, chuckling.

I wrote the title of my talk in chalk: "THE _____ & THE BEES." My title grabbed the audience's attention. The more advanced kids had already gotten the birds and the bees sex talk from one of their parents. Just about everyone else had heard about it and leaned forward in their chairs wondering if they were about to get "the Talk" from a stranger in a white lab coat standing next to a large field bag bulging with strange props and squeaking with the sound of live bats.

"Can anyone guess what we are here to talk about? The blank and the bees?"

An older-looking girl in the third row shouted, "Sex?"

"Close. The Bats and the Bees. This talk is more important than sex," I replied. Now I had my audience. Dr. Squealgood was a born performer. Like Alice Cooper, I used live creatures for effect. I paused so the class could hear the squeaking coming from my bat cage.

"After today's talk, you will all go home tonight. When dusk comes you will see your world as you have never seen it before. Before meeting me, most of you probably never noticed those winged little friends soaring through the sky to devour bugs. Tonight, though, will be a different story. Tonight, you will look in the sky and you will have appreciation for the job that bats do for us every single night. Tonight, you will look in the dusk and acknowledge our winged heroes. You will look skyward and say, 'You go, my little bat friend. You keep eating those bugs.

> *Like Alice Cooper, I used live bats for effect. I paused so the class could hear the squeaking coming from my bat cage.*

You make the world a better place, keep on winging.'"

I held up a paper globe of Earth. The globe was packed with a small explosive charge. A short fuse protuded from the bottom but the students couldn't see it.

"What's this?"

"Earth," everyone replied.

"That's right, Mother Earth. I have studied bats all over this planet. From Ecuador to Egypt. To do that you gotta do the old high-low. I have been low. So low that I have crawled five miles down into the center of Earth to find bats in caves. And I have been high. Real high. I have climbed one-hundred-fifty-foot-tall oaks to install bat houses in virgin pine forests. Our planet's really sick. What's wrong, Dr. Squeal-good? you say. Well, man created conditions that made it difficult for other species to live. Everywhere we went we destroyed habitats and wiped out species in the process. We chopped down forests and decreased the oxygen generated by trees. With no trees, Earth became hotter. Climates started changing. We had catastrophic tsunamis, floods, and heat waves. We drilled into Earth and plundered its core for minerals and fuels. When we ran out of fuels, countries panicked and fought each other for oil. Millions died. Economies suffered. Your parents cursed at the gas pump. Al Gore won an Oscar. We put dangerous nuclear plants around the globe and have had to suffer the consequences of the catastrophic damage of meltdowns. We're still not sure what the nuclear spillage will do to the planet. As I said, our planet is sick. It's hanging on by a thread. The problem is really bad. How bad? you ask. Well, if Earth has a time clock, that clock is winding down to the end of days." I reached into my bag and pulled out a large ticking alarm clock. In the second row, I spotted a wiry kid wearing a Misfits T-shirt adorned with an oversize button that read METH = DEATH. I put the alarm clock on his desk.

"So you may ask yourself, how much time do we have, Doctor?" I pointed to METH = DEATH boy to hit the top of the timer clock. The clock started ticking. All the students watched the clock. The clock bit was a decoy, and deftly using a magician's sleight of hand I took a lighter and lit the ten-second fuse on the bottom of the globe. The fuse and the clock were synced. The students hadn't noticed. "Watch the clock. Time for the countdown. How much time do we have, Doctor? The clock is ticking. Five, four, three, two, one." The globe burst apart with an earsplitting bang as paper shards flew through the classroom. Three students sought cover under their chairs. I asked them to take their seats again. "You can get back in your chairs. We're still here. But we've got work to do or we're going to wind up blown up. Here's what you need to know: the two most important animals that sustain this planet are . . . ?"

"The bats and the bees," the students replied.

"Yes. Let's start with the bees. Do you know what pollinates apples?"

"Bees."

"What about peanuts?"

"Bees."

"Yep, and that goes for avocados, celery, squash, cucumbers, oranges, peaches, and just about everything else. Bees pollinate one-third of the plants that create the food we eat. And guess what? Bees are sick. Just like Earth. Bees have a disease called colony collapse disorder. We've lost one-third of Earth's bee population in the last five years. If this keeps up, bees will go extinct and we will have no food.

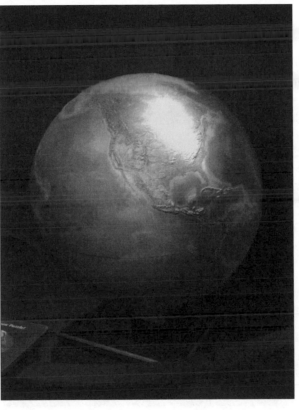

"Remember, I am Dr. Squealgood, not Dr. Goodbuzz. I know less about bees, but I know that bees pollinate during the day. Bats and bees work together. At night, the pest insects like mosquitoes come out, and that brings us to bats. A single bat colony, which is about thirty thousand bats, eats more than fifty tons of insects a year. That's ten semitrucks, like the ones you see on the highway, filled with mosquitoes and other insects. Now, bats have been dying off, too. Twenty-five percent of all bats have died off. We're struggling to find out why. To deal with the loss of bats, farmers have started using more pesticides. There we go, messing with the planet again. Many people think the pesticides are killing the bees. If there are no bats to eat the bugs, the bugs will ruin our crops and plants. And what's worse is that bugs carry disease. You've all heard of West Nile and malaria? Both carried by mosquitoes.

"Well, here we go. With no bats and bees, we're talking famine and plague. Earth blows up. You watch movies about zombie attacks and vampire bites, right? Forget that fairy-tale stuff. This is real. If bats don't protect crops and people from insect damage and disease, the world plunges into famine. If the United States stops exporting food, ninety-three countries will go hungry overnight. Those people will wind up eating each other for food. We'll all be zombies and vampires—we'll be feeding on each other to stay alive. Except you won't even be able to eat someone else because when the food runs out, insects will start eating us instead of crops.

"Malaria, West Nile, and other diseases will get ten times worse. Let me tell you, malaria is the most dangerous health crisis facing our world, and if we don't stop the bugs it's going to get worse. There were 247 million cases of malaria just last year. We have a million people a year dying from malaria right now. We don't see it much here in the States, but if we did see it we would all wake up. Bill Gates, the world's richest man, saw it in Africa and it changed his life. He pledged one billion dollars to try to solve it. You know why? Let me tell you why.

"Malaria ain't no picnic: spiked fever, chills, fatigue, muscle pain, a headache that by itself is painful enough to kill you. You sweat trying to rid yourself of the disease, drenching the sheets, only in the countries where they are dying of malaria right now there are no sheets, so they're drenching the streets, puking like frat boys that they'll never be and waiting for it to be over, waiting for the merciless microscopic malaria parasite that some vile mosquito injected into them to invade their system and choke off the last blood supply to major organs, resulting in seizures, then organ failure, and then you sit there praying that you go into a coma before the foam-at-the-mouth, convulsive death." The class watched me intently as I convulsed, foamed at the mouth, and collapsed to the floor in a dramatically reenacted tragedian stage death. As I got myself up, I approached the student in the Misfits T-shirt.

"So you see, Meth Boy, meth doesn't equal death. Bugs equals death. Here's the formula to take home: no bats equals more bugs equals death. No bats equals death. You see what we're up against, why I do what I do. I studied bats. I had the dedication. I had the discipline. You know, scientists like me, we don't call them bats. We call them *chiropterans*. They are the oldest species left on this planet. Bats were minipterodactyls. Descended from creatures called *therapsid reptiles*, bats first took flight in the Triassic period more than two hundred million years ago.

When dinosaurs went extinct sixty-five million years ago, bats witnessed what happened and kept on flying. These chiropterans won the ultimate game of survivor as they cheated the deadly game of species roulette longer than any other life-form. As scientists, we said to ourselves, if we could figure out how bats survived this long we could save ourselves. See, bats are mammals just like us. Then one day, we found a bat more like us than we ever thought possible: Bat Boy. Who knows about Bat Boy?"

Every student's hand went up. This was West Virginia, after all.

"Well, I have a surprise for you." This was my moment to cue the student Bat Boy I had hidden outside. I pointed to my car, and a figure with bat ears, a skin-colored skullcap, and a cape popped out of my Taurus. With their noses pressed against the window, the class cheered. They didn't know my setup: before each talk, I would pick a student and outfit him in my special Bat Boy costume. The costume wasn't much, really just a bald head cover, jeans shorts, some vampire teeth. The student skipped toward the school door.

"Students," I said, regarding them in the grand manner of a sideshow barker, "I present to you the legendary Bat Boy. Every great performer

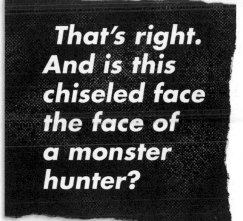

That's right. And is this chiseled face the face of a monster hunter?

has a little helper, Mr. Roarke had Tattoo, Kid Rock had Little Joe, and Dr. Squealgood has Bat Boy. This hybrid creature was discovered by my very own mentor, Dr. Ron Dillon. His discovery in the Lost World Caverns heralded a new dawn of scientific learning. When we found him, everything started coming together. With this little guy in a cage we were learning about our environment and about ourselves. We were closer than ever to solving the extinction problem. Then Bat Boy escaped. Then he was caught. Then he escaped again. Then I spent fifteen years looking for him. Then my wife left me (understandably). She called me a monster hunter."

The Bat Boy played by their fellow student now burst into the classroom to a round of applause. "Now I ask you, is this the face of a monster?"

"No. It's Darryl," a student responded.

"That's right. And is this chiseled face the face of a monster hunter?" I asked, pointing to my visage. The students were silent. "You don't have to answer that one."

"Let's get to work. Bat Boy, release the bats!" I pulled the curtain off the bat cage. "Release the bats!" I motioned for the student to open the cage. I hit the lights in the classroom.

The kids screamed. Now we had the classroom cooking. Bats were zipping back and forth. "See how close they get without touching you. It's called echolocation. It's a principle of sonar." The students were mesmerized.

Suddenly, Meth Boy shot out of his chair and pointed to the window. "Look! It's Bat Boy."

I grabbed his shoulder. "No, this is an act. Darryl is your classmate. He's playing Bat Boy. Are you on meth?"

"No, Squealdude. Look out the window."

I turned my head and there he was. Standing at the window watching this middle school mayhem was the very mutant that had eluded me over these many years. Bat Boy's ears pricked and his head tilted to observe me. For a second, his bulging eyes drew me in. We locked pupils. The mutant's pupils were bigger than quarters and reflected an emptiness that extended without end. It gave me the feeling of looking into a bottomless cave. I shivered. I was staring into an abyss.

I checked my transponder receiver. Nothing. Clearly it was busted. The kids all took off for the parking lot. I screamed after them, "No. Stay here. He'll kill you." My substitute teacher gig hung in the balance. I moved out to the parking lot to save the children. I was moving fast, trying to corral the kids back inside. I could hear Principal Victoria in the background screaming at me, "Doctor. You are finished."

As I stepped outside to get kids back inside, I looked to see if Bat Boy was lurking by the door. He had vanished as quick as he had come.

A pretty young woman emerged from the scene to speak with me. I was face-to-face with the daughter of a coal miner by the name of Betty Barnett. Miss Betty Barnett was rumored to be Bat Boy's girlfriend. She had a round, pretty face anchored by two of the saddest reddened brown eyes I had ever seen. She had been crying, this much was clear. Why was she crying? The difficulty of loving a bat mutant? Or, as I later learned, the fact that she had lost four generations of Barnett men to mine disasters? Betty's father, Jeb Barnett, died in a mine collapse. Her grandfather Jeb Barnett died in a mine collapse. Her great-grandfather Lump Barnett died in a mine collapse. Her great-great-grandfather Lucian Barnett died of a stroke and then got crushed in a mine collapse. Those, sadly, weren't the only deaths Betty had dealt with in her short life. She lost her mother, LuAnn, to secondhand black lung disease. Betty's grandmother Dolly died of grief after she caused the mine collapse that killed Jeb. From then on, no Barnett ever rode a horse named Willy, due to the fact that Willy had been a partial cause in Grandfather Jeb's mine collapse disaster. So there were the deaths. Betty Barnett was alone in the world, save her love of Bat Boy. She had found herself in the cruel cradle of the Appalachian Mountains, finding solace in her relationship with a bat mutant. She spoke to me in a hushed tone. "Bat Boy needs your help, he wanted me to give you this note. If you do what he says, you won't get hurt and he will meet with you. Here, read this." She handed me a piece of paper. The handwriting exhibited neat, feminine touches. Barnett had clearly written the note, possibly from Bat Boy's squeaktation. Still, I read it with great intent.

As I studied the letter, Betty Barnett walked away. It didn't matter. My mood had improved as I now learned Bat Boy didn't plan to pluck my eyes out. I looked up as Betty got in her car and drove off. I tried to see the plate but couldn't. But on the left bumper, the car had a bumper sticker that read GET FLAKY @ TIMBER FLAKE.

Timber Flake was a crummy ski resort up the mountain a ways. There had been rumors that Bat Boy could be spotted there during heavy snowfalls at the night skiing sessions doing insane aerials. I never gave it much thought, but this was now an important clue. Was he really living at the ski resort?

Someone shouted,

"Squealgood." I drifted back to the present scene: chaos everywhere. Kids were running all over the parking lot like banshees. An impromptu wrestling match had materialized in a ring bed of moldy fallen leaves. I was standing in the shadow of the General Boyd statue now. Principal Victoria emerged from a blur of wailing and running kids and shot right up to me. "You're finished, Dr. Squealgood."

"I am not Dr. Squealgood anymore, Miss Principal. I am the Mammal Messiah.

Dr. Leed

Quit this pathetic Squealgood circus act. Who do you think you are, Jungle Jack Hanna? Quit it. You were a good scientist. Your mother would be appalled. Go back to what you know best. We need you now. There's a disease that's wiping out bats. It's called white-nose syndrome and it's serious. I've been visiting all corners of the globe. We are in deep trouble and I need your help to stop the disease. With Dillon out of commission, you're the best scientist we have left and our only hope for solving it. Here's what I need you to do:

1.) Find out what the Feds know. DC is sending a Ranger named Corey Spivey to the ecology center to give a briefing tomorrow.

2.) Go to the briefing and take notes.

3.) Go check your cave—the Cavern Club—to see if white-nose has hit the cave yet.

4.) Get Dillon's files on me. I don't want those going public. They contain sensitive information and portray my intelligence in a negative light.

I will set up our next meeting. Bring with you the field samples from your cave, your notes from the Feds' ecology briefing, and Dillon's file.

Leed, I am counting on you. You don't want to wind up like Dillon.

Bat Boy

How would you like to be my first disciple? Climb in my Taurus. We've got an adventure brewing."

Years of dealing with intemperate schoolchildren must have short-circuited her wild side. She did not look amused. The principal chastised me: "Squealgood, you're sick. You're a freak. You just ran out into the parking lot chasing some imaginary mutant. You know I am not paying you for this crap." She turned like a cat to walk back to the school. With a twist of her head she looked back and said to me, "You know, the principal in Tetersburg said you knew what you were doing. Told me you have to book Dr. Squealgood. He called you a Bat Whisperer. What a mistake. You're a freak whisperer." Just then Meth Boy jumped out from a nearby tree. He had my Squealgood flyer in his hand and thrust it forward. "Doctor-dude, that was awesome. Can I get your autograph?"

"Sure, Meth Boy. Remember, bugs equal death. Science will need you someday." I wrote

BUGS = DEATH, YOUR PAL, DR. SQUEALGOOD.

Principal Victoria scurried back and chimed in, "Tommy, get away from that man. He's a freak show." The principal grabbed Meth Boy by his arm and turned to walk back to the school. I watched her butt bobble as she walked away, then yelled, "Hey, Principal, you forgot my bumper sticker."

"Paste it on your ass," she yelled with a turn of her head. She still looked good, even when angry and even from behind. I heard laughing and looked through the classroom window and saw that the kids were laughing at me. One of those numbskulls had opened the windows and my bats were flying away. They were chirping with delight to be freed from their cage. They were laughing at me too as they flew off toward the serrated West Virginia mountaintops huddled in the distance.

I averted my eyes from the ugly scene and looked toward the statue and up at the steely eyes of the Civil War hero General Boyd to see if his face would betray a reaction and laugh at me, too. The stone face of this great American hero didn't move. Then I noticed his ears. What wacky pointed ears on that General Boyd. I didn't give it much thought and climbed into my Taurus, my mind racing with all that had just happened. My heart pounded as I pulled out of the school parking lot to head for the Fed meeting. I was on a mission. I was the Mammal Messiah now.

CHAPTER 10

SMELL THE GUANO

The Feds had summoned an emergency press conference at the West Virginia Ecology Center. Corey Spivey, a federal FWS (Fish & Wildlife Service) ranger from Washington, had flown in for the meeting.

DC didn't just drop in on a regular basis, so I figured they had something to get off their chest, some new regulation or fine they wanted to impose. Ranger Corey's advance people had assembled practically every biologist, zoologist, specialist, researcher, scientist, wildlife bureaucrat, and university professor in the state.

Of course, DC didn't invite me to the press conference, but I found out about it just the same. As the founder of the ATEX Institute, I was too independent for the government's taste. I called my own shots. These scientists scoffed at my institute. Called me Dr. Squealgood behind my back, or Guano Boy, founder of the Ass-scratch Institute. Out of earshot, they would remark, "Dillon was the only other independent out there, and look what happened to him." They could scoff all they wanted for all I cared. If being an outcast was the price for being independent, then I gladly paid my price. Nobody owed me anything. I was the only independent body in the room.

The room was wall to wall with whitecoats—lab rats or beaker heads, as I called them. It was a beaker-headed speakgeeky.

The team from West Virginia's DNR (Department of Natural Resources) sat to the left of the podium. The team from West Virginia's WRS (Wildlife Resource Section) sat on the right. Those two state agencies never got along, always fighting for local, state, or federal grants to expand their offices or conduct some meaningless clinical study.

DNR was run by Tim Glenning, whose career took off after he found a fossilized alligator with a human-looking head. Carbon dating confirmed that the fossil dated back 150 million years (older than Regis Philbin, even). Glenning called the creature "manigator." Finding that mutant lump propelled Glenning to the head of the state agency. I heard on good authority that he discovered the mani-gator by accident, an accident involving an angry prostitute, a mint Trans-Am, a scuffle, and some underbrush that he relieved himself in after he came to.

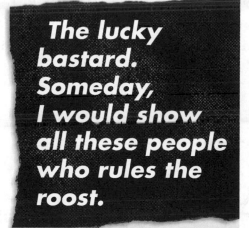

The lucky bastard. Someday, I would show all these people who rules the roost.

The lucky bastard. Someday, I would show all these people who rules the roost. Someday, I will roll into the West Virginia Ecology Center with a living, breathing mutant and knock this place on its ear. Then I'll march my mutant straight down to Washington and get a bright, new, shiny job from the man in DC. I'll get my respect, not from this group of quacks but from the president himself.

As I sat down in the front row, I turned to the back of the room and spotted the boys from FOW seated by themselves in the back left corner. That's when I knew we had deadly serious business ahead. FOW, which stood for Federation of Wildlife, had no state affiliation nor did they receive grants. Supported by the sale of animal pelts and small contributions from groups like the NRA, FOW advocated hunters' rights across the state. These guys slaughtered animals. Worse, they defended trappers' rights while referring to themselves as "sportsmen." Their three membership reps sat fidgeting in their chairs, waiting for the meeting to start. They were scruffier than the rest of the group and had the dark eyes of executioners. Sportsmen? Hardly. This was a regular coonskin cap killing crew. Giving this group a hall pass to the meeting was the equivalent of inviting three furriers to a PETA board meeting. If Federal Wildlife officials felt they had to open the circle of this meeting to include input from these

ACTUAL RELEASE
REPRINTED WITH PERMISSION

FOR IMMEDIATE RELEASE – U.S. FISH AND WILDLIFE SERVICE
U.S. BATS IN EXTREME PERIL
WASHINGTON

A rare disease is currently sweeping through caves from Maine to Pennsylvania claiming the lives of over 500,000 of our nation's bats in recent weeks. Federal Ranger Jay Ferguson discovered the viral disease and named it white-nose syndrome for the white powdery smudge that appears on the noses of affected bats.

The disease has spread so fast that scientists find themselves struggling against the clock to find the source of the disease and stop it before it's too late. As of today, all caves from Maine to North Carolina are closed to human visitors by order of the federal government.

killers, then the situation had certainly escalated way beyond desperation.

Ranger Spivey stood up to start the meeting. He looked wispy and pale for a ranger. From my vantage point, he lacked the ruddy complexion and musculature of a field general like me who had spent his life outdoors.

The ranger spoke. "Thank you for coming. The first thing we're going to do is circulate this press release. Make sure everyone gets a copy." I read the text under the government logo letterhead.

Ranger Spivey continued with his brief: "You can see from the headline that we have identified a serious syndrome that is currently afflicting Northeastern bats. I have officially classified the problem as white-nose syndrome. Here's what we know about it.

"Three weeks ago, a caver named Al Tibbits found a clump of dead bats outside a cave opening forty miles west of Albany, New York, in a town called Slingerlands. He photographed the cluster of dead bats. Tibbits sent the pics to the New York Department of Environmental Conservation biologists. NYDEC took a week to catalog and process the photos before they realized they didn't have a clue and called me. By the time I got the photos, we had numerous other reports coming out of Northern states into our alert center in Washington. We got a call from a woman in Pittsfield, Massachusetts, whose dog brought a dead bat into her house straight from her driveway. The dog was twelve

years old and had never got a bat before. She sent the bat to us. I looked at the photos from the Slingerlands' bats and compared them to the Pittsfield cadaver. I noticed something peculiar between the photo and the bat corpse. Both looked like they had an unusual white substance on their muzzles. The next day more calls hit the hotline. Same stories. 'Cat got a bat.' 'Dog got a bat.' 'Pile of dead bats by the shed.' 'Have never seen a dead bat before in the winter.' Calls started coming in now from parts more south: Winsted, Connecticut; Hackettstown, New Jersey; Fleetwood, Pennsylvania. Now, there's been nothing from West Viriginia yet. But that's why we came down here—to let you know we're on the case."

"Who you gonna call?" I said to myself, under my breath, I thought, but the ranger must have heard me because he shot me a glance like a teacher catching a kid mouthing off in class.

"Excuse me, I am going to open it up to questions in a second. What I am about to say is very important. We think that this is spreading cave to cave. There's evidence that it's affecting caves that have had cavers in the past.

"We believe that humans are the agents of the disease and are providing the conduit. As a result, we are now putting into place a federal ban on all people entering caves. Although the cause of WNS is still unknown, we have enough bat samples and bat corpses that we believe we can make a case to the government that funds should be released to allow us to study this and make recommendations. Keeping people out of caves buys us time while this process takes effect. This caving ban is an order endorsed by Bat Conservation International and even the White House itself. Anyone found in violation of the cave prohibition will be prosecuted to the full extent of the law. Questions?"

I popped up. "You don't need to know guano about bats to know that they just don't die in the winter. They're hibernators. How can you close the caves when you haven't checked hibernation spots yet?"

"Barry," Ranger Spivey said with more than a hint of exasperation, "we've examined thirty-seven hibernacula from Maine all the way down to Pennsylvania. Each one showed a significant loss of life. We called this meeting because we think we can draw the line at West Virginia and stop WNS in its tracks."

I answered, "Drawing the line at West Virginia may have worked in the Civil War, but that was a long time ago, and this thing sounds like it's spreading too fast."

"The first step in a crisis like this is to gather the scientists like yourself along with the news media to talk about how we are responding."

"Ranger, you mentioned a white smudge. White smudge to me means fungus. If there's a fungus among us, we all know what that means. Fungus spreads. Fungus in a cave kills. If we don't contain this, we're looking at a mass extinction."

"Well, the first thing we're going to do is write a proposal so we can secure some funding to monitor this thing and research it," the ranger said.

It was time to sound the alarm. "This thing sounds like AIDS for bats. Who called it a syndrome? This thing sounds like a pandemic. Why the hell are we calling it a syndrome?"

"Leed, you know the procedure here. We have to study this thing before we whip up a hysteria."

"How many species do we have to lose before you people get religion? If you've got white powder, then you've got a fungus. Fungus is the most dangerous thing facing species. This thing has spread five hundred miles across nine states practically overnight. You're calling this a 'syndrome'? You need to call it out for what it sounds like, a 'plague.' Before any of us ever heard of this we had four bat species on the federally endangered list. There are only forty-five species of bats in our whole country, out of a worldwide total of eleven hundred species. Half of those are in the Northeast. Ranger, you better call this the great bat plague because it sounds like you're going to have a million dead bats. When the bats are dead and the bugs are left to roam free and spike malaria, destroy crops, and wreak havoc on the entire country, we can all say Ranger C was on the case. If you're telling us that we have to close all the caves, this is a pandemic. Those are the words we

should be using right now: 'extinction' and 'pandemic.'"

"Okay, Leed. Calm down. Everyone will need to be calm. We want to coordinate task groups that address the various aspects of the investigation and can liaise with the WRS management's work."

"I'm not waiting around. I am going to check my caves and try to save West Virginia."

"Leed, that's not allowed. We have to follow the protocol, make sure the recommendations are correct. We're going to be holding regular conference calls to discuss and monitor the research before we jump to any conclusions."

Chatter in the room started bouncing off the walls. In small whispers in various parts of the room, I could hear the voices of those detractors who had hounded me from the beginning of my career. "Leed, who you gonna call? Bat Boy?" one of the FWS guys said with a chuckle. A professor from the university laughed. "Squealgood, you're going to wind up just like Doc Dillon."

Tim Glenning, the head of DNR, stood up. The room erupted in laughter because he had covered his ears with plastic halloween-style pointed bat ears to mock me. He had unbuttoned his shirt to reveal to the whole room that he was wearing a Bat Boy T-shirt with the classic BAT CHILD ESCAPES! cover. He stuck his pudgy belly forward and yelled, "Hey, Squealgood, where's Bat Boy when you need him?"

"I'm going to check the caves. If this thing is a fungus, and I think it is, then we need to evacuate every single cave right now."

Glenning replied like a schoolteacher chastising a student: "Barry, you can't go into the caves. Ranger Spivey told us they closed the caves. That order is supported by the White House itself. Time to put that old Bat Boy search on hold, Dr. Squealgood."

That's when I lost it. My frustration transformed into a Captain Quint moment. I needed to get their attention. It was time for my screech-on-the-blackboard moment. I took a glass vial of guano out of my field bag and smashed it on the floor.

That got the lab rats' attention. "Hey, beaker heads, do you smell that?" I shifted from a *Jaws* moment to a *Spinal Tap* moment. I picked up a shard of beaker glass and waved it in the room. "Smell the guano. Smell the guano." I walked it straight over to Glenning and put the jagged Pyrex shard right up to his nose. He raised his fat elbows from his sides in a nerdy attempt to push the shard away. For a second I thought of cutting his face wide open with the sharp end but gained my composure and pushed it right back near his nose and looked him straight in the eye to deliver a lecture he would not forget. "Hey, Glenning, if white-nose syndrome is a fungus, you have to warn the bats or we'll have fifty million dead bats. It'll be another Panamanian tree frog disaster. We can't close every cave. Even all the assembled resources in this room couldn't get that done fast enough to save the species. The only way out is to get Bat Boy to evacuate bats via sonar. I don't know why I'm even telling you this. Do you even remember what it smells like in the field? Or are you too busy counting your fat pension and getting tanked in the parking lot at Denny's? And by the way, take those damn ears off before I cut them off Van Gogh–style."

I turned from Glenning to address the larger group, including Ranger Spivey, who just looked at me mystified. "I am going to the caves," I said. "By the time you're done writing the reports, coordinating task groups, revisiting protocols, and asking permission to go to the bathroom, I'll have this thing cooked. Bats aren't going extinct on Barry Leed's watch."

"Tell Bat Boy we said, 'Hi,'" some dork with glasses jeered at me on my way out the door. I had exhausted every movie-inspired gesture I could think of, so I just dropped the jagged shard of glass and kept walking. On my way out into the parking lot, my esophagus contracted. It was different from the tingle that I felt in the field. It was a tingle I had never felt before, and it emanated from the new challenge ahead. The tingle was telling me that this group would regret their disrespect. The tingle was telling me that this was *my* time to prove them wrong.

CHAPTER 11

THE CAVERN CLUB

I descend on my rope into the cave shaft. To get to my lab, I drop twenty-seven feet down the shaft, then climb sideways fourteen feet up a wet water wall to a small, four-foot-wide passageway where I crawl crablike on kneepads for nearly two miles until I drop into the inner limestone cavern.

It's worth the trip. This is the famous cave where Dillon discovered Bat Boy. This was Bat Boy's home before Dillon plucked him out from the rock about a mile and a half down from where I am now.

As I emerge into the inner cavern, beneath all those layers of dissolving ancient limestone, I can hear my bats. The acoustics are so sharp that you can hear every squeak, peep, and tweet a bat makes. The sound always perks up my ears. I take my bag off my shoulder and drop it on the floor. It makes the same echo it always does. The bats hear my bag drop. I hear the change in their squeaks—a shriller note. The bats cheer. They know that their friend is near and that I always bring my bag with me. To the bats, I truly am Dr. Squealgood, and the bag I carry has medicine that can help them.

Most cavers name their caves. My handwriting in chalk on the right-hand limestone wall greets me:

WELCOME TO THE CAVERN CLUB

The acoustics led me to name it the Cavern Club after the famous music venue in Liverpool that hosted the Beatles, the Who, the Rolling Stones, and all the great bands. Bats squeaking melodies in perfect harmony every single night, and no cover charge. Some people observe bats in mines. It's not a natural habitat, though. Bridges and mines harbor a lot of bats, but I have always left those spots to the tourists. Those tourist traps are for fanny packer fudgies who would no more touch a bat than they would stick their head in a mountain lion's mouth. My cavern is the best bat observation area anyone has ever discovered. It has a low domed ceiling with natural sight lines. A small opening near the top of the ceiling allows the bats to enter and leave in the warmer months.

The Cavern Club has been my laboratory and my life. Finding this cave so many years ago ranked with the highlights of my career. Right up there with receiving the Lambert Schpronk Medal from the American Speleological Association for my cave habitat preservation work.

In this habitat, or hibernaculum as we call it, the bats cluster in groups of four to five on the ceiling. I named the groups of bats after the famous groups that played the Cavern Club. There's something human-looking about a bat's face, and naming them helps me to fix them in my mind and identify them each trip. There's the group that I call the Who over in the left corner. Roger is the furriest one, Peter is the skinniest, the Ox is the burliest, and Moonie has the most energy: he bounces in between the other three, never settling down or staying still. On the left wall, you have the Stones, grouped over on the right side of the wall. There're Mick, Keith, Ronnie, Charlie. I can always tell Mick because he never sits still. He prances back and forth almost using his wings like a bullfighter works a cape, just like

Mick did at Altamont. I hope they are okay. They should be okay here. If I can seal up their hole and just make sure they stay inside for the winter until we solve this syndrome, they should be fine. I snap pictures where I can on my cell phone.

I reach for my bag and unclick the fasteners. Digging around, I locate my most treasured tool—my camouflage Eveready 1,000,000 candle watt flashlight. This sucker has the power of a million candles burning at once. Seriously. That's what it says on the label. If the foredeck hands on the *Titanic* had had this light, they never would have hit that iceberg. I take off my fleece Grandoe gloves and clip the light to my belt with a shiny green Coleman camping clip (I love green—not only is it the color of nature, but I read somewhere that it is also the favorite color of geniuses). I power up the Eveready and turn off my headlamp to save its battery for the trip back up to the surface.

I pull out my forensic kit. It's really just a bunch of Q-Tips and petri dishes, but hey, you gotta put your evidence in something. I shine the stage lights up to the groups that I came to check on. Some of the bats blink back at me. That's not good. Their eyes shouldn't even be open at all. But the eyes are foggy, glassed over. These guys are definitely dying. Then it dawns on me. I realize what I am seeing. "So this is what it looks like in the flesh," I say out loud. Their noses are covered in the fine white powder. I am stunned.

Shaking off a momentary paralysis, the scientist in me gets to work. There is no time to waste and I know it. First I need to collect samples of the powder. I start with the Beatles. I hold up one of the long, thin wooden sticks with the cotton wrapped around the end. "George, this isn't going to hurt, I just need to wipe your nose," I say softly. I carefully swab around the nose. George shivers and gently weeps. I twist open a small, round plastic container with a clear, red substance on the bottom. In a back-and-forth motion, I rub the cotton on the dish, and the white powder smears from the cotton to the plastic dish. I replace the cap and write in black Sharpie marker on the top GEORGE. Methodically, I go down the line, repeating the procedure: "John, you're on deck," and so on. Then suddenly, something drops to the floor with a thud. "Ringo?" I cry. Frantically, I wave the flashlight trying to spot her. There she is. But I know she is gone. Bats don't just drop from the ceiling . . . unless, of course, they are dead.

Wait. The flashlight again. Pan past Ringo. She's not alone down there. No. There're more scattered on the floor. No! The Stones, the Who—they're dead. There's Mick, Keith, Ronnie, Charlie, Roger, Elton—all dead on the floor. My bats, bats discovered by me, bats named by me, bats tagged by me, bats raised by me. Others are now falling from the ceiling, weakened by dehydration. Shrieking, pulsing, and then falling. I can't bear the thuds. But they keep coming. On the cave floor, every bat

bears the same plague: a white, dusty mold around the nose. This is definitely a fungus.

I pick up Keith and do a quick exam to memorialize my worst fears. I pull my MP3 recorder out and start speaking.

EXAMINER: Dr. Squealgood

EXAMINATION: Keith Richards

SPECIES: *Myotis lucifugus* (Le Conte) aka little brown bat

LOCATION: Cavern Club Cave, West Virginia

SYMPTOMS: Geomyces fungus rampant. Appears to be recently classified white-nose syndrome. Body shape of deceased bat appears normal. No evidence of swelling or inflammation. However, profuse signs of white hyphae and conidia growing on bat muzzle. Conidia have spread to wing membranes and pinnae. Surface hyphae and conidia flake off skin surface easily but have clearly penetrated deep into bat tissue. Field microscoping of flaked-off areas reveals clogging of hair follicles and sebaceous glands.

REMARKS: This colony of geomyces is a powerful fungus that is branching quickly. Spreading fast. Close proximity of bats in group roosting and hibernation is accelerating the disease spread. Bats appear to have no resistance to the disease due to lowered immunity response during hibernation. This is bat cancer on steroids. It will wipe the species out.

I click off the recorder. I gather up and bag several bat corpses for later examination. I needed to get to Bat Boy at once. With Bat Boy's sonar, we could warn the bats to stay out of the caves until we solved this disease. Dillon, and only Dillon, would know where to find him. I hadn't spoken to him in years, not since he had fired me as his lab apprentice. This is no time for either of us to hold a grudge. We need to solve white-nose syndrome before it is too late. Scientists are inherently linear problem solvers. Scientists mobilize against a disease like this with a predictable linear logic: find fungus, fight fungus, foil fungus. Bat Boy, however, had demonstrated a propensity to proceed with less linear logicality: escape lab, attack girl, endorse Al Gore, attack girl, endorse John Kerry. He is a true wild card, and that made me nervous. Would he help us? I wasn't sure. But I knew enough to know that logic wouldn't be enough to fix this pandemic, and perhaps that's why I was instinctually drawn to him in this crisis. He would never be tamed. He would never apply for a government grant. His whole life was a series of illogical twists and turns beginning with his arrival into the world. I knew we would make an unlikely team, but something told me that was just the sort of team it would take to stop bats being led to extinction. We would be Crockett and Tubbs, if Tubbs were not an African-American cop with an Afro but a mutant bat; Felix and Oscar, if Oscar lived in caves and excreted guano from his rear; Cagney and Lacey in reverse drag, with Lacey keen at echolocation.

I rush to leave the cave. This is spreading faster than anyone knows. I had been in the cave two days ago and no sign of affliction was present. I say aloud to the surviving bats, "I am coming back, guys." On my past visits to the cave, the bats gave me a loud chorus of squeaks when I went to leave. Tonight, my cave sounds quiet. A muffled squeak of pain here and there. The Cavern Club is closed.

As I start to shimmy my way out of the inner limestone cavern, I hear a high-pitched cough. I turn my head in its direction and my headlamp light illuminates the faint outlines of a puff of white smoke trailing up toward the inner cavern exit hole. I look lower into the corner and there he is. Curled up in a ball in the corner of the Cavern Club is Bat Boy. At first glance, I don't recognize him.

I move closer. He is coated in a white dust. Cautiously, I move within arm's length. He is shivering and whimpering. It is clear he is nearly dead. It looks as though having been overcome by white-nose syndrome, he had returned to this familiar place of his origin to die.

I poke him gently with my finger. No response. I turn him over on his back. I am stunned. There he is. It has been seventeen years since I last saw him in Dillon's laboratory. I had been looking for him ever since. Here lies the creature I tracked up and down the West Virginia mountainsides.

While my heart pounds with engagement, Bat Boy's vital signs look severely compromised. His breathing is labored and irregular. Specks of white-spittled dust are coming out of his mouth as he makes weak attempts to cough. He is alabaster white and looks like a corpse. I had planned to rely on Bat Boy to warn the bats about white-nose syndrome, and now Bat Boy is afflicted. Intuition tells me he fled his burrow and crawled back to this cave to die. The scene reminds me of the death march of a white possum that I had observed as a child back home in Indiana. The summer I had turned seven years old, I was kneel-

ing on our driveway drawing out scientific formulas with a piece of chalk when a pale possum stumbled right in front of me. The possum was squinting in the bright sunlight as it limped across my chalk formula. At the other end of the driveway, it disappeared into a circle of bushes that surrounded our mailbox. Having reached its final resting place, the creature stretched out on its side across the flat dirt underneath the bushes, next to the mailbox post, and died. Just like

African elephants that file away to secret graveyards, Bat Boy had echo-located his own secret graveyard.

I pull out two vials of glucosamine and pour them into his mouth, careful to keep away from the fangs in the event the liquid doesn't agree with him or suddenly revives him. He takes the liquid and relaxes slightly. His hand unclenches and a slip of paper falls out. It is a prescription for a six-month supply of Viagra, or sildenafil citrate as it is known by its scientific name. I jam the scrip into my field bag and gather my things to move out of the cave.

I give myself a beaker full of glucosamine. It is going to be hell hauling Bat Boy up and out of this cave. I bend down to pick him up. Even in this frail and emaciated state, he weighs nearly eighty pounds. He is barely conscious. This is going to be a fireman's carry extraction. I am glad for my volunteer service to the Morgantown Fire Department. I lift him up and throw him over my back. It is going to be a tight squeeze. As I pull and corral him out of the cave, my mind is racing. Where should I take him?

Taking him to a lab is out of the question, given his past. Besides, I can't take him back to the ATEX Institute. The reality is that the good old Ass-scratch Institute was the spare bedroom in our condo until Marie threw me out when she initiated divorce proceedings five months ago. And so, the ATEX Institute had gone mobile. It was my station wagon. For all my false bravado I put on at the press conference, the truth is that I am *really* unattached. The good doctor has no fixed address. The only thing keeping the light on in my lantern is the trickle of cash coming in from my part-time teaching gigs. Outside the classroom, I have more credit inquiries than General Motors. I am a financial wreck. Well, I have to tell myself the middle of an important epidemiological battle is no time for personal problems to intrude.

CHAPTER 12
LIMBER SNAKE NIAGARA

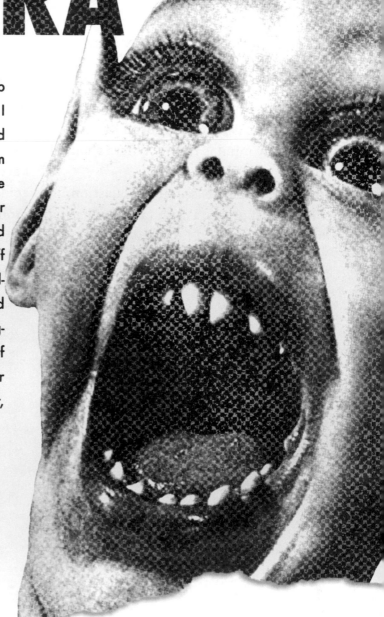

I finally crawled out of the Cavern Club with Bat Boy loaded over my shoulder. I put him down next to the cave entry and strapped my snowshoes on, then lifted him back up. It was a mad scramble down the mountain. Halfway down, I came under attack by a wall of mosquitoes. I swatted them with my hands and nearly slipped off the trail. The swarm flew on past me, heading in a southerly direction. I had squished one against my green parka. It looked bigger than normal and showed no trace of red blood, just a milky goop. Weird for mosquitoes to be out in the dead of winter, I thought, and kept hustling to my car.

When I reached my wagon, I popped off my snowshoes and laid Bat Boy across the backseat. I grabbed the roll of duct tape from my field bag and began to tape Bat Boy down for transport. Without warning, the little mutant strained to speak. I heard him say, "Niagara Limber Snake." I looked at him quizzically and I swear I could hear him mutter, "Niagara Limber Snake," again. He then conked out and was unconscious. I finished wrapping him to the seat. Figuring this opportunity would never come again, I went into my field bag and pulled out a transponder. I couldn't believe it. Only Dr. Ron Dillon had ever tagged Bat Boy before. Dillon had tagged the left ear. I examined the ear and found the mark where Bat Boy had forced out the tag. I examined the overgrown right ear and found the perfect place. I gently clipped it on.

Dr. Squealgood had just tagged Bat Boy! I checked the transponder receiver to verify that the signal was working. It was. Now I would always be able to locate him, unless he forced it off or unless the signal was blocked in a cave.

I hopped in the front seat and adjusted the rearview mirror at a severe angle so I could watch Bat Boy. He shone a ghostly white in the dark. It was like having Casper in the backseat. But this was no friendly ghost. This was a true

> **He shone a ghostly white in the dark. It was like having Casper in the backseat.**

American enigma and we were in a race against the clock.

As I peeled out onto the highway, I was unsure how it all would end, but I knew where to start. I needed Ron Dillon's help. If Dillon could move past the circumstances of his mauling, I knew he could be a valuable ally in the battle against this disease.

I kept checking the rearview mirror. Then, out of nowhere, my cell phone rang. It was Nigel Potts again. When he explained why he was calling, I nearly hung up on him.

"Squealgood, Tim Glenning tells me that you are very close to getting to Bat Boy," the reporter said.

"Hi, Nigel. You know you'd be the first call I'd make if I ever got close."

"My arse you would, old chap. What's going on with white-nose syndrome? We heard Bat Boy himself got white-nose, too?"

I couldn't let on to Potts. The last thing I needed right now on my tail was a meddling geriatric British reporter. I felt like screaming from every West Virginia mountaintop, "Barry Leed just tagged Bat Boy!" That would come later. For now, I had to play it cool. If I told Potts the truth, even *he* wouldn't believe me, and this was one journalist who wasn't afraid to go straight off the top of his head when he was on deadline and needed to wrap things up before happy hour. If I told Potts that I just found Bat Boy near death from white-nose syndrome in the Cavern Club cave, had stuffed him in the backseat of my Taurus, and was on my way to see Dr. Ron Dillon to try to figure out how to beat white-nose and what the meaning of the Viagra prescription was, the old codger would have had a heart attack right on the phone.

"White-nose is a killer. Anytime you have fungus in caves you risk extinction, Nigel. This disease could wipe bats out."

"That's what I hear. I also heard federal wild-life officials are on their way to testify to Congress. I'm surprised they didn't ask you along."

It was a standard journalism trick to tweak your interviewee to see if you could elicit an angry response from him by conveying a slight.

"Well, they should have asked me, but if Glenning had anything to do with it I'm sure he blacklisted me."

"You know, I know how serious this thing is. Do you remember the story I helped break for *WWN* back in 1999? We learned that the U.S. government was training insects to ruin crops. I should send you a copy. What's your address there at ATEX Institute?"

Bat Boy coughed from the backseat. Potts heard the cough. "Sounds like you're under the weather, Squealgood."

"Not feeling great, Nigel."

"I am sure you have been kicking around the caves. Probably down at that Cavern Club that you and Dillon used to go to. Do you think that you've got white-nose syndrome? That makes a great story."

"No. I don't have white-nose."

Bat Boy coughed again.

"Sounds like a denial to me. I'm going to print it. Let me know what the symptoms are like, chap. I can see the headline now 'LEADING BAT SCIENTIST SICKENED BY WHITE POWDER.'"

"Nigel, I don't have white-nose."

"Yeah, well, we're all a little fixated on any-thing involving white powder here after every-thing that went down."

"Seriously, though, stay out of caves. This thing sounds serious," Nigel said.

"Let's stay in touch."

That was a close call. If Bat Boy had made a squeak, Potts would have sent someone to investigate right away. Bat Boy coughed again. His condition worsened. Don't die on me, Bat Boy. What if he died right here in the car? What if I had to eulogize him here on the side of the road in West Virginia?

I would start with some humor. My impish backseat passenger would want it that way.

Something like:

Dearly beloved, Bat Boy soars no more. His final resting place awaits him in the cave in the sky. This is a sad day for bats everywhere. Mosquitoes, however, have just proclaimed today Mosquito Independence Day. But seriously, folks, Bat Boy has gone into eternal hibernation and our nation should mourn. While mosquitoes may be pleased that Bat Boy is no longer, bats are not. Our nation owes a debt of gratitude for Bat Boy's service and dedication to this country.

Out of necessity, there would be a public memorial. The governor would likely attend. Nelson Mandela would make an appearance, for he himself lived in a cave of sorts for so many years. Steven Seagal would come. It would cost West Virginia millions just to cover the memorial service, but the state would make up for it with all the tourists eager for a piece of the memorial service pie.

On the Celebrity Death Scale, the passing of Bat Boy would rank high. Not as high as Michael Jackson, certainly, but surely higher than the sudden deaths of other celebrities that could pass away at any time, people like Screech, and Ethan Hawke, and Tom Wopat, and the cast of *Two and a Half Men*, and Janet Reno, and Jennifer Love Hewitt, and Carrot Top, and Yahoo Serious (if he's still alive?!).

DEATH TO BATS

...white nose plague kills millions!

By NIGEL POTTS *Correspondent*

CAVE exploring is now banned in theNortheast United States.

The urgent government move comes after reports that a deadly fungus called white-nose syndrome has stricken the domestic bat population.

Alarm bells even rang in the halls of Congress after researchers warned that white-nose syndrome could ultimately cause the extinction of bats, one of the longest living species on earth.

"This may be the biggest health crisis we currently face," declared one concerned congressman when he learned about the disease. Many other leaders in Washington have since joined the outcry.

"This is a real and present danger, and our nation is at risk," said a government scientific adviser. "the president has been informed of the situation, and he is promising his support and attention in this matter."

"The health of this nation must be preserved at all costs, especially in the post-9/11 world, where life hangs in the balance more than ever."

No one knows how many bats have died in this country, although the CIA, FBI and NSA estimate that the number could be as high as three million.

"Even the president has serious doubts about the accuracy of those estimates," says a White House staffer. "We are getting intelligence that shows much higher numbers, perhaps three or four times that. To get to the bottom of this, the president has ordered all caves closed to the public population. The president has also called for the formation of a special task force to monitor the spread of the disease and to examine the pathology behind it. Those in violation

Researchers struggle to find a cure for a plague so severe it could wipe out all the bats on earth!

of cave trespassing will be prosecuted to the fullest extent of the law.

Congressional committees have been working overtime on a bat protection bill since scientific advisers first revealed the crippling effects of the disease.

"Bats eat millions of tons of harmful insects every year. The ecosystem that we currently enjoy will be irreparably destroyed should this plague eradicate the bat population," says an aide to the White House's scientific advisers. "We need to be more alarmist about white-nose. We have read at least two news reports on this risk, and I think the American people will thank us for our vigilance and for protecting them from something they had no idea they needed protection from.

"If the bug population takes over

at this critical junction we will experience problems far worse than we can imagine. I am talking about crop destruction, food shortages, and the rise of malaria."

The latest version of the bipartisan pro-bat bill includes a provision for $1.2 million to study bat health and another $7.7 million for a campaign educating the public about the importance of bats, "as soon as the science guys determine exactly what the public should know," says the White House staffer.

White House staffers did not rule out biological warfare or the involvement of terrorist groups like Al Qaeda as a possible cause of the disease. "We're mobilizing every agency at our disposal to find the cause of this disease," says the staffer.

I did not want that scenario to become a reality. I turned on the radio and sped toward Charleston. Air Supply's "The One That You Love" came on:

Here I am
The one that you love

The lyrics made me wistful. *Here I was* with Bat Boy in my backseat. We shared so little in common. Me, the fact-loving, linear, problem-solving scientist. Brought up in the Midwest. Always studied hard. Always worked hard. Probably too hard. Striving for new discoveries to stop this disease and save the race of bats from extinction. Lost my marriage along the way. But still striving. Striving for greatness, really. In some ways, trying to punish myself for my comfortable Indiana childhood.

And Bat Boy half dead. His fungus-addled brain likely hallucinating with visions of forearms to bite. The world locked him up and robbed him of a childhood. When he escaped, scientists and the government hounded him from sunup till sundown. From his earliest age he had been thrust into the center of our cultural spotlight. Stripped of his anonymity as a mere boy, he soldiered on. Had he ever learned to ride a bike? Seen a baseball game? Gone to a prom? Or even made a friend? Instead, what had he seen in his short lifetime? Captivity. War. The pain of confinement. The isolation from family (if he had any). And now affliction from a disease that could potentially wipe him out along with his entire species.

How could I not help? How could I not try to save him?

Were it not for that seventy-nine-pound mutant in the backseat, I would never have ventured into this mysterious land of West Virginia that I now called home. I would never have known the serpentine peaks, the miles of cave networks, the smoke-hole bergamot plant of this wonderful land. This was a land unlike any other part of the world. I had to help.

"Hang in there, Bat Boy," I urged. Bat Boy was feverish and sweating. I opened all the windows and turned on the air-conditioning in the middle of winter to try to cool him.

As the car zoomed along, I thought of Dr. Ron Dillon, about what it would take to beat white-nose syndrome. Dillon would have to open up. Dillon needed to hear what was happening. He would know if my plan to thwart white-nose would work. More important, he would have to tell me what makes Bat Boy tick and how I could get him to cooperate to solve this disease. Squealgood, you're going to need a miracle, I thought. *Drive.* If I could get Bat Boy to cooperate, he could alert the West Virginia bats about the cave fungus and save the species in our state. *Drive.* Bat Boy must cooperate—tearing another scientist's face off under the grave specter of white-nose would be highly inappropriate.

The lab rats at the federal press conference at the ecology center really didn't know what they were up against.

Speeding toward Charleston doing eighty-five miles an hour, my wagon rattled as though it would break apart at any minute. My hands and face started itching and I could see in the rearview that those mosquitoes had tagged me good outside of my cave. I didn't care. My focus now was laserlike. I had to get Dillon to talk. *Drive.*

Negotiating the narrow shoots and jagged ascents through the forest and between limestone cliffs, my soul slowly uncoils. It is the melancholic reality of middle age that allows a man to track the consequences of innocent decisions made twenty years ago with perfect objectivity and know that he is where he is because of youth's illusory passions, a victim, really, of possibilities that only the wisest fools of youth harbor. These mountains are my capitulation, my Zen, my six-second tube ride. Move me sixty miles from these foothills and I am the most forthright of atheists who wouldn't even deign to lament the toils postmodern Christianity has imposed on the human race. But drop my ass in a constipated-sounding station wagon stuffed with explorers' utensils, point me up a cold mountain in the dead of night, and all of a sudden I'm the Dalai Lama sucking hash through a hookah, a divine martyr whose intent transcends courage, transcends the need to overcome fear's insidious

beck when demise is certain. Life is a deathbed. This is my morphine drip.

Dillon's injuries were so severe he had required a life-flight chopper off the mountain to Charleston General Hospital. The surgeon on duty later told reporters that the bite marks were consistent with a bear. He even had a wildlife geneticist on hand to say that the DNA markers surrounding the tissue samples near the bite marks and the loose hairs from the site of the attack confirmed a bear mauling. The scientific community knew better.

Any zoologist knows that a bear would have dragged his victim off the trail, stomped the chest to collapse it, and then started the feast: fingers for the appetizer, then arms and legs the way Maine natives work a lobster. All ambush-hunter predatory animals from lions to bobcats find a remote area to consume their prey. Whatever creature did this mauling left Dillon right there on the trail. Whatever did this wanted everyone to see its handiwork. Dillon was served up as a warning symbol. Dillon was left alive on purpose. A greasy blood slick deposited straight in the middle of the trail by a spiteful attacker that made his point clear: no one will ever collar and tag me again. FEMUR must have paid the surgeon off to remove scrutiny from Bat Boy so they could capture him first.

CHAPTER 13

THE GIANT PEACH

The sun was coming up as I pulled off the highway into Charleston. I cased the hospital gift shop. I was in luck. The shop was open and they had West Virginia University caps. That would be my icebreaker. A die-hard West Virginia hoops fan, Dillon always bitched that he could never find the right West Virginia basketball hat. The hoops hat could get him to talk. It was early and the shop attendant was fidgeting opening up a case of soda to load into a display fridge. I swiped the hat from the display rack and put it on my head. She never looked up. I headed off to the ambulatory care wing of the hospital. It was a West Virginia football hat, but Dillon wouldn't know the difference.

I entered the room. Everything seemed a dull, moldy yellow. The stray shafts of winter sunlight that snuck into the room were muted by heavy vinyl washable shades that lined the two windows. The fluorescent light threw off more yellow. I was glad Dillon couldn't see this. This was not the type of place I wanted to hang out in and I certainly didn't have the time to dwell. I positioned myself so I could look out the window while talking to Dillon and keep an eye on my Taurus with Bat Boy duct-taped in the backseat. Looking at Dillon directly was out of the question.

In the corner of the room sat the patient and next to the patient sat a blood transfusion machine with tubes snaking out of a central computer cabinet into a large plastic bag of blood with warning labels on it. It looked like something a scientist had devised to create tomato soup. The transfusion machine gurgled, waiting for its next appointment with the patient, while making the bubbly, glooping, angry sound of an overheated stew.

I noticed the bags near the bottom of his wheelchair. Hooked to the sides of his chair were three large plastic bags of dripping liquid. It was hard to tell if the liquids were coming

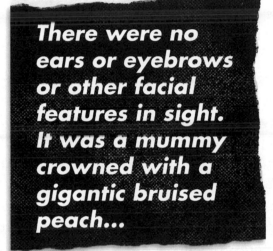

There were no ears or eyebrows or other facial features in sight. It was a mummy crowned with a gigantic bruised peach...

or going. One bag contained clear liquid, possibly glucosamine; the second bag contained a crimson collection of blood; and the third bag contained a yellowy pus, the by-product of heavy scabbing—all the right colors for a tequila sunrise if mixed together.

I looked upward slowly, to observe the extent of the mauling. The wheelchair contained a lifeless lump cross-sectioned by tattered gray bandages. At the ends of his extremities, where hands and feet once met limbs, now sat bulbous wraps of hospital gauze sodden with the persistent greasy ooze of pustule seepage.

At chest level, tubes poked out of either side, spilling gut juice into waiting bags. At the top of this bandaged heap rested a hairless, misshapen orb swollen beyond proportion, listing so hard to the left that it looked like it could tumble off at a moment's notice. There were no ears or eyebrows or other facial features in sight. It was a mummy crowned with a gigantic bruised peach showing color streak variations from red to yellow. This giant peach bowling ball had two dark finger holes where eyes had once been. Centered below the finger holes was a bigger thumb-hole-sized opening that now functioned as Dillon's nose. With each labored inhalation, the thumb-hole nose produced a wet wheeze similar to the sound made by stepping slowly on a dog's plastic chew toy. Below the "nose," a lipless straight line formed at mouth level as though it had been drawn by a Sharpie. It was not clear if the giant peach could talk.

"Hey, Doc, go Mountaineers."

"Who's that?" replied the Mammal Messiah in a pained voice. The Sharpie line could talk.

"Barry Leed, Doc."

"Leed. What the hell do you want? I am sure you didn't come to bring me flowers."

"No, I came to bring you a Mountaineers basketball hat. Here you go." I placed the hat in the mess of bandages furled in his lap.

"Put it on my head. But be gentle—those damn surgeons took most of my skull plate out. Make sure the cap is unhitched on the back, otherwise the littlest bit of pressure will cause unbearable pain." I got the cap on his head.

"Thanks, Leed. I've been trying to find a hat. Trying to cover up what's left of this melon of mine. You still screwing around trying to find Bat Boy?"

"Yeah. I got him in my trunk."

"That's funny, Barry," Dillon said.

"No, really, I got him in the trunk of my car," I said.

Dillon's voice intensified a touch. "Bring him to me and I will finish that mutant off."

I decided to quickly change my approach. "No. I wish I knew where he was. I'm no closer to finding him. Was looking for him up on your trail last night."

"You always had a sick sense of humor, Barry."

"Doc, the real the reason I came to visit you is white-nose syndrome."

"Heard about it. This sounds like the big one. Those clowns like Glenning don't know what they are up against. Fungus in a cave kills. Could wipe out the whole species."

I rubbed my palms together so Dillon could hear it was time to talk business. "Doc, how do we beat white-nose?" I asked. I then realized, thanks to Bat Boy, Dillon was now blind so it didn't matter what I did with my hands. I waved them emphatically just to see if it would draw a response from Dillon. Nothing.

Dillon replied, "First step is get the bats out of the caves. Then you'd have to treat them with some kind of circulatory enhancement so that they could ward off the fungus."

"Do you think a regular medicine like Viagra could work to beat the fungus?"

"Give Viagra to a bat? Well, that's interesting. From what I know about white-nose, it afflicts the central respiratory system and shuts down vessels, creating a lethal sort of lethargy in the bat. Viagra's a vasodilator. Pfizer originally made it as a chest pain alleviator. A bat is a mammal, so it would certainly be effective in halting the white-nose spread in an affected bat, plus it would have the benefit of pushing reproduction in bats so that this massive population loss could be reversed. It's a pretty solid idea,

Squealgood. But it's going to take a lot of Viagra and you're going to have to find a way to get into the caves and get the bats to consume it."

I decided to test my next theory on Dillon. "I was thinking if we secured Bat Boy's assistance, he could alert the bats to stay out of caves and we could figure out a way for Bat Boy to get the Viagra to the sick bats."

"Screw that shifty mutant. You find him and you bring him here. I should have wrung that bastard's neck when I had the chance. Now I don't have enough fingers to do it. I could just get him with my left hand and then use my forearm bar to try to choke him. Look what that bastard did to me. Look at my medical file."

Dillon nodded toward his lap. I saw the medical record atop the blood soup machine and picked it up.

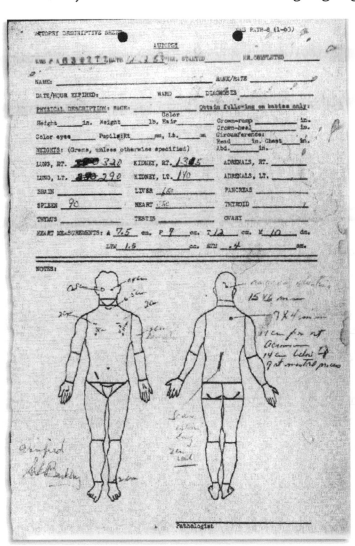

"Can you believe that? It's actually an autopsy report. He mauled me so bad the docs thought I was dead. I came to right before the coroner was going to get to work. That little bastard had me heading toward the light. I was way off base. That mountain trail is not where he lives. He lives over by the ski resort. He knew I got too close. I never should have let him escape." Dillon's mouth was going dry. I poured him a glass of water and tried to align the straw with the mouth line.

"Doc, here's some water. Which ski resort did you say it was?" I asked him while he took a sip of water. He wasn't listening. He was in vengeance mode.

"I would just choke him and never let up. I never should have let him out of my lab. If I had full use of my legs I would run to him and confront that mutant. If I had full use of both

BAT BOY'S FACEBOOK STATUS UPDATES

<Bat Boy is so hungry he's foaming at the mouth. Oh wait, that's the rabies.>

<Bat Boy wishes he didn't lack a claw on the second toe of his forelimb.>

<Bat Boy is sleeping . . . right side up. Just kidding!>

<Bat Boy continues to emit high-pitched sounds locating prey.>

<Bat Boy is happy it's Friday!>

<Bat Boy was born to shred.>

<Bat Boy can't believe how warm and sunny it is! Damn you, sun. Damn you.>

<Bat Boy will never fly near a wind turbine again. Scary!>

<Bat Boy wants a Bloody Mary.>

of my arms I would grab hold of him. If I had but three little fingers attached to two hands I would choke him. And then if I had just one opposable thumb I would ram it right into his eye. And if I had eyes, I would watch that little bastard squirm as I choked the life out of him." Dillon had now grabbed the West Virginia hat and was choking it.

"But which ski resort does he have his cave near, Doc?"

"You idiot. He's on Facebook. Just look him up. He's a snowboarder now. He works a chairlift part-time at the Timber Flake Ski Resort to make ends meet. He's even got a girlfriend. That little freak is getting smooth with a little lady and yet he took from me the one thing that I can't get back. I never should have let him leave my lab. Never should have untied him. I never should have let him go."

Dillon moved his head to motion to the dresser. There was a piece of paper on it. "Those are his last Facebook status updates before he got to me."

"I saw that on Facebook, but I figured it was some kid just playing around. Bat Boy snowboards?" I studied the paper printed out from a computer. Dillon had apparently friended Bat Boy on Facebook in an attempt to monitor his activities. He had compiled several status updates.

"He got his Bloody Mary, all right. Look at me. They say when the swelling goes down and the first facial scab layer peels off, I will start looking more normal. I can't wait to see that. You know, Leed. You could have been a good scientist. I thought you were genuine. You sold me out to the government. You were a mole."

Dillon was referring to my brief flirtation with the Defense Department. I hadn't always been independent and I had to learn the hard way. The department had contracted me to study bat wing movement for a new fighter jet. I had kept it a secret until Dillon busted me with a classified folder.

"Stupid me. I thought all those questions you asked about bats' flying abilities were legitimate. You were stealing my bat flight sim research and passing it off to the Feds as your own work."

"Yeah, but when you busted me, I offered to cut you in."

"You tarnished the whole lab. Everybody figured I was in on it already, and I wasn't."

"Ron, I was desperate. I was out of options. Had grad school debt up to my ears. Plus, Marie left me. She took every cent I had and my anime collection. I had to get Uncle Sam to pitch in."

"It was the principle, Barry. You lied to me."

"Once you fired me, I was cooked. Nobody would touch me. Who the hell gets fired from an eighteen-thousand-dollar-a-year job as a bat research assistant? I can't get a grant to save my life. I've changed. The limb I was hanging from broke years ago. I'm in this because I love bats. They still have so much to show us. I want to make a difference now. You showed me the way back then. I remember you told me, 'Find one mutant and get your name in the paper; find an entire new species and you're Charlie friggin' Darwin.' Hell, even Darwin, your hero, took money from his government. The king paid him to study butterflies. Paid for his trip to the Galápagos. Screw butterflies and that chrysalis crap. We study bats. We study mammals. Ron, help me figure out how to work with Bat Boy and we can find that whole race of Bat Boys. We can be famous. Lewis and Clark. Crick and Watson. Dillon and Leed."

"All right. Look, I'll tell you what makes Bat Boy tick. Surprised you haven't figured it out yet. But you have to promise me you will bring him to me alive. He's going to resist capture at all costs. So, ALIVE. That damn mutant needs to pay for what he did to me. I want him alive and I am going to do him a turn worse than that janitor ever did. He'll be begging for the business end of the broomstick when I'm done with him."

Dillon convulsed in his chair. "He's got a girlfriend now. You know, Barry, like anyone else, he's driven by the need to reproduce. Find his girlfriend. Make friends with her. If you can get her in your pocket, Bat Boy will follow. I was wrong hiring that speech therapist for him. He couldn't help himself. I should have hired him a girlfriend. But watch out for that trollop girlfriend of his, Betty Barnett. I think she's the one who set me up. The girlfriend lives with him at that Timber Flake Ski Resort." Dillon reached up to adjust his hat with a bandaged stump. He pushed the hat down farther over his eyes where his eyebrows used to be and said, "Leed, I want you to bring him to me alive. ALIVE."

Timber Flake, I thought to myself. That was it. That's what Bat Boy was saying to me in the car. Timber Flake, not Limber Snake. I had to get Bat Boy back home, back to his girlfriend. If I could get him healthy I could gain his trust and we could beat this disease.

"Hey, Doc. As a down payment on me bringing him back to you alive, how about you could loan me a few bucks until I capture him?"

"Are you kidding me? Taking money off a blind double-hand amputee! Have some respect, Squealgood."

"You want him alive, right? It's not going to be easy."

"All right. You did get me this hat. Grab a twenty out of my wallet. It's over there on the dresser."

"Oh, and one more thing. Do you happen to have any Viagra?"

"For Christ's sake, Leed. Kick a guy when he's down. I do have a leftover scrip. I sure as hell won't be using it, given my condition." Dillon nodded over to the sink, and I picked up a vial of the pills.

I split in a hurry. I didn't want to linger with Dillon, and I needed to get back to make sure Bat Boy hadn't gone anywhere. I had gotten what I needed from Dillon. Fortunately, he didn't know my secret, that Bat Boy was in the back of my wagon. The (supposed) West Virginia hoops hat had broken the ice, but it didn't close the deal. Only Dillon's misguided desire for revenge on Bat Boy got me his access and trust. I checked with the floor nurse as I exited the care center to see what freedom of movement Dillon's doctors prescribed. She told me that under no circumstances was Dillon allowed to leave the premises. She told me with clinical certainty that the only way he would leave the center was feet first.

The field scientist in me knew why Dillon wanted to be free. He wanted to get back on the trail. It would never happen. The Mammal Messiah was the Mammal Maulee. Bat Boy had trapped his trapper.

CHAPTER 14

TIMBER FLAKE VIAGRA

The Timber Flake Ski Resort stood on the outskirts of Davis, fairly close to the Spruce Knob area. After a long drive through the mountains, I arrived at the resort with Bat Boy safely in tow, semiconscious in the backseat.

The guidebook called the resort "quirky," which in guidebookspeak meant the place would be uneven, to say the least. The guidebook also mentioned that the resort, despite its location in a national park, had received numerous citations for environmental violations. The National Green Ski Association had singled out the resort for having the worst ecological record in ski resort history.

The first thing that struck me about the place was that they made the parking lot way too big. A six-acre eyesore spread of asphalt with maybe nine cars in the lot. Some contractor swindled someone to lay down a lot of asphalt. There was a horrible, loud whine of engines in the air. I counted eight large four-stroke snowmobiles traversing every which way, belching smoke as they moved. There were bulldozers, dump trucks, and mover trucks lying about. Judging by the heavy construction machinery, it looked like they hadn't finished building the resort, though it was thirty years old. The roads looked as though they were in a permanent state of construction. The landscape bore the scars of a mining state's approach to ski resort construction.

It was nearly dusk by the time I pulled into the parking lot. I looked around. Bat Boy had

fallen asleep. I had tried to wake him, but he was very weak. I would need a hand hauling him to his cave if this was indeed the place that Dillon's file pointed out was his true home.

I needed to find someone who could be trusted and could give me the intelligence on where exactly Bat Boy lived. The sound of a Lynyrd Skynyrd song drifted into earshot. It seemed to be coming from a lone lift ticket booth. I walked toward the music and found a young man with a beard who was closing up the booth and singing along to "That Smell." His name tag read BRUCE, TICKET PROFESSIONAL, DAVIS, WV. He was a local.

"Hi, Bruce. My name's Barry Leed. I am a bat research scientist. Have you ever seen Bat Boy around here?" Bruce casually produced the trail map and showed me the area on the mountain where Bat Boy normally liked to hang.

Bruce pointed to a small hut on the map and said, "That feller dwell right up here."

I pulled out the twenty dollars that Dillon had given to me and put it on the counter. "Bruce, could you come over to my car for a second? I need to ask you a big favor." Bruce grabbed the twenty-dollar bill off the counter and said, "Sure, whatever you need." We walked over to my car. I pointed to the dazed Bat Boy in the backseat. "Is this the same little guy you've seen around here?"

"Yep. That's him. Little guy. Pointy ears. Sharp teeth. Always wears jeans shorts, no matter how cold it gets."

"Okay. I need your help hauling him up to his hut. Can you help?"

"Um . . . I got a snowmobile. Maybe we can hook him up in one of these ski patrol rescue sleds." He pointed to an orange sled lying next to his ticket sales area. "We should be able haul him straight up in this. Get him out of your wagon and meet me right here."

"You got it." I pulled Bat Boy out of the backseat, lifted him up onto my shoulders, and walked him over to the snowmobile. We loaded Bat Boy into the gurney sled and climbed on the snowmobile. It took off slowly up the mountain. I kept looking back to make sure Bat Boy was secure in the sled trailing behind us. As we headed up the hill, each of us was curious to find out what the other knew about Bat Boy.

Bruce called back to me, "So where did you find him? We hadn't seen him in a while."

"I found him in a cave about ninety miles away. It was the cave that the scientist Ron Dillon originally found him in. I think it's the same cave he was born in. He got real sick. He was going back there to die when I saved him."

"I saw in the car that he looks really pale. Does he have that white-nose thing that's killing all the bats?"

"That's my diagnosis. I've got some medicine with me that I think will help him. How long's he been here at Timber Flake?"

"I first saw him last winter. My uncle was working a blast job up on the mountain when they found him."

"A blast job?"

"Yeah. They was widening that green bunny slope at Spruce Knob and had to blow about half the mountain away just to make room for it. I was working that day. Man, that was the biggest blast I think they ever had here."

"So how did they find Bat Boy?"

"Like I said, my uncle was the assistant foreman on the job and he told me the blast goes off and all these rocks and shale go shooting everywhere. As the debris starts to settle, this shirtless little bald kid comes walking out of a gigantic cloud of black smoke. Kid is coughing dust and looks pissed. In his hand he has a half-eaten squirrel. None of the fellers up there could believe it. They must have set too much dynamite into the rock and blown his cave to bits."

"Did he attack them?"

"No. So what happened was the fellas was scared the little guy would go to the EPA on us and that we would get fined for putting too much TNT into the mountain. So my uncle had someone go down the mountain to the shop and buy him a hat, shirt, a pair of boots, and bring some food up from the kitchen. The guy came back up to the blast site with the clothes, a twelve-pack of Bud, and a frozen rack of ribs. Man, that kid loved those ribs. The whole crew watched him eat the whole rack, bones and all. Then my uncle had one of the guys open up this out-of-the-way warming hut for him. That's where I showed you on the map. They figured they would get him a proper roof on his head and let him sleep the whole thing off."

"And he slept it off, no problem?"

"Yeah, and here was the natural-born genius part of it. So the next day my uncle sends this chairlift operator named Betty Barnett up into the warming hut with a hundred bucks and a brand-new snowboard to give him to keep him quiet. Well, he didn't even take the money. He pointed to her ribs and she figured out that he just wanted some more ribs. She kept him quiet, all right. She started hanging out with the kid. She runs the top chairlift kind of near his shack, and every morning when she would start her shift she would bring him some ribs."

"Did she teach him how to snowboard?"

"Nah. He taught himself. You should see the kid. The crazy thing is he doesn't even wear boots. Just curls his toes around the board and takes off from the top of the hill. He don't even use a chairlift to get back up the hill. What he does is, when he gets down to the bottom of the hill he does this thing where he drops his head and sort of accelerates into a U-turn that gives him this crazy momentum that shoots him back up to the top of the ski run almost like he can fly. Then he just does the run again. He always lets out a squeal at the top and the bottom."

"He doesn't bother the other skiers?"

"You kidding me? That kid is so rad on the board that every kid here tries to copy him or ski with him. His girlfriend, Betty, was saying they was trying to get him a tryout for the Olympic snowboard team. Some of the kids would try to keep up with him and meet him, but he'd be too fast. Kids would even try to get his autograph. But he's not the most friendly guy. Just kept to himself."

The snowmobile arrived in front of a small green hut. There was a light coming from the inside; someone was home. Bruce unhitched the sled and I knocked on the door.

The door opened and there she was: Miss Betty Barnett.

She wore Timberland work boots and a beat-up old Timber Flake Ski Company green ski parka with a name tag that read BETTY, CHAIR-LIFT OPERATOR, DAVIS, WV.

> BETTY
> CHAIRLIFT OPERATOR
> DAVIS, WV

Betty gazed down into the ski stretcher, and at the instant she caught sight of the pale, ghostlike invalid wheezing in my stretcher, those sad red eyes changed their expression to joyous relief.

"Hi, Betty. We met at General Boyd Middle School in the parking lot. I think I have something that belongs to you."

"You found Bat Boy. Thank you, Doctor. Thank you." She kissed Bat Boy's head and noticed right away that he was nonresponsive and warm to the touch. "He looks sick. Is he okay?"

I didn't want to get into more details with Bruce hovering on the scene. "Thanks for the ride, Bruce." Bruce took the hint and unattached Bat Boy's sled. Then he started up the snowmobile and headed back down the mountain, leaving the two of us alone.

"Betty, there is a very serious disease attacking bats right now called white-nose syndrome. Bat Boy shows early symptoms of the disease, but I think I found him in time to cure him. I am going to need your help."

"Of course, Doctor. I know about white-nose syndrome. I was worried sick for him. I sent him on an errand last week. He never came back. I didn't know what to do."

"Is there somewhere we can take him?"

"Can I trust you, Doctor?"

"Betty, you can trust me. I don't want to see Bat Boy in captivity. I know what happened to him when they locked him up before. That's why I brought him back here when I found him. It wasn't easy to find you. I have some medicine for him that I think will cure him."

"Okay, Doctor. Follow me." She stooped to grab Bat Boy's feet. I grabbed him underneath the shoulders. Betty lowered her shoulder to lean against a section of the wooden hut, and a panel moved away. The warming hut harbored a secret entrance to Bat Boy's cave. She began walking down a series of rocks that formed a natural staircase. We descended for thirty feet and then banked into a central hallway. This first cave entry point looked like a vanity chamber. On the walls were posters from *Bat Boy: The Musical*. I could begin to see that his cave had the layout of a New York City tenement railroad flat—a central hallway with rooms on either side. Large candles along the hallway provided a minimal amount of light.

Betty could see me making mental notes of the cave. She spoke up, "Bat Boy would kill me if he knew I was doing this. You can never tell anyone about this cave location, Doctor. I am the only one who knows."

"Don't worry, Betty. I won't tell anyone. Also, it looks like this cave is safe from white-nose syndrome. I don't see any signs of the fungus on the walls or corners."

"I like to keep a clean cave, Doctor. Bat Boy likes it that way," Betty said.

As we moved down the hallway, I noticed rock grottoes on either side that formed the rooms. There was what looked like a home gym on one side, and a home office on the other side. I paused briefly to look into the gym and saw large posters of the Bush twins Jenna and Barbara. As we went farther down the hall, I wondered why every secret male lair contains weights and photos of the Bush twins. On another side of the cave, I noticed a home recording studio. Farther down the corridor, I could see a garage that looked like it had a car inside it. One room on the left side of the hallway looked bigger than the others. An interesting modern sculpture of metal protruded into my line of sight, drawing my eyes toward what looked to be a gallery extending deeper into the cave. Was it possible that Bat Boy had an art gallery down here? We kept moving, and finally Betty reached another cave opening, and as we descended a few more feet I could see that this was Bat Boy's bedchamber. We laid Bat Boy on the bed.

In the darkness, I couldn't make the room out entirely. My head bumped into a swinging device attached to the ceiling. It appeared that there was a figure on top of the swing. Did Bat Boy employ a swing to sleep hanging upside down while Betty slept in a regular bed? I couldn't be sure. I would have to come back

> **Bat Boy would kill me if he knew I was doing this. You can never tell anyone about this cave location...**

and check this area again with a headlamp. We laid Bat Boy down on the bed. I reached into my pocket and pulled out the vial of Viagra that I had gotten from Dillon. If Bat Boy could read, he would certainly have gotten a kick out of knowing that he was now in possession of Ron Dillon's Viagra supply. I gave the vial to Betty and said, "Here's the medicine that I think can help Bat Boy. It's Viagra. You may have seen their ads on TV."

"Doctor, that's what I sent Bat Boy out of the cave last week to go and get. We ran out."

"This is a vasodilator that should counteract the effect of the white-nose syndrome fungus. There are of course side effects, but we can talk about that later."

She grabbed the vial of pills and began feeding them to Bat Boy one after another.

"I think just one should do, Betty."

"No, doc. He eats these like M&Ms."

The effect of the pills was immediate. The Snuggie blanket got a little too snug. There were visible signs that Bat Boy was stirring. Lust and must swirled in the dank cave air, causing a damp electricity to charge the air of this grotto of love. I figured it would be safer to leave now than run the risk of frightening Bat Boy in a vasodilated state. "I'll come back in a few hours to bring Bat Boy some bugs." Bat Boy's eyes began to blink quickly. There was no telling how he'd respond to my presence, and I didn't want to end up like Dillon.

"He would love that," Betty said as she rubbed his forehead. "If he's feeling better he may even want some wasps."

"I know. He loves wasps," I said, thinking back to the days in Dillon's lab. The sudden intimacy of the situation made me uneasy. I had no interest in being a third wing. It was time to go. As I left the cave, I turned back and saw that Betty had already stripped down to reveal lingerie. Against my better judgment, I snapped a photo from my cell on my way out. She hadn't noticed the picture. Her glance focused squarely upon her tumescent mutant. Her almond eyes had taken on a different appearance. In place of the reddened sadness there now shone a glint of pure happiness.

Betty Barnett

CHAPTER 15

BAT BOY'S CAVE

I made my way back through the cave and attempted to use my cell phone to take pictures, but the light was too low to make much sense of anything. I got out to the hut and descended back down the mountain. I rounded up a supply of insects along with some bees that I got from a local honey grower. I went back up to the hut and pushed the wood panel and went down into the cave. I called out for Bat Boy and Betty, but nobody responded. I went all the way down the hallway to the bedroom and found no one. Probably fearing that I might compromise their location, they had flown the coop and cleared out.

I decided to get some photos. I had brought my camera and had the headlamp on to illuminate what I saw. I opted not to use my tape recorder. I needed it to be quiet in case Bat Boy and Betty came back. I started in the room with the sculpture. Upon closer examination, it looked as though Bat Boy had taken bits of disused ski lift machinery and assembled them into mobiles. Bat Boy's precise arrangement of discarded metal made a bold statement about the dehumanizing intrusion of the machinery of our modern age. Bat Boy, after all, did not use chairlifts. As I explored, I discovered a gallery of artwork by Bat Boy. The technical range of paintings was incredible. At his young age, Bat Boy could draw like an Italian master, and some of his works displayed the expert tone of Botticelli or Caravaggio. There was also evidence that Bat Boy was well versed in modern techniques such as airbrushing and could replicate photo depictions as well as Chuck Close. Bat Boy was a Renaissance mutant.

While his range of technique was quite broad, his subject matter was ludicrously limited. Bat Boy drew only self-portraits or images that contained his own image. I took photos of the canvases that lined this room. Without ever having studied at the École des Beaux-Arts in Paris, Bat Boy had done a supremely passable version of the famous Cupid and Psyche portrait *Le Premier Baiser* by the mid-nineteenth-century French master William-Adolphe Bouguereau. Bat Boy had taken the liberty of replacing Psyche with his own image. What that meant in terms of his own identity I could not formulate. I snapped a photo and moved on.

The gallery went from the dreamy romanticism of the picture above to a disturbing head decapitation. I felt as though I had stumbled off an Amsterdam dock into Rembrandt's studio. In the next wall painting, Bat Boy had knocked off the great Italian master Caravaggio's *Medusa* from 1597. Bat Boy had replaced Medusa's head with his own face. The effect was chilling. In Greek mythology, Perseus had used the image of Medusa's severed head as a shield to ward off enemies. Bat Boy's version would certainly ward off enemies—as well as friends. The symbolism of the painting was not lost on me. It was definitely a warning signal of some kind.

For his next painting, Bat Boy turned to the expressionist anguish of the primal scream that the Norwegian painter Edvard Munch had so brilliantly depicted in his masterwork of 1893. Munch's painting had attained iconic cult status within our modern culture, appearing in TV ads, on dorm room posters, book covers, and even bumper stickers. Anyone could clearly see that by making this version of the scream autobiographical, Bat Boy drew a sharp parallel to his own situation as an iconic figure trapped by society's expectations. The tortured anguish inherent in this piece nearly brought me to tears. I had to move on to the next work.

Included in this portion of the gallery was a version of an old master portrait that Bat Boy had incongruously put next to a much more modern portrait that he had airbrushed in the style of the Shepard Fairey street art graphic.

I was amazed at how deftly he could copy styles through different movements and centuries. The next group of paintings revealed that Bat Boy had an equally assured understanding of the imagery that surrounds our culture. Rather than working with oils, now he was working in airbrush, gouache, black and white, and possibly even using Photoshop, though I saw no sign of a computer.

The first image was a redo of the imagery of the movie *Bad Boys*. In Bat Boy's version, he doubled the trouble. He followed up his macho theme by modifying the movie artwork from the smash motion picture hit *300*.

Moving back in time, Bat Boy showed his comic side by

linking himself to the comedic greats Laurel and Hardy (with Bat Boy's apologies to Laurel, of course).

There were still other images that prompted questions about Bat Boy's identity and offered a stirring glimpse into his own soul. Bat Boy had completed a tribute image to the Dutch artist M. C. Escher. The picture's superb rendering of the head trapped within a ball spoke to the isolation that Bat Boy must have felt living in his cave.

I turned my attention to two other portraits in the gallery. The composition in these pieces felt more original, but sadly they illustrated Bat Boy's feeling of a loss of control in his life. I would have not thought of Bat Boy as a victim of "puppet syndrome," but these deeply personal works made it clear that in some way Bat Boy felt that someone else was pulling his strings. As a mutant, Bat Boy certainly lived with the fear that he could never be himself if he wanted to be accepted and loved. It was as if he had put his own identity aside to play "Bat Boy" for the world. That he was acting to fill a role that society needed him to fulfill. That if he were to look up and see who was pulling his strings, it might actually be the men in black, the government. Or perhaps these were latent feelings that sprang from his dark days in captivity where he was caged and literally manipulated by scientists to discover answers that their research demanded. The torment in these pictures made it clear that Bat Boy still had work to do if he was to truly cut the strings and live independently.

Other images showed delusions of grandeur. Bat Boy placing his image in the center of grand parades both in China (where he was virtually unknown) as part of a Mulan celebration and in an antiquated New York City.

The last image in his gallery was perhaps the most telling. There was a special indentation in the cave rock formation that Bat Boy saved for this large-scale self-portrait. Bat Boy had depicted himself as a superhero with a new sort of costume. Yet his photorealistic portrait underscores all of the self-doubt that must fill his conscious mind. Bat Boy is shown with lame, outstretched cloth wings. Bat Boy depicts himself completely devoid of musculature. Even the crotch area, which usually

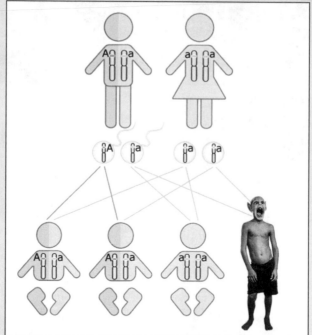
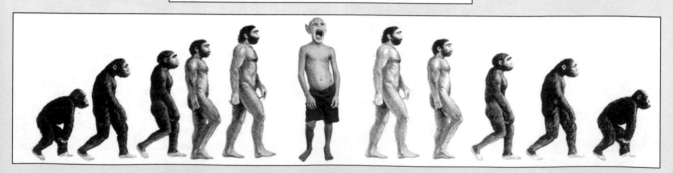

bulges with virility for nearly all superheroes, appears flat and unpronounced. Rather than portray himself as a capable superhero, he had sent the message in this last depiction that "I am a powerless hero, an empty shell, a costume only and nothing more."

I explored the other rooms and took pictures as well. Bat Boy had a media room with a television. He had DVDs of the movies *Men in Black*, *Twelve Monkeys*, and *Trapped in Paradise*, and DVD television episodes from *Roseanne* and *Weird Science*. All of these had featured Bat Boy at some point and so they became favorites of his. Bat Boy had also apparently scrawled into the side of the cave wall a list titled SHOWS I WANT TO SEE. Underneath in a crude scribble were the following shows:

TV SHOWS FOR ME

Batt Houston
Battlestar Galactica
Little Bat House on the Prairie
Grey's Anatomy, Particularly the Neck Region
Batman
CSI: Bat Cave in Rural America
Batlock

Next to that was another scrawled list:

JEOPARDY SUBJECTS TAILOR-MADE FOR ME

Rabies
Bram Stoker's Most Famous Novel
Bats
Fun with Frugivores
Movies Based on Bram Stoker's Most Famous Novel
Yippee for Yinpterochiroptera
Bible Quotes

There was also a bumper sticker in his media room for the Southern California radio station KROQ 106.7, which frequently interviewed Bat Boy and would, from time to time, pose the question to its listeners, "What would Bat Boy do?" I also found a piece of notebook paper in this room that read:

MY PLAYLIST BANDS

Bat Power
Vampire Weekend
Bat Rebel Motorcycle Club
What Made Milwaukee Famous Were Flying Mammals
The Good, the Bat & the Queen

Fleet Flying Foxes
Bats Domino
The Bats
Bat for Lashes
Clap Your Hands Say Yeah Bats Are Cool
Bat Stevens
'N Sync
Nine Inch Bats
Bat the Wet Sprocket
Bat Hole Surfers
Lisa Loeb

When I reached the bedroom, I was astonished. I couldn't believe what I found there. It didn't seem to jibe with the introspection of his gallery works. It appeared that within this chamber Bat Boy's confidence flourished. With my headlamp I was able to get clarity from what I had seen earlier in the darkened chamber. It was most disturbing and would take me some time to process.

As I headed out of the cave, I happened to take one last look in Bat Boy's office chamber. My headlamp scanned the wall and caught a leather-bound book that was slid into a rock opening. It was Bat Boy's photo album. I blew some dust off the top of the book and started reading. What I saw stunned me. This book contained the private photos of Bat Boy from his birth to adulthood, along with numerous handwritten notes.

It started with his baby photo and went from there. I read through the book and put it into my field bag. I had second thoughts about taking Bat Boy's photo album but figured I could likely sneak back in and return it after I had scanned it at a local Kinko's. The photos were of the most personal nature, and the album began with the most telling phrase concerning Bat Boy's identity. In the margins there were handwritten notes that offered unusual commentary.

"WHO AM I?" This section contained a genetic diagram of the mutation that likely caused him. It showed the DNA helix pathway that created Bat Boy. In the margins, someone had written, "MUTATION IS NORMAL! Mutations happen every day. Blue eyes, color blindness, vestigial tails."

The next page captured Bat Boy's view of evolution. The image seemed to indicate that the era of man began with Bat Boy and ended with Bat Boy.

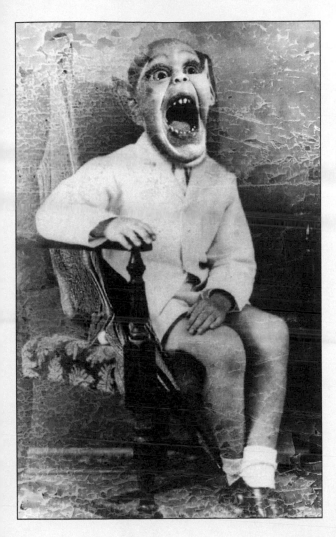

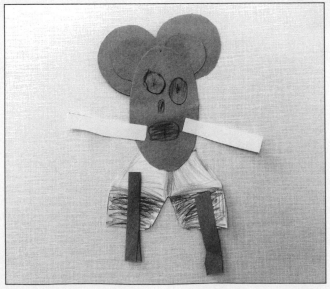

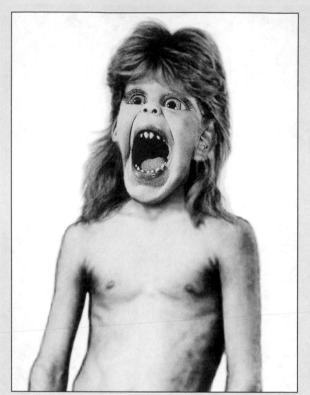
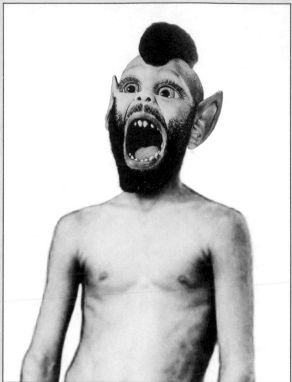
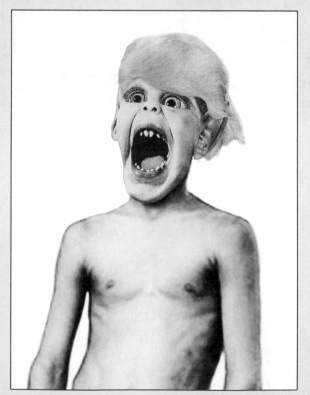
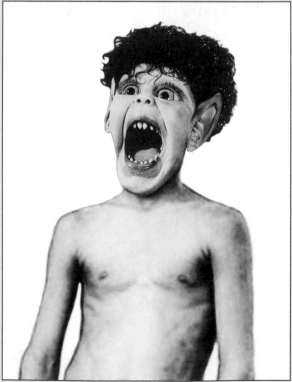

There was then a startling ultrasound image of Bat Boy in utero. The clarity of image that these gleaming, big white machines can reproduce at such an early phase of the life cycle was amazing. Thank you, General Electric, I thought.

The book moved on to his baptism, or as it was written in his photo album: "BAT-TISM." There was a "baptismal" certificate signed from the Seventh-Day Batventist church. There was a delivery photo of Bat Boy nude with swaddling covering his privates. In one picture, Baby Bat Boy was teething on what appears to be a femur bone. There was also a photo of what I presumed was Bat Boy's favorite toy. It was a Mr. Potato Head, only this version had been modified so that it looked like a Mr. Bat Boy Head.

There was a photo from a pediatric dentistry office in Wheeling, West Virginia, that outlined Bat Boy's unique tooth configuration. Similar to a shark's mouth, Bat Boy's mouth had rows of impacted teeth that were able to spring up if one of the front teeth got dislodged or came out.

There were pictures of two drawings. One a childhood self-portrait and the other a crude stick figure drawing of a mosquito. On the self-portrait someone had written "Age 4" and on the mosquito drawing someone had written "Age 2." Neither showed any evidence of any intuitive drawing capability that the later paintings in Bat Boy's gallery suggested. However, I was excited to take these handwriting samples back for analysis, as they could ultimately provide clues as to Bat Boy's mysterious parentage.

The next heading in his album read, "MY BAT-HOOD."

After that was a section title, "BAT HAIR DAZE." There were images of Bat Boy through many phases of hair styling. There was a picture of the Bat Boy comb-over, where Bat Boy sported a moppy, Trump-like do.

There was Bat Boy Mr. T, with Mohawk Afro.

And there was the Bat Boy *Thriller*—Bat Boy with a Michael Jackson–style Jheri curl. In the margin someone had written, "Experimenting with your hair is normal. All kids do it."

"BAT REBEL." There was a picture of Bat Boy in

BAT BOY FAMILY TREE

1953–1986 – Herbert Hoover Boy Jr., like his dad, worked in the mines until, it is said, "a hippie" dropped five hits of potent LSD 25 in his coffee. He was last known to be living in a yurt in the Pacific Northwest, eating mushrooms and "thinking about stuff."

1944–1972 – Herbert Hoover Boy, Margaret's son, went to work in the coal mines of West Virginia as a child of 12, not of financial necessity, but because he liked caves – and the job.

1910–1983 – Margaret Boy, Horace's only child, dropped the "e" from the family name and added a "y," so people wouldn't associate her with her mobster dad. She left The Windy City and moved to West Virginia, it is said, "for a fresh start."

1875–1930 – Marcus Boe, first-born son of Archibald, established himself as a respected "bug man" with a successful exterminating business. There were rumors that he didn't use flypaper or traps but caught them with his mouth.

1954–? – Susan Boy, Herbert Sr.'s daughter, achieved regional success as a country singer with a persona that has been likened to that of mountain songbird Dolly Parton. Susan's liaisons with an unnamed country legend produced two children: Ruth Carter Cash Boy and "the one they call Bat."

1982–? – Bat Boy, sister of Ruth Carter Cash Boy, is a decorated U.S. Marine who has confounded the authorities by stealing cars and biting children after serving his country as a "super patriot" on the front lines in Afghanistan and Iraq. Elusive and reclusive, where he will pop up next is anybody's guess.

1890–1931 – Horace "Joe Ears" Boe, Archibald's youngest son, left California at an early age – 13 – hopping an eastbound train to Chicago. He was befriended, it is said, by mobster Al Capone. Horace was shot dead in a shootout with famed federal agent Eliot Ness in 1931.

1972–? – Ruth Carter Cash Boy was "a quick learner who was able to quit school after the sixth grade." It is unclear where she is today.

1785–1866 – Andrew Jackson Boie made the study of bats, owls and other nighttime predators his life's work. Like owners and their dogs, it is said he began to resemble the leather-winged fliers.

1825 – 1911– Archibald Boe, Rodney's first born, left the family's ancestral home in Massachusetts and moved to California where people were "more tolerant" of unusual looking people.

1682 – 1776– David Boee is remembered as the oldest soldier to fight for American independence. He fought with valor and, tragically, was killed the day the British surrendered.

1787–1869 – Rodney Boe, Catherine's youngest, was an inattentive speller who inadvertently dropped the "i" from the family name. Family friends believed Rodney's poor scholarship was an attempt to focus attention on his smarter siblings, to divert eyes from his short stature, excessively oversized eyes and large, pointy ears.

1661–1692 – Susannah Boee, John and Rebecca's daughter, gave birth to two children, Alexander and David, before townspeople, spooked perhaps by their pointy ears, accused the woman of "consorting with Satan" during the Salem witch trials and burned her at the stake. The boys were spared.

1591–1622 – Artemis "Pip" Boee arrived in the New World just days after the landing of the Mayflower at Plymouth Rock on the lesser known, leakier and much lower-brow vessel, The June Bug. Little is known of his life.

1735 –1815 – Alexander's daughter, Catherine Boie, was best known for her work with wildlife. She studied animals and kept many unusual species as pets, including bats. Her eldest child, Andrew, was particularly fascinated with these nocturnal creatures.

1679 – 1769– Alexander Boee is remembered for having changed the spelling of his last name to Boie "because he wanted people to think he was French." He also was the shortest family member on record, standing just 28 inches tall.

1658–1722 – John "Little Cotton" Boee, Charles' firstborn, was deeply religious, "a preacher of the gospel," and he was devoted to his wife Rebecca. It is noted that her own birth was hard and long, resulting in slightly elongated ears.

1612–1591 – Charles Alexander "Cotton" Boee, Artemis' son, appears to have been a prosperous farmer in Massachusetts. He fathered, it is said, 23 children, but only one is recorded on the family tree.

leather in a rebel pose. In the margin someone wrote, "BAT TO THE BONE!"

The next chapter was "BAT-TOON." In this section were images of Bat Boy during his Special Forces days. The pictures revealed how a boy became a man fighting for his country overseas. There were band of brothers–style action photos from the trenches. They pumped fists and won medals, all the glory of combat with none of the bloody mess.

Next there was a folder of what looked to be very old parchments from more than a hundred years ago. I was holding Bat Boy's family tree.

Someone had clipped in this section an old, yellowed daguerreotype along with pages from a diary. Underneath it was written: "Bat Boy: You owe it all to him. Your great-great-great-grandfather, THE GENERAL. He would be so proud of you in the Middle East."

It struck me that these were primary-source documents from the Civil War. Bat Boy was in possession of the diary of General Bartholomeuw "Bat" Boyd. Not since the diary of Mary Chesnut had a document of such historical significance been located. I looked at the daguerreotype closer, and even in the muted sepia tones of that ancient image-reproduction technology I could tell at once that General Bat Boyd bore a deep resemblance to Bat Boy. The general had one of those massive Jefferson Davis–style undergrowths, which threw me off at first. But once I looked at the picture a second time, taking into account the wildly different facial grooming standards of that era, I could focus in on the pointed ears and bulging eyes. Those distinct features gave it away. This was Bat Boy's great-great-great-grandfather. Dillon was right all along that there was a race of these little people and it stretched back hundreds of years. More important, as I read on into the diary, Bat Boy's ancestor had played a pivotal role in the formation of our modern nation during our most turbulent era of civil bloodshed.

It appeared that Bat Boyd was a son of Virginia before the state was torn apart by the Richmond Convention of 1860 that led to Virginia's Ordinance of Secession in April 1861. General Bat Boyd was a true Southern dissenter. He was antislavery and loyal to the Union. As an observer at the Richmond Convention, he withdrew immediately following the vote and fled west into the mountains with a group of sympathetic Virginians. On May 13, 1861, Bat Boyd helped call a meeting of delegates from Northwestern Virginia in the town of Wheeling. Bat Boyd attended the meeting as temporary undersecretary. That day,

in Wheeling's Washington Hall, Bat Boyd was passionately vocal in criticizing the actions taken by the Virginia government a month earlier in Richmond. While others debated a legislative approach that might bandage the state back together, Bat Boyd defiantly took the podium and addressed his statesmen. I was holding the torn fragment of the speech in my hand. It was written in an elaborate script: "My fellow Virginians, let us act and let us act now. We must repudiate these monstrous usurpers; let us show our loyalty to Virginia and the Union at every hazard. It is useless to cry peace when there is no peace; and I for one will re-

peat what was said by one of Virginia's noblest sons and greatest statesmen, "Give me mosquitoes and liberty or give me death!" The next day a resolution was adopted for the creation of the new state of New Virginia. The rest was history. A map outlining what took place was enclosed in Boyd's diary.

A northern rebel was born. When the regular Virginia Army attempted to conscript Boyd into Confederate service, he deserted at once and fled to live in a cave up in the Allegheny Mountains. The general organized a small band of supporters called Boyd's Boys. Boyd's Boys became one of the Union Army's most effective assault teams. Boyd's band of brothers would make deep forays into Confederate territory and then hide out in swamps and bogs, where the high incidence of bugs and malaria prevented any militia from following them. Word spread among both sides of the war that Boyd's men were so determined in their efforts that their rations consisted entirely of mosquitoes and bog tadpoles. Neither side could believe that they drew such mighty sustenance from that grizzly diet.

Boyd's Boys spent the remainder of the war

Clement Battles

Lee Batwater

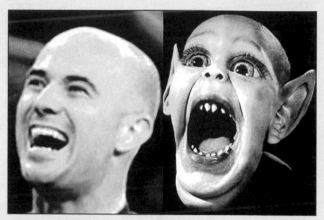

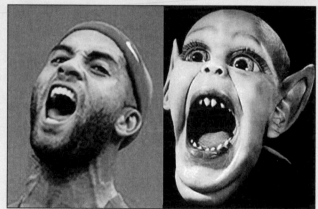

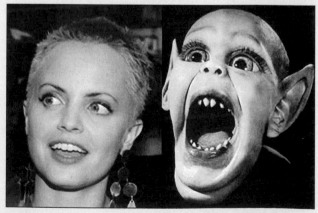

confounding Confederate troops with guerrilla-like nighttime raids featuring the earliest use of sonic warfare devices. Confederate troops under attack from Boyd's Boys would regularly cite ear-bursting screams as the harbinger of an upcoming vicious attack. One old-time soldier, lucky enough to survive a Boyd raid, commented in his journal that the screeching was so loud that he'd give anything to be back fighting the Indians again. Another wounded veteran had suffered bite marks over 78 percent of his body. Before passing away from a subsequent onset of rabies, the wounded soldier whispered his last words into his nurse's ear: "The pain is unbearable. I wish Boyd's Boys had just bayoneted me."

Boyd's Boys quickly proved themselves to be a very pointy thorn in the side of the South. With Grant and Sherman lurking to the north, the last thing Confederate soldiers needed to be worrying about was westerly incursions from a ragtag bunch of unkempt screamers who would bite you into submission.

Boyd was also a tireless antislavery fighter. Many of the raids from Boyd's Boys were

Battila the Hun

designed to free slaves. It would later be questioned as to whether Boyd's motives were purely moral or religious on this count. An informal census of his private cave from 1862 revealed Boyd to be cohabitating with fourteen freed slave women, twelve freed Mississippi natives, and two Alabamans. The census also noted copious amounts of an expensive cognac from France called Courvoisier.

Boyd died tragically at the age of twenty-seven in the Battle of Shepherdstown. Battle observers reported seeing a Union soldier staggering unsteadily into the Confederate line, foaming at the mouth and asking for a drink. At a distance of no more than thirteen feet, Boyd was pulverized by a close-range musket shot, and his tattered remains were quickly hauled off the battlefield. Many soldiers believed that Boyd had gotten drunk and lost his mind. However the autopsy revealed that Boyd was gravely ill with rabies and cited the awful disease as the cause of his death. In the end, it was not the pointed barb of a bayonet that felled Boyd, but rather the pointed barb of a mosquito. But sure as cotton is white, Boyd gave it to those mosquitoes worse than they ever gave it to him.

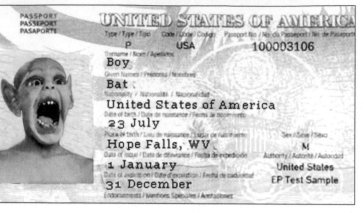

Bat Boyd's heroism became the stuff of West Virginia legend. Citing his bravery, the Union Army awarded Boyd a bronze star and posthumously elevated Boyd's rank to general. The army also paid out a substantial pension to his fourteen common-law wives still residing in his Allegheny cave, with the strict stipulation that the pension funds could not be spent on cognac.

Boyd's service during the painful crucible that forged our modern nation provided a clear pattern for other brave Americans to follow. From what I had now learned about a familial connection between Boyd and Bat Boy, it appeared that Boyd's legacy of freedom fighting was preserved through generations in conflicts that stretched from the bogs of antebellum Virginia territory all the way to the sands of Saudi Arabia.

So there it was in primary-source detail. All these years people asked who was his father. But they were asking the wrong question. As it turned out, Bat Boy through his ancestors was the real father of West Virginia. I remembered the statue at Boyd Middle School and the unusual ears. It looked just like Bat Boy.

That explained why Bat Boy had come to be a symbol in West Virginia in the same way that certain animals wield symbolic power in a country like China. In China, for instance, the dragon represents good fortune and is so revered that it became a symbol for China itself. To natives, the dragon is regarded as the mythical ancestor of all Chinese people. Similarly, among West Virginians, Bat Boy had come to be regarded as a communal ancestor because that's exactly what he was. Bat Boy was West Virginia's daddy.

There were other documents that showed Bat Boy's commitment to his country. Some of these volumes appeared to be highly classified and unusual reading. There was a treatise on Afghan tribal autonomy that was highly annotated in a scrawly hand. There was

Bailout Boy with Treasury Secretary Paulson

a book titled, *Ex-Guerrillas Out of the Mist: The New Leftist Leaders of Latin America*. There was a book on the destabilization of Chad and the troubling tome *How to Overthrow a Sub-Saharan African Despot in Ten Easy Steps*. There also was a report marked classified: *Progress Update: The Denuclearization of the Korean Peninsula*.

The next section was called, "FOOTLIGHTS." It showed Bat Boy at rehearsals of his musical. There were pictures of Bat Boy rubbing shoulders with other great theater luminaries and a picture of him hanging out at a few of his favorite musicals.

Someone had written in the margin, "ALL THE WORLD'S A CAVE." A little lower, someone had written, "Break a wing."

In the next section, Bat Boy's call to service was profiled. There were images of Bat Boy's public life, including the famous picture of him receiving his wings from NASA on becoming an astronaut.

Someone had written, "BAT BOY FOR PRESIDENT."

Bat Boy's passport was in the album, along with a handwritten note that said, "REMEMBER YOU ARE REGISTERED TO VOTE IN 48 STATES. SO ROCK THAT VOTE!"

The next section was "BAILOUT BOY." It featured an image of Bat Boy with Treasury Secretary Henry Paulson. Tucked in on another page was the thank-you note from Paulson to Bat Boy for his service.

"PEOPLE AND PLACES" was the next section. There were candids of Bat Boy with celebs and pictures that were arranged to make it look like Bat Boy was with a celebrity.

MY FAVORITE MOVIE IS *AMERICAN BEAUTY*
MY FAVORITE BAND IS FALL OUT BOY
MY FAVORITE SPORT IS TENNIS
Go, James Blake
Go, Andre Agassi

Dear Bat Boy,

Your service to your country in a tremendous time of need will not be forgotten.

The advice you gave to me both formally and informally proved highly valuable as we wrestled this financial crisis to the mat.

As you now turn your efforts to solving the nation's energy crisis, I know your counsel will prove as valuable to the Department of Energy as your counsel here at Treasury.

Please find the enclosed picture that the press pool delivered upon your appointment as undersecretary. Hopefully, it will provide you with fond memories of your time of service for years to come.

Faithfully yours,
Henry Paulson

MY OWN PERSONAL HEROES THROUGH
HISTORY

Battila the Hun
Clement Battlee
Republican strategist Lee Batwater
Yasser Arabat

These pages were followed by a section titled
"BETTY." There was a picture of Betty, and,
underneath, someone, most likely Bat Boy, had
written various romantic lines to her. There
were five handwritten lines, but the first one
was crossed out. They read as follows:

Dear Betty,
~~Guano have sex?~~

Dear Betty,
If I could rearrange the alphabet, I
would put U and I together. Then I
would bite you.

Dear Betty,
Did the sun come out or did you just
smile at me? Either way, I'm nocturnal
so, you know, stop.

Dear Betty,
I'm foaming at the mouth, you're so
beautiful. You're foaming at the mouth
because I just gave you rabies.

Dear Betty,
Let's echolocate back to my place.

Inside the notebook, I found other poignant
notes and printed pages. One was a printout
showing the lineup from Bat Boy's rotisserie
fantasy baseball team:

Batlanta Braves.
GM: Bat Boy
Manager: Joe Battin
C: Earl Battey
1B: Don Battingly
2B: Howdy Baton
3B: John Battig
SS: Ed "Batty" Abbaticchio
RF: Batsy Donovan
CF: Batty Alou
LF: Bat Burrell
DH: Batsy Dougherty
SP: Batt Holliday
RP: Batfish Hunter

The album ended on a heart-rending note.
It simply said, "SCREAMS FOR MY FATHER."
There was a picture of Batman and a question

mark next to it, along with a picture from the courtroom trial in which Bat Boy had unsuccessfully sued Batman for paternity. The case was thrown out by a lower appellate circuit at a county level. The judge ordered summary judgment and that was that. Someone had written in that section, "HANG IN THERE."

Then I discovered two critical documents. The first was a letter to the governor of West Virginia.

A second piece of paper tucked into the album contained a handwritten verse, "Bat Boy's Sonnet." The verse was ragged, but the poem expressed the deep struggle within Bat Boy to come to terms with his mortality. The lines also indicated that Bat Boy knew that white-nose syndrome was close to killing him. The reality of the disease had clearly caused a brooding melancholy to overtake his soul.

BIRTH CERTIFICATE

Born on this day

BAT BOY

This child is recognized as a member of the

SEVENTH DAY BATVENTIST CHURCH

Stony Creek, West Virginia

Dear Governor,

We have not met, though I am the unofficial mascot for our noble state of West Virginia. In these tough economic times, we need to create new revenue opportunities.

I write to you today with such a solution.

Over 100 million visitors a year visit Mount Rushmore in South Dakota. The visitors contribute roughly $50 million annually to the state's economy. West Virginia has no such monument, despite our more central location and better proximity to larger urban areas.

Therefore, I hereby propose the creation of Mount Batmore. This new monument shall serve as a granite shrine to the four most important cultural heroes in West Virginia history. The attached artist's rendition will allow you to visualize the monument. The lineup will be as follows, from left to right:

- CLARICE STARLING, a cannibal-chasin', serial-killer-arrestin', haunted-by-lambs-screamin' young West Virginian gal
- JOHN HENRY, a rock-drillin', steel-drivin', steam-power-beatin' C&O man
- AUNT BEA, an Opie-raisin', scalawag romancin', pork-chop-cookin' West Virginian lady
- BAT BOY, a bug-chompin', eponymous-musical-starrin', mountain-lovin' native boy

I have it on good counsel from a local engineer at the Timber Flake Ski Resort that this Mount Batmore chisel operation could utilize old strip mine equipment and would cost taxpayers no more than $27 million. Again, please refer to the attached drawing illustrating the carved granite in Burkham's ridge.

Awaiting your reply,

Bat Boy

BAT BOY'S SONNET
Montani Semper Liberi:
Mountaineers Are Always Free

I long for when I was a carefree child
Still hidden in my Stony Bottom cave.
Nightly roving the Appalachian wild
Devouring the mosquitoes I crave.

Now white powder has seized my darkened mind
It binds my wings such that I cannot fly;
Mortality to disease now aligned.
Few are my years, am I too young to die?

Once, in a dream, came visionary bliss,
Soaring through the air my mouth open wide.
Chomping millions of bugs to tiny bits,
I ruled the West Virginia mountainside.

I fear the world was not designed for me.
Fate conceals the hour when I cease to be.

CHAPTER 16

FREAKY-DEAK

I was leaving Bat Boy's dank lair when something on the floor near the entrance caught my eye. I bent to pick it up and was stunned to find that it was the most recent issue of *Time Out: Appalachia*. I must have just missed Bat Boy and Betty.

The pages were a blur of listings of upcoming events: bluegrass festivals and hog roasts and tent revivals and quilting lectures and tractor pulls and even a Dolly Parton look-alike competition at the Coalminer's Daughter Gentleman's Club near Pigeon Forge, Tennessee. But what seized my attention was a dog-eared, half-torn page near the back; on it, one of the listings was circled with a smear of what appeared to be guano. "See *Bat Boy: The Musical*," it said. "One night only!" The performance, at a high school gymnasium in the Smoky Mountains, was scheduled for the following evening.

I arrived just as the curtain was going up and slid into my seat as quietly as I could. I'd seen the musical before; done right it was a masterpiece. But this was an amateur performance, and there was no sign that Bat Boy was even in the audience. When intermission came, I was about to sneak away, maybe grab an early dinner at the Motel 8. But then I saw a group of young guys in fatigues near the back of the gym, talking with great animation, and I wandered over, intrigued. It turned out that they were a Kentucky-based handful of Bat Boy's war buddies, and they welcomed me into their circle, happy to share stories of their friend's military exploits.

In the early days of the war on terror right after 9/11, they told me, Bat Boy had been recruited into a top secret Special Forces unit assigned to what the military was then calling "target-rich environments." He was posted to Afghanistan, and at first he had trouble adjusting, recalled a cheerful, lumbering fellow who said I should call him Slick.

"Tell you the truth," Slick said, "I thought he was a freaky-deak. But know what? That little mutant bastard has more heart than the whole lot of us."

Time Out Appalachia

Harley Learns Us How: To Handel That Snake

Effie-May's Latest Quilting Tips

It's That Time Ya'll
Bluegrass and Pig Roasts
We'll tell ya the wheres and whens

"THE" Dolly Look-a-Like
That's What The Coalminer's Daughter
Gentleman's Club Says Anyway

Slick pulled a cell phone out of his pocket and clicked through some photos till he found the one he was looking for. Against a breathtaking panoramic backdrop of the Himalayas, this same group of guys had formed a human pyramid. Perched at the pinnacle was what at first glance, incongruously, appeared to be a member of Hamas. On closer inspection, I saw that it was Bat Boy, wearing a kaffiyeh to thwart the desert sun and firing an AK-47 into the air.

Bat Boy rapidly became indispensable to the unit.

Whenever the sun set over the Hindu Kush, and the men dug in to get some sleep, it was Bat Boy who would stay awake and lead night watch. His ability to penetrate the dark with his nocturnal vision was uncanny. Where a regular unit member might see a movement and dismiss it as a moth or a cloud, Bat Boy could pick out three Taliban moving along a ridgeline.

Other times, when the unit had to keep moving and couldn't afford to stop for some shut-eye, Bat Boy would rouse the somnambulant crew with a well-timed, ear-piercing shriek. "Used to annoy the heck out of me," Jed, a pimply kid with a harelip, told me. "But you know what doesn't annoy the heck out of me? Being alive. And I got to give props to B Bo on that one."

Jed's eyes misted over, and he stared down at his feet. "That's what we called the little guy," he said, his voice almost a whisper. "B Bo. You know, like J Lo?"

During the platoon's stealthy trek through Waziristan, Bat Boy proved himself an epic insect-killing machine, sucking down mosquitoes faster than Takeru Kobayashi eats hot dogs. The unit was so grateful for his bug-gobbling prowess that on his birthday they engineered a surprise detour to a malarial swamp, where Bat Boy enjoyed a full-on skeeter chow down. When they returned to base, his comrades were so free of the red welts that normally made Operation Enduring Freedom soldiers look like human blood blisters that they faced skepticism that they'd really been out on a mission.

But where Bat Boy most heroically showed his mettle was in his cave work. Raised in one of the Shenandoah Valley's most labyrinthine cave systems, with miles of unmapped passages full of traps for the unwary—spear-sharp stalagmites and spidering tributaries that a man could get lost in and never be heard from again —Bat Boy had grown up to be a master spelunker. And when the army developed intelligence that Osama bin Laden might be hiding out in the Tora Bora cave complex in the eastern border region near Pakistan, it was to Bat Boy that they turned.

The jihadists were no match for the mutant. Surfing the underground thermals of the cave system, he could achieve cruising speeds of sixty miles per hour and, with the merest twitch of a wing, make split-second dogleg

turns. With his unique built-in echolocation capability, he could fling sound waves against the limestone tunnel walls and use the feedback to instantly triangulate his position. With his operatically high-pitched voice, he was able to emit sudden sonic blasts that spooked the cave-dwelling Al Qaeda elite and reportedly led to at least one instance of self-soiling by a frightened bin Laden, who had been a nervous

child who always insisted on leaving a light on when he slept.

Personally, all I remembered of those early days of the conflict was what I'd seen on CNN: fireballs and smoke rising up out of the mountains. What I learned now was that every one of those thunderous explosions was the result of painstaking wing work by Bat Boy. "A lot of people thought that the U.S.A. had some kind of predator-drone geological X-ray-vision majiggy," a stumpy redhead named Doolittle told me. "But you want to know how they targeted those smart bombs? B Bo is how."

Just then, the lights in the gymnasium started to blink, and we all returned to our seats, but when the performance was finally, thankfully, over, we eagerly regrouped, and the fellows told more war stories.

In Iraq, Bat Boy had proved even more versatile than in Afghanistan. "I was at Abu Ghraib with him," a young soldier who barely had peach fuzz admitted. The Red Cross, Jethro said, might be focused on waterboarding and stress positions, but the best "enhanced interrogation methods," as he insisted on calling them, had been Bat Boy's. Hard cases who didn't blink in the face of humiliation by female guards, silly photos involving black hoods, and electrodes attached to their genitals, were reduced to slobbering little girls after an hour with Bat Boy, who deployed grating high-pitched squeals and liquefied-burrito guano showers to drive the prisoners to the very brink of madness. "They sure talked then," said Jethro, spitting a brown stream of tobacco juice onto the floor. "Say what you like about our methods, but they got the job done."

Bat Boy's most glorious moment had come in late December 2003. At the time, nothing seemed right with the world. American GIs were racking up a body count not seen since Vietnam, and George W. Bush's approval numbers were in free fall. Keiko the whale, star of *Free Willy*, had just died. It was a grim time. But it would have seemed even grimmer if the public had known that the hunt for Saddam, the despot who had provoked America into the conflict, was all but abandoned.

"Look, we just weren't getting anywhere," said the one soldier who hadn't spoken this whole time, a kid named Carlos. "It was a lose-lose situation." He paused. "And then B Bo showed up."

Informants had led American troops to a sheep farm near Tikrit, on the Tigris River, and the soldiers had scoured the place for signs of the fugitive tyrant. They had come up empty-handed and were about to move out when the commanding officer decided, just to play it safe, to call in a bat strike. Bat Boy, who'd been on R & R in Bangkok, trying to forget the ghosts of Abu Ghraib amid a haze of opium smoke and barely legal prostitutes, flew in the next day, riding in a cargo plane's wheel well in order to preserve his energy for the mission.

Well, mission might be an overstatement. It took him almost no time at all to accomplish what whole regiments of his 100 percent human fellow grunts had not managed to do over several months.

Bat Boy waited until nightfall and then began circling the farm in ever widening loops, his high, keening wail ringing through the valley for miles. Villagers eating dinner stopped, hummus-smeared pita in midair, to listen to Bat Boy's haunting melody.

He flew all night—singing, gathering information, stealthily using his sonar to develop a high-resolution 3-D mental model of the landscape. And then, finally, he got what he needed.

As Bat Boy glided over a narrow gap in the earth around 3 A.M., his sonar showed it to conceal a human-sized object with shaggy hair orbited by gnats. When dawn broke, he led his platoon straight to the spider hole. Saddam Hussein had been captured.

"It was something else," recalled Carlos, laughing. "And damn it if B Bo didn't go straight back to Bangkok."

At that moment, we were interrupted by yelling. It was coming from a kid who couldn't have been more than eleven. "It was Bat Boy! It was Bat Boy!" the kid shouted, pointing at a small pile of steaming guano on one of the folding chairs set up in the gym. A few other people stepped forward and said they'd seen the same thing: a shadow on the wall, a fluttering movement near the ceiling, and then a gust of air as something fast and dark flew out of the room. Well, well. Bat Boy had been there the whole time, hanging upside down from a rafter. Listening. Watching.

CHAPTER 17

Bat Boy had gone AWOL. White-nose syndrome continued to spread. The effects were devastating. U.S. crops were overrun by bugs, and food exports stopped. Overnight the crisis went global, as sixty-three nations plunged into famine. As bugs took over, bodies piled up. Mammoth mosquitoes invaded Florida. Americans had taken to wearing insect-repelling suits.

BAT CRISIS MANAGEMENT

Internationally, the country of Botswana was hit the hardest. Bugs brought famine and pestilence and wiped out the whole place. From a population of two million, the nation was reduced to one dictator and three female concubines, two of whom had AIDS. The foursome was trapped in the dictator's marble palace surrounded by large African carrion birds. Their water supply was running low. The UN was alerted.

Lacking Bat Boy's assistance, I turned to the brightest minds I knew to share my theory and to see if we could spur a breakthrough. For years, I had run a bat-geek Listserv called Give Me the Bat News First, and I used it now to call an emergency joint meeting of the American Speleological Association and BITC, the leading cave-and-bat expert organizations in the world. In a matter of hours, my e-mail box was filling with responses faster than I could open them. I was heartened. B 'n' Cers, as the bat-and-cave community is known, aren't your common run of person, and it was nice to have this confirmed once again by how quickly we all could join together in the face of a crisis.

When we gathered three nights later in an auditorium in Morgantown, a Who's Who of the bat-and-cave world was there: Lars van Sprungen, the sixteen-year-old prodigy from Antwerp whose work on the nano-acoustics of bat sonar had turned the field on its ears; Rob Mies, the Michigan mammalist who had wowed Leno on a recent *Tonight Show* appearance; Clem Lazarus, a second-rate scholar who had plagiarized my work on more than one occasion (and who, at more than three hundred pounds, was often referred to as Bat Fastard), was waddling around near the door; and even Dr. Ron Dillon, the legend who had first found Bat Boy and who had practically invented bat studies as we know it. Dillon had gone AWOL from his ambulatory care facility in order to make it there.

Because of the mosquito attack I had suffered, a number of people made comments about my appearance, which was that of a puffy human welt. "Did you have an allergic reaction to something?" was a common refrain. Lazarus snidely asked if I had a coke problem, I suppose because I kept scratching myself.

I called the meeting to order. This wouldn't be a press brief. This was show-and-tell. The lights dimmed, and with the push of a button, I launched my slide show, which in its depth, range, and production values made Al Gore's *An Inconvenient Truth* show-and-tell look like a kindergarten crafts project. Slide by slide, I outlined the crisis. I began, rather shrewdly I thought, with an appeal to the heart:

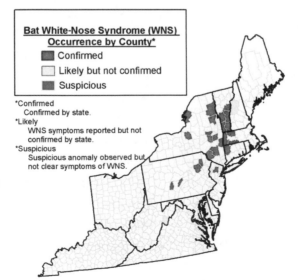

I clicked through images of bats in various stages of white-nose disease, each poor little critter covered with more of the fungus than the preceding one. The last bat I showed looked made of alabaster, so thoroughly had the fungus enveloped his muzzle, ears, and wings.

I displayed an epidemiological map depicting the disease's origination point, along the New York/Vermont border, as well as its main trajectory, down the banks of the Hudson River, then down through the Mid-Atlantic Corridor and into West Virginia. I explained that not only would the White Death be hard to control if it was allowed to spread through the state, given the complexity of West Virginia's cave system and the biodiversity of its bat population, but also it was worth remember-

ing that the state was home to more than a few heritage sites: I clicked through slides of Amish people driving buggies, Harpers Ferry, some of the most impressive mountaintop-removal mining operations anywhere, and the legendary Lost World Caverns.

At this point in the slide show, I paused. I knew that the LWC would be familiar to my audience as the reported home of Bat Boy. I let a few dramatic seconds pass before I dropped my bombshell on them.

"My friends," I said, "I am here today to tell you that while the Lost World Caverns are a wonderful tourist attraction, they are no more the home of Bat Boy than Area 51 is merely a top secret Air Force facility where secret weapons are tested."

There was a collective intake of breath, and despite the gravity of the situation, I must admit that I relished the moment.

I explained that the cave Bat Boy actually lived in was a previous-

Bat White-Nose Syndrome (WNS) Occurrence by County*

- ■ Confirmed
- □ Likely but not confirmed
- ■ Suspicious

*Confirmed
  Confirmed by state.
*Likely
  WNS symptoms reported but not confirmed by state.
*Suspicious
  Suspicious anomaly observed but not clear symptoms of WNS.

ly unmapped limestone ramiform cave I'd discovered near the western edge of the Monongahela National Forest or the MNF as we called it. Everybody in West Virginia knows that when we say MNF, we're not talking Monday Night Football. This forest comprises nearly one million acres of forest. It is so big that back in '43 the army used the MNF as a practice artillery and mortar range. Even today you can still find artillery and mortar shells in the area. Of course, the exact location needed to remain vague, for obvious reasons, but I had taken a number of pictures and had assembled them into a slide show for the benefit of this august crowd.

I'd gotten kind of ambitious with PowerPoint and began this second phase of my presentation with a cover slide that read, "Yo, MTV Caves," while I played a funky Busta Rhymes track in the background.

I began by showing a photograph of a chamber I had found that appeared to be a sort of vanity room, wallpapered as it was with play-

bills from dozens of different productions of *Bat Boy: The Musical* from all over the United States and quite a few foreign countries as well. It appeared to be especially popular in Eastern Europe, and several of the posters were in the Magyar and Romanian tongues.

Next, I showed a compact little room near the entrance, which seemed to function as a garage and contained an Austin MINI Cooper. This was the same MINI Cooper that Bat Boy had famously stolen from a shopping mall parking lot.

Then came a huge walk-in closet with endless rows of identical denim shorts and a section filled with knitted wool wing warmers, lined with cedar to protect them from moths when Bat Boy wasn't home to eat them himself.

There was a home gym, featuring Gravity Boots and clip-on weights that apparently Bat Boy attached to his wings in an effort to build wing muscle. "I suppose bats, too, want to be able to say, 'Check out the guns,'" I observed.

Bat'sHealth

THINK SMART, LIVE LARGE!

CARVE OUT YOUR OWN NICHE IN THE DELUXE CAVE MARKET

STRETCH YOUR WINGS

20 bat-friendly vacation spots within wings' reach

TEST YOUR ECHO DOES YOUR NAVIGATION NEED A TUNE-UP?

PLUS:

Colony Coming to Visit? How to make room for 1,000 of your closest relatives

I clicked to an image of a rather futuristic-looking office. On a desk were stacks of magazines and books—*Bat's Health, Bugs & Blood, Cave Beautiful, Chiropterology Week, Belfries of New England*. It was in this room that I had also found several boxes of documents, of which I had chosen a selection to show to this gathering. When I displayed a photo of baby Bat Boy in denim diapers and with only two fangs, a chorus of otherwise hard-boiled scientists said, "Aw." There were poignant letters, too, addressed in crayon in a child's hand to Batman and returned unopened.

Not all of the material was from Bat Boy's sad childhood. A fair amount seemed to date from more recent years, when he was earnestly struggling to come to terms with his hybrid identity. There were highly technical textbooks on mutation, elaborate genealogical charts, and a scrapbook filled with *Weekly World News* articles about him.

One of the more surprising slides was a picture of Bat Boy's home recording studio, with special sound baffles custom fit to co-ordinate with his sonar, and a pile of demo tapes. I explained that they featured Bat Boy's covers of popular tunes, including "Bat Out of Hell," "Wind Beneath My Wings," and "Cry Little Sister" from the vampire classic *The Lost Boys*. I played a quick medley for the audience. It all sounded pretty much alike: just a series of tuneless squeaks over instrumental tracks. Imagine a mouse doing karaoke.

Then I unveiled my plan of action to help. I made the case that Bat Boy was the only hope we had to warn bats to stay out of infested caves. If Bat Boy could use his sonar to warn the bats to get out of the caves until they could be cleaned, we could save the bats.

Finally, as a kind of kicker to bring the presentation to a close, I said, coyly, "You know, I didn't show you every room in Bat Boy's lair. I saved one for last. This," I said, clicking the remote one last time, bringing up a slide, "is where the magic happens."

On the screen was Bat Boy's bedchamber. A sex swing was suspended from the cave ceiling, and seated in it was one of those anatomically meticulous RealDolls. This one looked exactly like Miley Cyrus.

The applause was thunderous. I was taking my third bow when, suddenly, an unholy squeal issued from the back of the room. As everyone turned to see its source, I looked over their heads and saw only a small fellow who looked like an even more severe Peter Dinklage. But the sound from his throat, an inchoate mix of pain and rage, was not human.

Whoever it was, he was angry. His eyes burned red, like oversized diodes. Spittle bubbled from the corners of his mouth. And as he started toward me in a kind of mad rush, I realized it was none other than Bat Boy in disguise. He came at me in a movement that was neither walk nor flight but a headlong scramble. I tried to think fast. What could he be so angry about? I didn't say squeak about his asthma. Was it the public display of his Miley Cyrus RealDoll? Before I had figured it out, Bat Boy hissed a slap of warm goo across my face. Anticoagulant! A high-decibel scream pierced the hall, nearly bursting my eardrums. Then he was on me, sinking his fangs into one of my arms and then a leg. I could feel his weight on my chest. Keep your stomach to the ground, I thought, so he can't slit your gut. Trying to turtle, I pulled my knees up and struggled to roll over. I threw my hands in front of my face, trying to save my eyes. In the mauling, darkness took over. Rational, scientific thought fled my mind. I mustered a mental appeal to a higher power, a prayer from the dying to let me survive.

As my colleagues in the audience realized what was happening, a good number of them—Ron Dillon, wheeling forward in his wheelchair, and even, to his credit, Clem Lazarus—closed in on Bat Boy, who became very anxious, backing away from me and hopping from one leg to the other, flapping his wings, and squealing incoherently.

Over the years, Bat Boy had developed some fine-tuned survival skills, and the minute he saw Dillon, he spied an opportunity. I don't think he had any idea that this was his former captor and the chairman emeritus of the American Speleological Association. What Bat Boy saw was a blind, defenseless old man in his wheelchair. Grabbing Dillon in a kind of headlock with one of his wings, Bat Boy yanked the doctor from his wheelchair, placed his fangs near the poor codger's jugular, and made an unmistakable shrieking sound that could mean only one thing: "Get back, or else." Dillon asked his colleagues to comply, and Bat Boy retreated toward the exit using Dillon as a shield. When he was through the door, Bat Boy dropped Dillon and fled. Dillon collapsed in a frightened seizure. His giant peach of a head hit the floor and made a muted thud that sounded like someone had just attempted to dribble a water-logged NERF basketball. The West Virginia football hat that I'd given him fell to the side of his head on the ground. A watery substance began to leak out from

Dillon's head, following the slanted contour of the auditorium down toward the podium. Dillon sure didn't look good was the last thought I had before I lost consciousness.

When I came to, the ambulances had arrived to take Dillon and me to a hospital. I was rushed straight into surgery to have a severed artery reattached, while Ron, who seemed to have suffered a heart attack, was sent to the ICU. All afternoon, through a fog of Demerol and Percocet, I asked how Ron was. The nurses all said they were sure he was fine; I should focus on my own recovery.

That night, from my hospital bed, I was half watching *America's Most Wanted* when I experienced a tremendous shock. The news crawl on the bottom of the screen was announcing that Bat Boy was now wanted for murder. As the implications sank in, I found myself weeping for the first time in years. I was grieving for Ron. I was grieving for Bat Boy. I was grieving for bats. I was grieving for the world.

CHAPTER 18

The man calling on my cell phone spoke with a low-class British accent. It was Nigel Potts, *Weekly World News*'s crackpot journalist.

A BUG WING CONSPIRACY

On the phone now, though, the hack said something that grabbed my attention. Florida found itself under invasion by mammoth mosquitoes. Compounding matters, Ahmet Farouk, *Weekly World News*'s Middle East correspondent, had just returned from conducting undercover reporting in Afghanistan. While there, Farouk had discovered an Al Qaeda plot to terrorize the world by breeding killer mosquitoes capable of spreading deadly diseases like malaria. Upon his return from Afghanistan, Farouk met with Potts and shared with him the shocking details of the bug terror plot. In turn, Potts shared information on the bat crisis caused by white-nose syndrome and its impact on Bat Boy. The U.S. bat population stood alone as the last line of defense against a full-blown mosquito invasion. Farouk and Potts both agreed that Al Qaeda must somehow be behind the sudden onset of white-nose syndrome. Al Qaeda well understood the importance of taking out high-value targets.

On top of all this, Potts had recently received several calls from sources saying that

Bat Boy had taken refuge from authorities in the Florida Everglades. That wasn't all. Potts also told me that he had received additional tips from individuals claiming to have seen another mysterious creature in the swamp. The tales were consistent. All featured a monster mosquito—bigger even than the double-wide trailer home Potts said he himself lived in— that locals were calling the Bossquito.

Now, as I sat up in my hospital bed, the chain of events started to connect. There were evil entities that wanted to spread the deadly terror of disease through bugs. To do this, they needed to eliminate bats and even Bat Boy himself. I flexed my arm and leg to gauge the healing of the bite wounds. The stitches produced a tender pain that constricted my movement. This pain would not stop me from fighting the fight to save bats. Gather your strength, Squealgood, I told myself as I pulled out the IV from my arm and continued the conversation with Potts. "Nigel, you might be onto something. When I found Bat Boy in the secret cave, something really unusual happened on my way out. As I was leaving I was swarmed by a pack of mosquitoes. That's unheard of for winter around here. The Feds think the agent spreading white-nose is human related. I think these mosquitoes are spreading it. There's no reason for them to be up this far north this time of year."

"I'm always onto something, old chum. Get your arse down here and we'll get to the tail of the matter," was Nigel's gruff reply.

During the nurse's break, I snuck out of the hospital and flew to Fort Lauderdale. I thought the Bossquito discovery had the whiff of legend, like Mexico's Chupacabra or Scotland's Loch Ness Monster. Normally, I would have dismissed it as a fairy tale concocted by a checkout-line rag in order to sell papers. But while I disagreed with their methods, it was undeniable that Potts and his colleagues, unlike the lemmings in the mainstream media, were the only journalists to have given the Bat Boy story the attention and credibility it was due. And the truth was, I was desperate for answers. When Potts said he thought I should pursue Bat Boy and check out the mosquito story for myself,

something in my head clicked. At the ASA meeting, I had intended to advance the theory that the Feds were wrong about the contact point of white-nose. My theory was that the main agent was insect related. I had one final slide that I had wanted to show the group before Bat Boy attacked and all hell broke loose.

Potts picked me up at the airport in an AMC Gremlin. Dog-eared copies of *Oui* and *Black Tail* were strewn about the floor of the car, and I peeled what looked like a desiccated chicken drumstick off the passenger seat before settling in beside Potts. The car's faint smell of throw-up was masked only by a cloying piña colada air freshener that dangled from the rearview mirror.

On the phone, Potts had said he was about my age, but the guy driving his car looked like he was in his seventies. His skin, after years under a tropical sun, had long ago passed bronze and was now a deep and unsettlingly jaundiced-looking chestnut color; it was cross-hatched with so many lines that it looked almost like one of those leathery alligators that sporadically turn up on the Sunshine State's

WEEKLY WORLD NEWS

NEWS BREAK

THE WORLD'S ONLY RELIABLE NEWS

MAMMOTH MOSQUITOES INVADE FLORIDA

By NIGEL POTTS
Weekly World News

ORLANDO, FLORIDA — The skies over the vast Florida Everglades are black with swarms of huge mosquitoes, the result of a strange bug conclave in the Everglades.

An air-boat tour operator inadvertently stumbled onto a mutant strain of a particularly aggressive form of the common backyard mosquito.

Some of these mosquitoes weigh 14 pounds, with a wingspan of 90 inches and a ravenous appetite for the blood of animals and human beings.

The carnage caused by these monster-sized insects has forced the government to declare a national state of emergency in some areas, including curfews during the hours of dawn and dusk, when mosquitoes are most active.

Dozens of human lives have been lost to the relentless predator so far, but the major impact has been on Florida's citrus industry. Swarms of mosquitoes have also carried off entire flocks of sheep and individual oversized insects have drained an entire cow of its blood in less than 90 seconds.

"The normal way to deal with an infestation of mosquitoes is to kill them en masse with pesticides," says Bruce Buckle, of the Department of Agriculture and Animal Husbandry (DAAH).

"But these mosquitoes are far too big for poisons to do them much harm. The only way to deal with these giants is to shoot them, a very inefficient method of extermination."

In order to encourage the rural population to massacre the mosquitoes, the government has put a bounty on the creatures — $25 per stinger bagged and redeemed.

"Not that we need much additional encouragement," Buckle says. "Floridians are tough men who love their guns, just like the settlers in Wild West America.

"They'll love to load up and cut loose when it comes to protecting their livelihoods."

A special $100 bounty has been placed on the leader of the mosquito pack. A bloodthirsty giant that some locals have taken to calling, "Boss-squito". Buckle warns that anyone coming into contact with the Bossquito should ignore the bounty and alert officials.

BRUCE BUCKLE says the huge mosquitoes are too big for poison.

Mutant bloodsuckers are as big as eagles!

SWARMS of the oversized mosquitoes can drain a cow of its blood in less than 90 seconds.

golf courses. Silver hairs sprouted from his ears. His Hawaiian shirt made me think of pizza. The daiquiri in his hand, as we changed lanes haphazardly and without signaling, made me extremely nervous.

Potts had hired a stunning bronze beauty of an airboat captain named Hiawatha Brown who he said was essential to our mission. Brown stood six foot two inches tall and was descended from a Seminole shaman. Locals called her the Bug Whisperer, for her almost supernatural connection with mosquitoes. Potts had found her at a strip club in

Dana, Florida, called the Body Shop. She took him out back and showed him how she could communicate with the bugs of the night. The article said she could stop a mosquito in its tracks with a simple hum. She stopped me in my tracks the minute I saw her. Potts immortalized Hiawatha when *WWN* did a cover story, "The Seventh Sense: 'Bug Girl' Speaks Creepy-Crawlese!" With a lone alligator tooth dangling above her breast from a leather-string neck-

lace, our tall, dark, Amazonian captain pushed us off and sent us gliding over water lilies and swamp grass. Sitting above us, Hiawatha straddled a large Lear aircraft prop engine that powered her shallow-draft craft. It wasn't long before the jungle became thicker and less penetrable. Captain Brown throttled down on the stick to reduce our speed. Slowly, but expertly, Hiawatha steered the craft through a gauntlet of skinny, prodding cattails. Then we came upon a mangrove forest full of huge fallen logs. I looked up over my shoulder to glimpse the captain's determination as she worked the stick, inching us safely around one huge lumber projectile after another. I was smitten with this swamp mama.

As night fell, the swamp came alive with the whoops of birds and the croaks of caiman lizards. A few times, a submerged cypress branch would poke Hiawatha's boat deck and give us a start. Potts nodded off, but I couldn't sleep, I was so jittery with anticipation and confusing feelings about our captain. Feelings I hadn't felt since my innocent youth with Marie back in Broad Ripple.

Perhaps to control my nerves, or just pass the time, I mustered the courage to talk to her. Hiawatha Brown had a mesmerizing green lazy eye and didn't say much, but she was a good listener. When I complained about my ex-wife Marie's sleazy lawyer and even, at a length that some might consider oversharing, revealed some of the topics that had come up in mediation near the end of our marriage, including Marie's accusation that I had "sadistically bored [her] to the brink of madness with

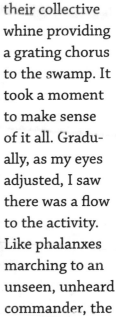

Bat drinking Swoop

[my] incessant and self-involved preoccupation with bats," the good captain merely nodded and said, "I guess that's how she rides," which I didn't entirely understand, but it suggested to me a deep, attentive understanding born of a childhood among tribal elders on the reservation.

On the third day, the bugs got denser, and the distant whine of what sounded like a chain saw grew louder. Around midday, when we rounded a bend in the tributary we'd been following, we came upon a low-lying building. It looked like one of those trailers you've seen on the six o'clock news, where a high school science teacher is being led away in handcuffs and a mustachioed cop is talking half-wittedly about the scourge of methamphetamine.

Clouds of insects swarmed around the trailer, their collective whine providing a grating chorus to the swamp. It took a moment to make sense of it all. Gradually, as my eyes adjusted, I saw there was a flow to the activity. Like phalanxes marching to an unseen, unheard commander, the clouds were entering the far side of the trailer one at a time; each time one cloud entered, another seemed to be expelled from the front. The cloud leaving looked just like the one entering, with one difference. As if they had just flown through a blizzard, each was coated in a snowy, diaphanous fuzz. They had more powdery white stuff on their noses than Richard Pryor did after his freebase explosion.

Potts was out cold, but I stepped on his hand,

grinding my Timberland boot heel into it until he woke up. I knew he'd want to get pictures of this.

Captain Brown closed her eyes and began to rock back and forth, all while emitting a loud and incredibly annoying high-pitched sound that was pretty much what you'd think a mosquito would sound like if it was jacked into a Marshall stack that had been surgically implanted inside your skull.

Then, in an almost oracular tone, the Captain began to speak. "The bug spirit is making the whiteness here," she said. It seemed Brown was channeling something larger than herself, larger than any of us. "The bug spirit has a holy vision: a dark world filled with bugs, death, martyrdom, and destruction. The bats must go, the bug spirit says. It is not personal. It is war. Jihad. This whiteness that you call white-nose disease, it is just the mechanism, the means for the bug spirit to realize the vision."

So the mosquitoes were manufacturing white-nose syndrome right here in the Florida Everglades, and this was their laboratory.

Focusing back on the trailer, I forced my eyes

to trace the roofline. A strange spire protruded. It was a makeshift minaret. This was, after all, an Al Qaeda outpost.

Until now, the captain had seemed in control, but suddenly she turned white with terror. Her lazy green eye snapped to attention. A small puddle formed beneath her. Quivering, she slowly raised her head toward a craggy hill behind the trailer's minaret. I looked in the direction she seemed to be looking in. The hill looked like some sort of rock formation, but as our eyes adjusted to the subtropical glare, we saw that it was alive. There were two oversized eyes, and two extra-long wings, and not one but two giant stingers that attached to the creature's forehead like the curved horns of an African Watusi bull. But the vast bulk of the creature was an enormous red ball, an engorged sac pulsing like a heart. The creature looked at us through heavy-lidded eyes. He seemed kind of sick, like he'd had too much to eat or drink.

On his back was perched a human-sized Camelbak backpack, with what looked like a large can of beer attached to each side. I brought binoculars to my eyes and zoomed in. What I saw chilled me to the bone. Those cans of Milwaukee's Best were actually glass beakers filled with a ruby-red liquid that could be only one thing: blood. From each beaker, a straw ascended to the creature's mouth.

The whole while, each newly albino mosquito swarm was taking off toward the vine canopy, rising en masse above the tree line, hovering in the air for a few seconds, and then seeming to scatter in every direction.

"They are taking the whiteness to caves," Captain Brown explained. "They are bringing death to the bats."

CHAPTER 19

BATS ARE BACK

While Captain Brown struggled to find her composure, Potts and I trolled for bass off the rear of the airboat. We had grown hungry. The exploration into the Everglades' interior had taken longer than any of us planned, and our expedition had run out of food. We had all also lost a fair amount of blood from constant mosquito bites, despite Captain Brown's amazing ability to keep the majority of the bugs at bay by using her bug sense.

From the east, the hum of an approaching motor tore through the air. As it neared us, the boat produced a reverberating river wake that rocked our small airboat. The wobble nearly sent me overboard but Captain Brown grabbed me. We hugged in an awkward embrace, my head cradled against her bosom and my ear pressed against her sharp alligator tooth necklace. Potts pointed at the boat's approaching hull and said, "Look at the SB stencil on the bow. It's a swift boat. And it's armed." The boat idled its engine and two sailors mounted its bow with guns pointing straight at us.

"This is Captain Hiawatha Brown. You are trespassing on Seminole land. This is a sacred place. Put down your guns."

The soldiers did not comply and kept their guns pointed right at us. I glimpsed their faces. The young men looked familiar. They were Jed and Carlos, two of the Special Forces soldiers I had befriended at the Bat Boy musical.

"Hey, guys, it's me, Dr. Barry Leed, we met at the Bat Boy musical." The soldiers did a double take but kept their eyes fixed in a cautious glare on Potts.

One of the soldiers barked out at us, "What's with Pocahontas? Is she a real Indian?"

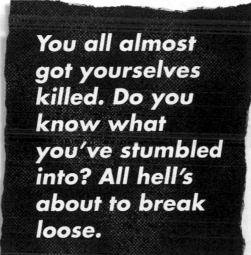

You all almost got yourselves killed. Do you know what you've stumbled into? All hell's about to break loose.

It occurred to me that Potts's chestnut skin coloring likely caused the soldiers to think he might be Al Qaeda. The soldiers also eyed Hiawatha suspiciously. It was racial profiling in the Everglades, of all places. The situation tensed. Then a female moved toward the bow. I recognized her almond-shaped eyes immediately. It was Bat Boy's paramour, Betty Barnett.

Betty Barnett defused the situation. "Jed and Carlos, they're okay. I know them." The soldiers lowered their guns. Betty invited us to board. Jed and Carlos helped our group onto the deck.

Jed grinned at us as he spoke. "You all almost got yourselves killed. Do you know what you've stumbled into? All hell's about to break loose." The captain of the boat, a tall, lanky, elderly man with a senatorial, wooden face came forward holding three bulletproof vests. "Here, put these on. When the lead starts flying, you can get injured on these swift boats. I should know, it's happened to me." The captain looked like one of the trees from *The Wizard of Oz*. It was none other than John Kerry. He was still serving, still fighting, and bravely piloting his craft into this swampy heart of darkness.

I rushed over to Betty. "What's happening?"

"Sink your fangs into a new SWOOP!"

SWOOP

ENERGY DRINK FOR BATS

Now with 75% REAL VIAGRA!*

*25% same old carbonated sugar water

16 OZ

Betty wasn't sure she should be talking, but she also knew she owed me an explanation, as I had saved Bat Boy. She looked nervously toward the sky as she spoke. "From the moment of Bat Boy's recovery, I had known that the only way to reverse the progress of white-nose syndrome would be to somehow get afflicted bats to ingest Viagra for vasodilation. And I had known that such a thing would be all but impossible. The logistics of distributing pills to millions of far-flung bats was a nonstarter. The only approach that might work would be somehow to create an enormous and tasty reservoir of liquefied Viagra and bring the bats to drink from it. My friend Bruce's brother is a Viagra rep, so he was able to get me source pills. My plan, therefore, was to mass-produce a bat reproductive energy drink called Swoop. I spent the next week furiously liquefying those magic pills that had been the source of Bat Boy's miraculous recovery. The biochemistry was only half the challenge. The beverage had to taste good to bats, or they wouldn't drink it, so I involved Bat Boy every step of the way. And I have to say, Bat Boy became a bit snobby about the whole thing, developing a number of affectations: he took to twirling a gold-tipped cane, smoking hand-rolled cigarettes in a long ivory holder, and wearing an ascot, which he would remove and tie around his head like a blindfold before tasting his way through rows of sample Swoop blends. He would ostentatiously swirl each batch around in a tulip glass, inhale deeply, not say anything for a minute, then take a tiny sip, slosh it around in his mouth, and spit it out. And finally, in a barely legible hand, he'd scribble down his thoughts. They were mostly florid and, frankly, unnecessary. I was quite sure bats didn't care whether the stuff had 'aggressive cedar base notes' or 'a haunting whisper of rotten pomegranate.' At the end of each note, he would assign a numerical score, on a hundred-point scale. He was consuming so much Viagra at this point that I admit I had grown weary of his affections and renewed energy." Betty reflexively grabbed her stomach at this point.

"Just as we were nearing production, Bat Boy vanished. At first I was alarmed. There was much work still to do. We had our energy drink, but we needed to let bats know about it and somehow bring them to it. I had been counting on Bat Boy to head up this part of the operation. Fortunately, I had taken precautions against just such a turn of events."

Betty looked skyward again and then continued. "Before Bat Boy's recovery, I had taken the opportunity to inject a transponder pellet into his wing, and now I activated it. I could track his movements on my GPS phone. As soon as I turned it on, I saw a blinking bat-shaped light moving north through Maryland. At first, I could make no sense of Bat Boy's movements. Over the course of about a week, he went to New Jersey and Massachusetts, cross-country to Nevada, and then southeast to Texas. But

then it hit me. The pattern was obvious. Each place Bat Boy went is a known population center for bats. Cape Cod is the home of a small but influential colony of little brown bats, Nevada has an important roosting site for pallid bats, and a mine shaft in northwestern New Jersey is popular with Indiana bats. And Texas—hell, Texas is bat central. Austin is home to the largest urban bat colony in the United States, with as many as 1.5 million Mexican free-tails summering beneath the city's Congress Avenue Bridge. San Antonio is near Bracken Cave, which draws an astonishing twenty million bats every year. Bat Boy, I realized with growing excitement, was way ahead of me, already meeting with his winged brethren and letting them know, using his sonar, that they needed to drink Swoop. The transponder recorded Bat Boy's flight all the way to Botswana, where he worked to save the struggling nation."

She continued, "At the same time, my various bat-related Google alerts began filling my in-box with news dispatches out of these very same datelines, reporting enormous evacuations of swarms of bats. On my smartphone transponder receiver, the bat blip hopscotched across the country, stopping and starting, until I saw it begin to move down through Texas, crossing into Louisiana. Extrapolating from Bat Boy's trajectory, I calculated that he was heading directly toward the Everglades! Bat Boy called me and said that the bats were going to Florida. And they were on a due course for Bossquito's lair. He told me to get in touch with Jed and Carlos and they would know what to do. I called Jed and Carlos, and they contacted their friends in the government, including Senator Kerry. A C-130 military transport plane picked me up along with the four liquid tons of Swoop that we had brewed in West Virginia, and here we are. Look to the stern: we are towing a four-ton barge of Swoop for the bats."

I asked, "So he's not suffering from PTSD?"

"He's still as heroic as he's ever been. It's in his blood. He will never stop serving his country, just like his great-granddaddy Bat Boyee." Betty pulled out her cell phone GPS. "In fact, if this transponder's working, my little freedom fighter should be zoning in here any second now."

"What about the murder charges for Dillon?"

"Well, first of all, the maulings that were committed were part of the Al Qaeda plot to set up Bat Boy. Bat Boy never touched Dillon or anybody else. We had Devon Pickstock look at the bite radius again. I will guarantee you that Bossquito was responsible for the maulings once we get his big old bug head on a plate."

A shrieking came across the sky.

Then the sky darkened. Rain began to fall. At first we thought it was one of those tropical showers common in south Florida, but then we heard the sound: instead of the low rumble of thunder, it was a shrill, birdlike noise at the upper limits of human hearing. And then, as an acrid stench rose off the swamp, and a sour taste puckered our mouths, and our vision began to blur, we realized that this was not rain, no, but a fecal monsoon, *the fecal monsoon*, perhaps the greatest guano torrent ever known to man.

"I guess you could say it's raining bats and dogs," Potts said, gray green slime dribbling off his chin. Like an anxious schoolboy, he looked at me for a reaction.

"Good one, Nige," I said, offering a chuckle, which seemed to please him no end. The limey was starting to grow on me, but he had the corniest sense of humor.

In sheer numbers, it was the biggest army the world had ever seen, greater than Caesar's legions or Napoleon's Grand Army. Tora Bora had nothing on the shock-and-awe display of winged might that unfurled now in south Florida. The bats came in low, swarming Bossquito's wetland's redoubt from all sides, battering the trailer lab into a pulp of scrap metal while circling Bossquito in ever faster, tighter loops. Bossquito, who was so fat he couldn't move, just sat there looking queasy. Since he was essentially a tiny little bug atop a freakishly large blood sac—picture a midget riding a Hippity Hop—all the bats needed to do was puncture the sac. Carlos and Jed threw down a withering cover of assault rifle fire.

The bats attacked from every direction, bulleting toward Bossquito with fangs bared, subjecting the monster to ten thousand pinpricks. Each made only the slightest perforation in his enormous, disgusting carapace, but collectively they turned him into a spherical sprinkler head, spraying laser-thin jets of blood in every direction.

Bossquito deflated, sagging like a lopsided waterbed. He began to look pathetic, until there was nothing there but a hedgehog-sized mosquito attached to what looked like a Trojan Magnum condom. Bat Boy tore his wings off and ate him.

Then Bat Boy led the bats to the Swoop-filled barge tanker. While the Bossquito pile-on had been taking place, Betty Barnett had busied herself, flipping open the tanker's hinged lid. The tanker was now effectively a floating swimming pool filled with Swoop. The bats lapped it up thirstily. Even as they drank, we could see the white fungus flaking off their noses.

Bats who had been rendered weak and passive by the disease now regained their strength, and then the strangest thing happened. Imagine Woodstock, *Caligula*, and Plato's Retreat rolled into one, then add wings, fangs, and squeaks. The bats were having a bat orgy. Right then and there these bats were conceiving a new generation, a bat baby boom that would reverse all of the recent population decline.

As the orgy raged, I looked at Captain Hiawatha Brown. She was smiling. We hugged. She hugged me back harder, rearranging several loose vertebrae in the process. Everyone was happy. The bats were back.

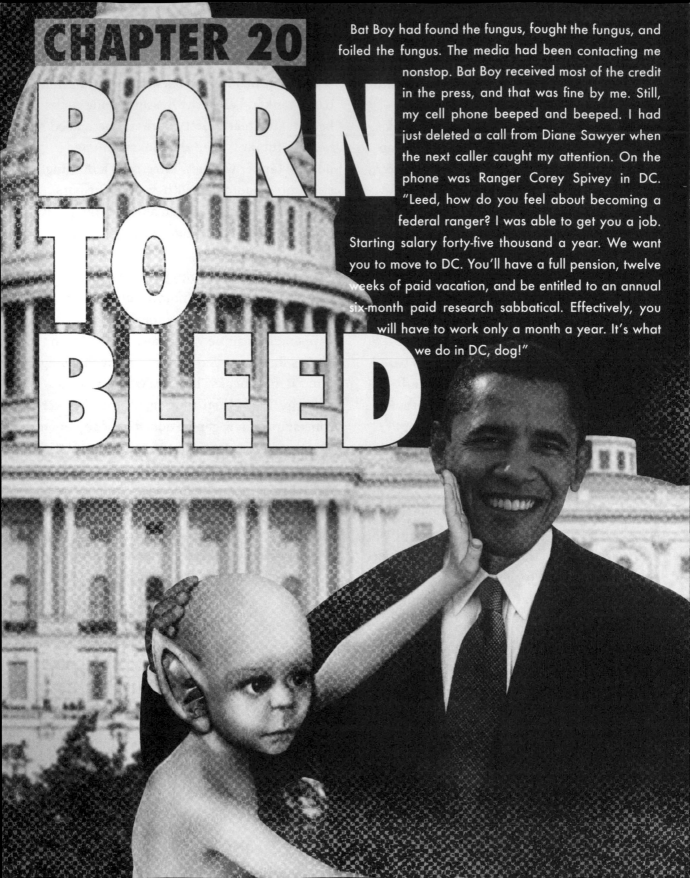

CHAPTER 20
BORN TO BLEED

Bat Boy had found the fungus, fought the fungus, and foiled the fungus. The media had been contacting me nonstop. Bat Boy received most of the credit in the press, and that was fine by me. Still, my cell phone beeped and beeped. I had just deleted a call from Diane Sawyer when the next caller caught my attention. On the phone was Ranger Corey Spivey in DC. "Leed, how do you feel about becoming a federal ranger? I was able to get you a job. Starting salary forty-five thousand a year. We want you to move to DC. You'll have a full pension, twelve weeks of paid vacation, and be entitled to an annual six-month paid research sabbatical. Effectively, you will have to work only a month a year. It's what we do in DC, dog!"

"Sounds like a dream," I said. I was thinking that Corey was probably making $85K, and if I could get down there and work a little harder than the next guy, four or five weeks a year vs. three weeks, I could bump him out and have the division to myself.

"Leed, there's one more thing. The president wants you down here for a presentation. They're giving you a medal. I put you up for it."

"Well, I'd be honored," I said to the ranger while turning my head over to Hiawatha Brown, who lay in the bed with me, her size-twelve feet sticking off the edge. We had decamped to her trailer to celebrate our success in defeating white-nose syndrome.

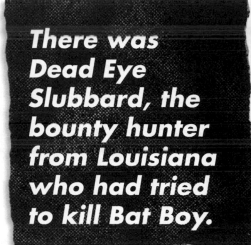

There was Dead Eye Slubbard, the bounty hunter from Louisiana who had tried to kill Bat Boy.

"One last thing. The president's office asked me if you could get Bat Boy to join the ceremony. Look, we all know that you're the guy who beat white-nose, but the media is all about Bat Boy, so I told them at the White House that I would ask. I know the real score. That was an amazing thing you did. I know the media gave Bat Boy all the credit, but you're our guy."

I told him I couldn't make any promises for Bat Boy, but I would look into it.

It was a sunny winter day when I went down to DC. The protocol office had decided to hold the medal ceremony outdoors. The president strode to the microphone and addressed the crowd.

Bat Boy fans filled the seats, and sprinkled among them were people Bat Boy had touched in other ways. I took a minute to scan the crowd and was overwhelmed with the turnout of support. Everyone had showed up. From the B 'n' C crowd there was Lars van Sprungen and Clem Lazarus (the Bat Fastard). From DNR, Tim Glenning made it to the presentation. He showed up wearing his Bat Boy T-shirt. Bat Boy's old war buddies from Saudi were there. I noticed many of the same faces that I had seen in the auditorium. There was that young soldier with peach fuzz, Jethro, I think his name was. There was Eric Riccardi, the Las Vegas businessman who had found Bat Boy in his pool and nourished him back to health with Spam and table scraps. There was Dead Eye Slubbard, the bounty hunter from Louisiana who had tried to kill Bat Boy. I was thankful that the crowd had gone through metal detection and that Slubbard was presumably unarmed.

Even Bat Boy's critics were sprinkled in

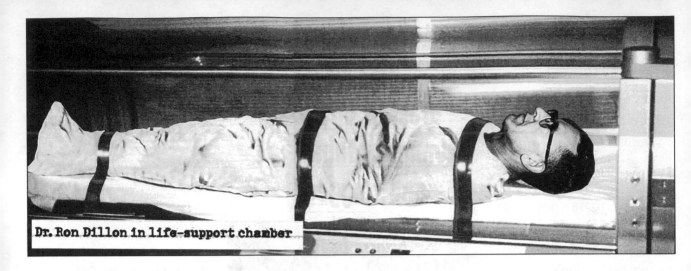

Dr. Ron Dillon in life-support chamber

the audience. There was Mitt Romney, the presidential candidate and former governor of Massachusetts who had shamelessly stunt-stumped outside Bat Boy's cave calling Bat Boy a threat to mining safety. Amy Mikelly, the little girl from Orlando whom Bat Boy had nearly ripped to shreds years earlier when she was in fifth grade, came to the ceremony. She had grown into a healthy young woman. Her wounds appeared fully healed. Dressed patriotically for the occasion, Ms. Mikelly sported a red, white, and blue skirt-blouse combo.

In the crowd, I spotted Nigel Potts wearing his trademark Hawaiian shirt. He flashed me a thumbs-up.

Then I caught the familiar mottled and bruised giant peach face of my mentor, Dr. Ron Dillon. He had recuperated in a life-support chamber. I learned later that like the bats, he, too, had started drinking Swoop following his unfortunate tumble in the auditorium caused by Bat Boy. His condition improved considerably. Blood flow had returned to what was

left of his extremities. He was perched in his wheelchair with his West Virginia cap attached. Resting in the cup holder of his wheelchair was a tall boy can of Swoop. From the can opening extended a long custom straw that reached to his mouth. DNA gathered at the mauling scene had exonerated Bat Boy. It turned out that a runaway chimp, escaped from a residence in Wheeling, had been responsible. FEMUR quickly matched the DNA and put the unruly monkey down. Dillon's mauling was likely FEMUR all along. I was too tired to raise that issue now, especially since I would soon be a federal employee myself. Dillon didn't seem to bear any ill will toward anyone. He looked comfortable in his wheelchair, visibly aroused and sippin' Swoop as he awaited the proceedings. Everyone in attendance could see that he still had one good appendage left.

But for all the familiar faces there was one that meant more to me than all the rest: Captain Hiawatha Brown, the exotic one-eighth Seminole, one-eighth Creole, one-eighth

African-American, one-eighth Korean, one-eighth Haitian, one-eighth Caucasian, one-eighth Scottish, one-eighth Aleutian Islander Bug Whisperer. Hiawatha had dressed in her finest reptile skins. We had been dating since she helped me foil white-nose, and I had never before known the happiness of human comfort I had found within her solid frame. I had a Zales engagement ring in my pocket and would be dining with her later that night at the famous Queen Bee Vietnamese restaurant in Arlington, Virginia. I had arranged with the management that we would be presented with their legendary Hanoi beef soup. In Hiawatha's soup, an engagement ring would encircle a chunk of beef. If everything went as planned, my green-eyed "bug girl" would soon be my Queen Bee. Hopefully, the symbolism in my choice of restaurant would not be lost on my sexy shaman. As her dutiful drone, it would be my obligation to follow her mating dance back to the Key Bridge Marriott. I glanced down at the take-out menu in my hand.

The president strode to the microphone.

QUEEN BEE RESTAURANT

3181 Wilson Blvd. • Arlington, VA 22201 • (703) 527-3444

SOUP

1.	HANOI BEEF SOUP - (Pho An Choi)	.2.95
	The most popular of Vietnamese soup. It's sliced beef on rice noodle in delicate beef broth.	
2.	ASPARAGUS WITH CRABMEAT SOUP - (Soup Mang Cua)	.2.95
3.	WONTON SOUP - (Hoanh Thanh)	.2.25
4.	SHRIMP & PORK VEGETABLE SOUP - (Canh Thap Cam)	for 2 . .6.95 / for 4 . .9.95
5.	SPICY & SHRIMP SOUP - (Canh Chua Tom)	for 2 . .6.95 / for 4 . .9.95
6.	SPICY & CHICKEN SOUP - (Canh Chua Ga)	for 2 . .6.95 / for 4 . .9.95
7.	SPICY & SOUR FISH SOUP - (Canh Chua Ca)	for 2 . .6.95 / for 4 . .9.95
8.	TOFU & TOMATO SOUP - (Canh Dau Hu Ca Chua)	for 2 . .6.95 / for 4 . .9.95

APPETIZERS

11.	QUEEN BEE SPRING ROLLS - (Cha Gio) (2)	.3.50

"Ladies and gentlemen, we are honored to have Dr. Barry Leed with us today. Dr. Leed convinced Bat Boy to join the fight against white-nose syndrome and eradicate a disease that crippled our nation. Getting a mutant to do anything is difficult. I should know. As the press reported, I have a half-bat half brother named Obatma who was rescued from a Kenyan cave and brought here to Washington. While we love him, Obatma can be shifty and elusive." Hearing his name mentioned, Obatma honked the horn of the Capitol Police cruiser that he was trying to hot-wire and raised his fist outside the car. I snapped a photo of the unusual sight. The president, clearly annoyed, interrupted his speech and called out to him, "Obatma, please get out of that squad car." Security personnel forced Obatma out.

The president resumed his presentation, ruffled but unbowed. "Let us turn our attention to the man, er, mutant at hand. I am sure you all know Bat Boy's story by now. We asked him to attend today's ceremony, but he is one busy little batriot. Orphaned in a West Virginia cave, Bat Boy has grown to become the most famous cryptozoological celebrity in America. He survived a childhood marked by adversity, thanks to his indomitable will to succeed, in the process developing a burning passion for helping the less fortunate. After being in and out of research laboratories, Bat Boy volunteered to join the U.S. Marines as a civilian in 2001. In 2004, he successfully led troops in Iraq to evil dictator Saddam Hussein's 'spider hole.' This is a true American hero—the rare young man who 'bites for your rights.'"

Obatna

The president asked me to step forward. He shook my hand. As he was hanging the Medal of Freedom around my neck, my cell phone rang. It was Diane Sawyer, pleading for an exclusive. I told her to lose my number. I turned back to the president and apologized. The president gave me a look of understanding and said, "I understand. Diane Sawyer never quits. Let's get down to business. Dr. Barry Leed, due to your service to this nation and your defeat of white-nose syndrome in the battlefield state of West Virginia and the saving of millions of bat colonies of the United States, we hereby by order of official proclamation declare you a recipient of the Presidential Medal of Freedom."

The president finished hanging the medal around my neck. News cameras popped and flashed. Then the president introduced a man named Bobas Basimbi, the president of Botswana. Basimbi spoke of the situation in his country and the malaria spike and how Bat Boy had saved them all from the bugs, malaria, and AIDS. He then proudly announced in halting English that his congress had recently ratified a measure during a session in his bedroom the previous night to change the name of the country from Botswana to Batswana. He unveiled the new flag of Batswana. Basimbi modified the tricolor so that Bat Boy's iconic face sat in the middle of the flag.

Next, the president did something that none of us expected. Not to be outdone by Botswana changing its name to Batswana, he announced to the assembled crowd that because of his work defeating the evil Everglades bug colony and saving our country's food and vegetable supply, the U.S. government would honor Bat Boy in a special way. In solemn tones, the president mentioned that he had known differentness in his life. "Today I hereby decree upon special order from the United States Treasury, under my command, that our government will officially replace Abraham Lincoln's image on the five-dollar bill with Bat Boy's image." The president unveiled a large check, similar to the ones that sponsors give to the winners of golf and tennis tournaments at the conclusion of the event. The government had decided that it would not be appropriate to have a shirtless figure on the bill, so they dressed Bat Boy in a suit and bow tie. He had never looked more dapper.

The president looked at me and said, "I only wish Bat Boy were here to see this."

Dumbfounded, I replied, "Me, too, Mr. President."

Just then, a kid in the audience pointed up to the sky and screamed, "Look! It's Bat Boy." Sure enough, there he was, flying low, almost too low. As he grew closer, I could see an impish look on his face. He was moving fast. I knew what he was doing. The little mutant was going to buzz the White House!

A cheer rose from the audience. He swooped in low, wings beating. I noticed a commotion on the roof of the White House. Security officers scrambled to their posts, with guns drawn. A man on the ground signaled them back. And then Bat Boy whizzed by so low we could almost smell him.

The president looked on in awe. Then, almost by instinct, he saluted Bat Boy. Later, I was told that this marked the only time in our nation's history that the president of the United States had saluted a mutant former soldier. Though Bat Boy was flying very fast, everyone on the ground could see that he returned the salute along with an almost eardrum-bursting, high-pitched squeal. The squeal had to register 120 decibels. The crowd roared. Sounds at 160 decibels can cause permanent hearing loss, but no one seemed to care. All assembled heads turned to watch Bat Boy's flight. His silhouette struck a sharp

contrast against the DC sky—a friendly witch atop America's broomstick. How far, I thought, he had come from his days of captivity and the beatings of a broomstick of a different kind. Just then, I noticed Sayer Schming, the sadistic janitor who beat Bat Boy with a broomstick—some speculated he may have even sodomized Bat Boy—pointing toward Bat Boy. Schming was standing next to the president and whispering in his ear. What was he doing on the grounds of the White House and how did he wind up on the president's advance team? On the other side of the president stood Alan Thrush, the former security guard for Dillon. It turned out that a forensics team found splinters in Dillon's skull consistent with Thrush's souvenir Cooperstown bat. Bat Boy had not mauled Dillon. Thrush had been working with FEMUR, and the agency had put the hit on Dillon to frame Bat Boy and keep their federal

funding alive. Thrush's reward for his participation appeared to be a Washington assignment. Now these lowlifes were presidential confidants? I shook my head and pretended not to see either one of them.

Bat Boy was soaring due southwest now, back to his native West Virginia, his fatherland, literally. Back to carving snowboard turns and keeping America safe.

But wait. Bat Boy spotted a flock of twelve Canada geese flying south for the winter. One by one he grabbed them by the neck from their formation. Canadians in attendance sighed in alarm, uncertain as to the fate of their beloved bird. A hissing sound was heard. Was it the geese? Was it the Canadians in the audience? Or was it Bat Boy hissing before he shot his anticoagulant?

As Bat Boy circled back around DC gathering steam, he bit the head off the first goose and started flying in a predetermined pattern. He was skywriting—in blood, no less. Then the heads of the geese popped one by one as his bloodred ink formed his indelible message in the afternoon sky:

BAT BOY
4
GUV
WVA

BORN 2 LEED

Having entered Bat Boy's cave, I knew "LEED" was intentional and a tip of his hat to me. The vast crowd ducked as one by one the bloodless skin sacs of the Canada geese started dropping left and right from the sky.

Then, in a final gesture, clutching the neck of the remaining blood-sputtering fowl, Bat Boy circled back and put a "B" in front of "LEED" so that it read:

BORN 2 BLEED

The message sank in: Bat Boy's patriotism ran so deep that he could not resist making reference to his selfless sense of obligation for national military service one last time. Just like his noble ancestor Bartholomeuw Boyd, Bat Boy was born to fight for his state of West Virginia, the state that his forebears founded. In his upcoming gubernatorial campaign, he would run on those principles as surely as he lived by them. I hoped there would be room for me in his administration. I watched him take off again, gliding westward: a comet of American heroism blazing his trail back home to West Virginia. Flying faster now, with the wind at his ears. Now his swooping silhouette shrinking in size: smaller . . . smaller . . . smaller. Now a minuscule, barely visible speck diminishing upon the horizon, the ghosted trail of our last true American hero.